The International Political Economy of the BRICS

Exploring to what extent the BRICS group is a significant actor challenging the global order, this book focuses on the degree and consequence of their emergence and explores how important cooperation is to individual BRICS members' foreign policy strategies and potential relevance as leaders in regional and global governance.

The BRICS countries (Brazil, Russia, India, China, South Africa) have come to play an important role on the global political scene. As a group, and as individual countries, they have taken initiatives to establish new institutions, and have engaged in yearly summits that coordinate their voice and focus on intra-BRICS cooperation. In this sense, the BRICS may be seen as a "balancing coalition", and often the main opposing force to Western powers. Looking at the debate around the role of the BRICS as an actor, expert contributors also explore the international political economy (IPE) of individual BRICS countries as systemically important countries with highly asymmetrical individual power capacities.

The comprehensive theoretical and empirical coverage of this timely volume will be especially useful to students, researchers and professionals interested in ongoing academic debates around the IPE of emerging powers, and those researching global governance and globalization.

Li Xing is Professor and Director of the Research Centre on Development and International Relations, Department of Culture and Global Studies, Aalborg University, Denmark. He is also the Editor in Chief of *Journal of China and International Relations*.

The International Political Economy of New Regionalisms Series
Series Editor: Timothy M. Shaw

The International Political Economy of New Regionalisms Series presents innovative analyses of a range of novel regional relations and institutions. Going beyond established, formal, interstate economic organizations, this essential series provides informed interdisciplinary and international research and debate about myriad heterogeneous intermediate-level interactions. Reflective of its cosmopolitan and creative orientation, this series is developed by an international editorial team of established and emerging scholars in both the South and North. It reinforces ongoing networks of analysts in both academia and think tanks as well as international agencies concerned with micro-, meso-and macro-level regionalisms.

Understanding Mega-Free Trade Agreements
The Political and Economic Governance of New Cross-Regionalism
Edited by Jean-Baptiste Velut, Louise Dalingwater, Vanessa Boullet & Valérie Peyronel

Pan-Caribbean Integration
Beyond CARICOM
Edited by Patsy Lewis, Terri-Ann Gilbert-Roberts and Jessica Byron

Global Economic Governance and Human Development
Edited by Simone Raudino and Arlo Poletti

The Relevance of Regions in a Globalized World
Bridging the Social Sciences-Humanities Gap
Edited by Galia Press-Barnathan, Ruth Fine and Arie Kacowicz

Expanding Perspectives on Human Rights in Africa
Edited by M. Raymond Izarali, Oliver Masakure and Bonny Ibhawoh

The International Political Economy of the BRICS
Edited by Li Xing

For more information about this series, please visit: www.routledge.com/ASHSER-1146

The International Political Economy of the BRICS

Edited by Li Xing

Routledge
Taylor & Francis Group
LONDON AND NEW YORK

First published 2019
by Routledge
2 Park Square, Milton Park, Abingdon, Oxon OX14 4RN

and by Routledge
52 Vanderbilt Avenue, New York, NY 10017

Routledge is an imprint of the Taylor & Francis Group, an informa business

First issued in paperback 2021

British Library Cataloguing-in-Publication Data
A catalogue record for this book is available from the British Library

Library of Congress Cataloging-in-Publication Data
A catalog record for this book has been requested

ISBN: 978-1-138-57957-6 (hbk)
ISBN: 978-1-03-209380-2 (pbk)
ISBN: 978-0-429-50794-6 (ebk)

Typeset in Times New Roman
by Apex CoVantage, LLC

To the memory of Steen Fryba Christensen.
May his spirit remain with us and encourage
us to continue our work and life.

Contents

Tables

Figures

Contributors

Ana Flávia Barros-Platiau is Associate Professor at the Institute of International Relations, University of Brasília, Brazil.

Danielly Silva Ramos Becard is Associate Professor at the Institute of International Relations, University of Brasília, Brazil.

Raúl Bernal-Meza is Professor at University Arturo Prat (Chile), Universidad Nacional del Centro de la Provincia de Buenos Aires (Argentina), and Universidad de Buenos Aires, Argentina.

Peter Marcus Kristensen is Associate Professor at the Department of Political Science, University of Copenhagen, Denmark.

Antônio Carlos Lessa is Professor at the Institute of International Relations, University of Brasília, Brazil.

Laura C. Mahrenbach is a Postdoctoral Fellow at the Bavarian School of Public Policy at the Technical University of Munich, Germany.

Jørgen Dige Pedersen is Associate Professor (emeritus) at the Department of Political Science, Aarhus University, Denmark.

Leonardo Ramos is Associate Professor of International Relations at Pontifical Catholic University of Minas Gerais, Brazil. He is also the Editor of *Conjuntura Internacional*.

Mette Skak is Associate Professor at the Department of Political Science, Aarhus University, Denmark. She is also the Denmark-editor of *Nordisk Østforum*, a Nordic-language journal.

Javier Vadell is Associate Professor of International Relations at Pontifical Catholic University of Minas Gerais, Brazil. He is also the Head of Graduate Studies, and the Editor of *Estudos Internacionais*.

Justin van der Merwe is Senior Researcher at the Centre for Military Studies of the University of Stellenbosch, South Africa.

Li Xing is Professor and Director of the Research Centre on Development and International Relations, Aalborg University, Denmark. He is also the Editor in Chief of *Journal of China and International Relations*.

Xiao Alvin Yang is currently a PhD candidate in Political Science, subdivision Globalization & Politics, at the University of Kassel, Germany.

Editor's note

The idea for this volume was jointly initiated by the Routledge IPE book series and I, with the support of my colleague Steen Fryba Christensen. Together, Steen and I made the book proposal and together we signed the book contract with Routledge, with him as the co-editor of this book.

Sadly and unfortunately, Steen, my closest and dearest colleague and friend, suddenly died in April 2018 shortly after signing the contract for this book. His passing is a great loss to me, my research group, my department, and Aalborg University. In particular, it is a great loss to Brazilian studies in Denmark, an area to which Steen made significant contributions.

Steen Fryba Christensen was Associate Professor of the Research Center on Development and International Relations in the Department of Culture and Global Studies at Aalborg University, Denmark. His teaching and research interests and areas included development studies, foreign policy studies, international relations, international political economy, emerging power analysis, Latin American studies, and the world order. His main research focus was on Brazilian and Latin American engagement in the global political economy, China-Latin America relations, and analyses on the changing global order. He acted as advisor to the Danish Foreign Ministry and received a grant from the Danish Agency for Science, Technology and Innovation for research collaboration between Brazilian and Danish scholars. This same Agency invited him to participate in research network activities in São Paulo. He had been very active in the Danish media, giving expert commentary on Brazilian and other Latin American issues.

In recent years, Steen had been extensively working on China-Latin America relations in general, and China-Brazil relations in particular. I have had the honor of working with him on two previous book projects: Christensen, Steen Fryba and Li Xing (eds.) (2016) *Emerging Powers, Emerging Markets, Emerging Societies: Global Responses*. London: Palgrave Macmillan; and Li, Xing and Steen Fryba Christensen (eds.) (2012) *The Rise of China and the Impact on Semi-periphery and Periphery Countries*. Aalborg-Denmark: Aalborg University Press.

I wish to have this book devoted in special memory to Steen. I am sure that he would be very happy to see this book project completed, since the book's theme and the chapters' topics were of great interest to him. I wish to thank him for his friendship, support, passion and collegial relationship for two decades (1998–2018). May his spirit remain with us and encourage us to continue our work and life.

1 The international political economy of the BRICS in a changing world order

Attitudes and actualities

Li Xing

Conceptual discussions

In recent years, terms such as "emerging power", "rising power", "emerging market", "BRICS" (a grouping which contains Brazil, Russia, India, China, and South Africa), etc., have become conceptually interchangeable and have gained special attention as a thematic topic of research (Fonseca et al., 2016; Tank, 2012). The term "emerging power" is a broad and somewhat vague concept. It refers to those countries that are perceived to be in the process of increasing their share of global economic and political power comparatively faster than that of the rest. The implicit implication behind the concept is that emerging power is desirable and is optimistic in its development outlook.

However, there is no agreement on the boundaries of the concept or on which countries belong to the category of "emerging power". According to Fonseca et al. (2016: 65) the concept of "emerging power" indicates those ascent powers who are able to make a *hierarchical transition* to the core in international politics and economics, and they are identified as "a country that observes a positional improvement in the distribution and accumulation of global wealth and converts it into political power" (Fonseca et al. 2016).

For some scholars, countries that qualify themselves as emerging powers are very few, namely those countries that realistically may have the potential to make a hierarchical transition to the core in international politics and economics. In this usage, the terms "emerging power", "rising power", and "BRICs" or "BRICS" are almost conceptually interchangeable. This could mean that, for instance, only the BRIC or BRICS countries would count as emerging powers. The BRICS grouping, which consists of Brazil, Russia, India, China, and South Africa, has gained special attention as a thematic topic of research.

Across various literature and media reports, the concept of "emerging power" has been overly and extensively used. Some scholars would include more countries by looking to the financial G20, which consists of both developing and developed countries, and even includes the EU. Apart from BRICS, other developing countries such as Argentina, Indonesia, Mexico, Saudi Arabia, and Turkey could be considered as second-tier powers because they are becoming successful "emerging markets" outside the group of traditional powers led by US hegemony. Some analysts might want to include other periphery countries such as Nigeria, and perhaps Chile and Colombia, which form the next layer of developing country "emerging markets". These countries would count as second-tier regional powers positioned below the regionally dominant or most powerful countries. Yet others might include still more countries as emerging powers based on a broader understanding, where "emerging power" is almost synonymous with the concept of "emerging market".

There is no real objective way of making the cutoff on the list to say which states or countries should be considered emerging powers and which should not. As Cooper (2013: 966) argues:

> Even if the exact composition of the cluster cannot be precisely pinned down, what a broadening out nonetheless does to an extended 'rising middle' is to turn the focus towards the form of the diplomatic activities associated with emerging powers.

Regardless of the number of states on the list of emerging powers, there are major asymmetries amongst these states. This is even true within the BRICS group. South Africa is, thus, an outlier in the group, as it is much smaller than the other countries. O'Neill, the inventor of the term "BRIC" (O'Neill, 2001), even commented that "for South Africa to be treated as part of BRIC doesn't make any sense to me", but, he also added that "South Africa as a representative of the African continent is a different story" (*The Guardian*, April 19, 2011).

Many international journalists and analysts see China as an upcoming superpower, rather than as an emerging middle power from the Global South. From this perspective, China has already emerged as a great power and has thus made the transition to the core of the global system. Some analysts even find that China is the only candidate that may be a potential competitor for the US in terms of global hegemony, even though China does not seem to be seeking to subvert the liberal world order (Christensen and Bernal-Meza, 2014: 43).

Along with the concept of "emerging power", "emerging market" and "rising power" are also widely applied nowadays. Antoine van Agtmael coined the concept of an "emerging market" in the 1980s. At the time, van Agtmael was working for the International Finance Corporation and wanted to create a concept for the promising stock markets in the developing world which would interest international investors. This concept has come to refer to a large number of developing countries, of which some by now have emerged as belonging to the world's high-income countries – a category used by the World Bank – while others are at different stages of development in terms of average per capita income. The point here is that an "emerging market" is not necessarily an "emerging power" in terms of its political weight and influence.

Kenneth Waltz's definition of "rising powers" is much narrower than the broad "emerging market" concept. It has much in common with the concept of an "emerging power", which is not strange since "rising" and "emerging" are almost synonymous words. This may explain why analysts at times use them interchangeably when talking about "rising power" and "emerging power". For Waltz, "rising powers" are those countries that could realistically become great powers. Writing on this, shortly after the end of the Cold War, he found that only three countries qualified as "rising powers", namely Germany, Japan, and China (Waltz, 1993: 50).

"Emerging power", in its most narrow conceptualization, is similar to Waltz's understanding of "rising power". The difference is that Waltz was interested in any country that might make this transition, whereas the concept of "emerging power" would not include traditional Western powers, but only the most powerful countries from the developing world or outside the traditional Western powers. In this connection, Russia is not really an "emerging" power. Clarisa Giaccaglia (2016) refers to "new" countries from the Global South when delimiting the meaning of the concept, treating Russia as a "re-emerging" power that does not belong to the Global South (Lechini and Giaccaglia, 2016: 9). This would leave Brazil, India, and China in a category of their own amongst other "emerging powers", a category which Samuel Pinheiro Guimarães (2005: 15–17; Giaccaglia, 2016: 28) and others see as the "great peripheral states" based on their relative material capacities. In other words, size matters.

Considering the dimension of international activism, more states may be added to the list of emerging powers. For instance, Giaccaglia (2016: 28) points out that South Africa, along with the other BRICS countries, is participating actively in a number of significant arenas. Her argument is that Brazil, India, China, and South Africa are a subset of states between traditional core powers and the rest of the developing world due to their power resources. Amongst developing countries, they belong to a set of "regional powers" and "middle powers" that are more powerful than other developing countries. At the same time, she points out that emerging powers and re-emerging powers may pursue their rise jointly through the formation of coalitions in international politics (Giaccaglia, 2016: 19). She singles out Brazil, India, China, and South Africa, i.e. BRICS from the South of the global system. However, for many academics, the BRIC or BRICS group, including Russia, is synonymous with the concept of "emerging power", or at least the most evident examples of countries that qualify as belonging to the category.

The BRICS concept, like the concept of emerging market, is a product of the imagination of the international financial community. Fonseca, Paes, and Cunha point out (2016: 47) that Goldman Sachs' reports "redefined the discussion of emerging markets, indicating, among them, those who in fact could perform the hierarchical transition to the center, from the economic and institutional point of view". They similarly argue that the BRIC acronym has come to bequeath "a stronger political sense to the idea of an emerging actor in a wider sense". The BRIC or BRICS group, which emerged as a kind of coalition or network in the global system with the first BRIC Summit in 2009, is at the heart of discussions and controversies about the challenge to traditional dominant countries and possibly to the hegemony of the United States. These discussions relate to theoretical discussions within the international relations (IR) discipline on the balance of power, polarity, and hegemony.

In their synthesis of the concept of "emerging power" in the IR discipline, Fonseca et al. (2016: 61) present a conceptual prototype of the concept, identifying it as "a country with a set of material and ideational attributes along with a specific political behaviour, a reformist or revisionist activism in international order". They further establish that claiming protagonism is not enough in itself, since a country needs to have "other material attributes that connote its effectiveness". Finally, they argue that "emerging powers" usually have anti-hegemonic status-quo values.

Carlos R. S. Milani et al. (2017: 588) are critical of this last point. They find that countries that are labeled as "emerging powers" should not necessarily be viewed as "the new challengers to the West and the status quo" and they similarly criticize the tendency in the literature on emerging powers to describe them as countries that experience dynamic economic growth. Instead, the foreign policies of these countries may go through changes both in terms of foreign policy strategies and in terms of their ambitions in the global system, and economic growth may, at times, falter. Brazil after 2014 would exemplify this possibility. Similarly, while some emerging powers such as China may emerge as great powers, others may find themselves stuck in a second-tier position. With the issues of the potential for setbacks and the existence of asymmetry in power attributes amongst the BRICS countries, these authors – instead of focusing on a model of power transition or systemic change as much of the BRICS-oriented emerging power literature does – aim "to propose a foreign policy analytical tool for second-tier non-nuclear states". This arguably enriches the debate on the importance and consequences of the diffusion of power in the global system and the rise of "emerging powers", as the world is entering a new conjuncture different from the early 2000s.

Historically, the concept of "emerging power", with various degrees of variation and contextual specification, has been expressed in different terms. For example, "middle powers" and "regional powers" are often used by politicians and scholars, despite the fact that both expressions remain vague and their meanings are contentious. Literally, "middle powers" often refers to states that occupy a middle-level position in the international power spectrum. Middle powers, regional powers, and regional patterns of security are becoming increasingly prominent in shaping international politics. Nevertheless, discussions of middle powers in the IR literature still lacks a consensus about what the term "middle power" actually means.

These conceptual discussions imply, on the one hand, the complexities and difficulties in making a clear conceptual definition of "emerging power" and, on the other hand, the author attempts to sort out the varieties of claims, terms, concepts, usages, and definitions in order to identify the most applicable one(s) that can best reflect the current situation (actuality) with regard to the notion of "emerging power".

Emerging power and BRICS: attitudes and interpretations

Literature on emerging powers are wide and highly diverse in terms of structure, scope, and focus (see Table 1.1). IR and international political economy (IPE) literature has, in recent years, concentrated on debating the contributions, challenges, and "instabilities" brought about by emerging powers, particularly China, to the existing US-led world order (Mearsheimer, 2006, 2014; Layne, 2009, 2012; Ikenberry, 2008, 2011; Buzan, 2011). In addition to scholarly academic literature, a large

Table 1.1 IR/IPE theories on the rise of China/emerging powers

Liberalism/neo-liberalism	*Different schools of realism*	*English school and constructivism*	*Different strands of Marxist and critical theory*
The rise of emerging powers is within, not without, the capitalist world order. It is a byproduct of the existing system. BRICS is and will be conditioned and shaped by their integration with the existing capitalist world system. The BRICS bloc is not a counter-hegemonic force. The rise of emerging powers symbolizes the resiliency of the existing system to accommodate the catching up of other states.	The rise of emerging powers will not be peaceful, and it will unavoidably challenge the existing US-led world order. Power transition leads to adversarial relationships and may further lead to interstate warfare. China's rise, for example, will not be peaceful due to the mistrust between the revisionist hegemon (China) and the defensive hegemon (the US).	It is important to emphasize the mutual generation between material capacity and ideas, a mutually enforcing relationship. Emerging powers have a shared creed in their transformative potential to make changes in the world order in general and global institutions in particular. China is rising as a global actor in norm-diffusion and norm-setting, especially in global financial governance.	The BRICS phenomenon demonstrates that the world's capitalist system has been expanding beyond its core territories and incorporating new centers of capital accumulation and new spaces for capitalist relocation and investment. It is perhaps a good representation of an emerging consensual order driven by alternative ideas and norms.

number of writings on the subject by policymakers, think tanks, and journalists can be characterized as being more speculative and forecasting. Some pieces of literature deal with the concept of "emerging power" as a unit of analysis, others tend to focus on specific emerging powers (most frequently China). Much of the literature reveals a great deal of either fascination or irritation with emerging powers that have influenced Western scholarship and journalism, often producing abrupt sentiments ranging from excessive approval and unqualified optimism to unwarranted revulsion and deep pessimism.

Opinions of fascination, irritation, optimism, and pessimism – driven by contending theoretical perspectives – reflect the disagreement on conceptualizing BRICS as a counter-hegemonic socio-economic and socio-political force. On the one hand, it is counter-hegemonic, seen from a Gramscian perspective, because hegemony can never be taken for granted once and for all but, rather, it is constantly struggled over and challenged by competing socio-political forces. There are also potential conflicts over trade, and geopolitical and security issues between the existing powers and the core BRICS powers, China and Russia. On the other hand, although BRICS all claim to deviate from the neoliberal Washington Consensus, nevertheless, their economic achievement and prosperity relies on integration with the global economy, and they do not have the intention of representing a fundamental challenge to the neoliberal world order, at least in economic terms (Worth, 2015)

Some literature on BRICS takes its point of departure as discussing and assessing the impact generated by emerging powers on countries located in the different stratifications of the world system – the core, semi-periphery, and periphery. They argue that the emerging powers such as BRICS are on a course to reshape and transform the global economy (Cai, 2009; Gu et al., 2016; Marr and Reynard, 2010; O'Neill, 2013; Stuenkel, 2015). While some books by Chinese authors focus on intra-BRICS dynamics (Li and Wang, 2010; Li, 2011; Sun, 2010; Wang, 2010), others study intra-BRICS country comparisons (Fan et al., 2007; Lin and Zhou, 2011; Velloso, 2009; Velloso and Roberto, 2009).

It is recognized that the debate is still going on regarding the appropriation of the concept of emerging power to the fields of IR and IPE, regarding the theoretical impact it inflicts on the discipline, and regarding the duality of its formation as a theoretical category (Paes et al., 2017). It is also necessary to relate the "emerging power" concept to the earlier IR/IPE "intermediate states" category, as well as world system theory's "semi-periphery" concept. Another recently popular term is the "Second World" (Khanna, 2008, 2009, 2012). It is an extensively fluid concept that draws a new terrain constituted by the three most important global power centers – USA, Europe, and China. The so-called G3 are competing to forge relationships with the "Second World", which covers the pivotal regions of Eastern Europe, Central Asia, South America, the Middle East, and East Asia. Khanna's depiction of a Second World refers to the regions and countries that are in transition and which are growing in influence and economic strength (Khanna, 2009). Interestingly, China, seen from Khanna's perspective, is both a Second World country in terms of some internal features, and a superpower in its own right in terms of its geopolitical and geo-economic activities and its global influence and impact.

If "world order" is defined as the general acceptance of international "norms, values, rules and practices" that are historically and culturally shaped, often imposed by the hegemonic powers (the West in general, and the United States in particular), then it is not difficult to understand why the existing hegemonic powers are today watching carefully how emerging powers are applying their power, because historical lessons suggest that emerging powers can generate a dramatic and even violent impact on the existing order. International scholarship tends to focus on the debates amongst the different schools of IR in hypothesizing and theorizing the binary choice faced by both the existing and emerging powers: the existing powers are struggling to assimilate the emerging powers into the existing order, while the emerging powers are endeavoring to benefit from challenging and changing the established structure. In recent years, academic debates on world order transformations have revolved around the theme of emerging powers vis-à-vis the existing world order (see Figure 1).

It is important to point out that the author of this chapter co-edited a book on emerging power and emerging market by turning the perspective 180 degrees around and focusing on how countries in different regions such as Asia, Africa,

Latin America, Europe, etc., are reacting to the rise of new powers and the rebalancing of the world economy (Christensen and Li, 2016). Rebalancing, here, is understood as a change in the distribution of economic power (structural power) in the current world order.

BRICS in an era of emerging world order: wither actualities?

The picture of an emerging world reorder in 2018 looks very disturbing to the whole world. The China-US trade war shows that the competition between rising power and existing power is actually less about "trade" itself and the growing military confrontation in the South China Sea and other geopolitical and geopolitical arenas than it is conventionally perceived, but more about rising China-US competition over the leadership or dominance in the future of innovation – intellectual property and design, electric vehicles, self-driving cars, and artificial intelligence – the battle for the future (Elen, 2018)!

The great failure of the G7 meeting in Charlevoix, Quebec on June 10, 2018 was globally seen as a turning point for the 21st century Western democracies, when US President Donald Trump disrupted the international economic order by unilaterally imposing US tariffs on steel and aluminum imports. The US also refused to sign the G7 joint communique that advocated a "rules-based trading system". Dismayed by the Trump Administration's "American First" protectionism, some Western leaders and media outlets called for the unity of the remaining democracies in standing together against the US unilateralism that threatened to remove the cornerstone of the international order (*The Guardian*, June 10, 2018). German Chancellor Angela Merkel emphasized her line several times after her summit with Trump and the NATO meeting in May 2017 that "we in Europe have to take our fate into our own hands" (CNBC, May 28, 2017). "The Group of Seven has become increasingly irrelevant in a world of new emerging powers", Jim O'Neill, who famously coined "BRIC" in 2001, wrote in a blog post that "an institution that excludes the BRICs while still including economic basket cases like Italy cannot possibly claim the legitimacy required to exercise global economic leadership" (Bartenstein, 2018).

In retrospect, a few years after the invention of the acronym "BRIC", the grouping had already become a common concept in IR jargon. With the inclusion of South Africa, "BRICS" have come to play an important role on the global political scene, as they have coordinated foreign policy positions on key issues in different international institutions that provide direction to different aspects of global and regional governance. Many of their policy positions on, amongst others, climate change, poverty reduction, nuclear proliferation, etc., can be legitimized as an active voice in the claim for a transition toward a multilateralism in global governance. In particular, the rise of BRICS as a new actor within the international system accelerates the evolution of a *new agenda* within global governance, such as the G20, the International Monetary Fund, etc. (Duggan, 2015). Since 2009, BRICS has been engaged in yearly summit, focusing on coordinating their voices within international institutions. In addition to their coordination on global affairs, intra-BRICS cooperation has also become institutionalized through a steady process of holding regular ministerial meetings on areas such as education, health, finance, agriculture, energy, science, and technology and security.

The rapid global attention on BRICS was organically followed by the world financial crisis in 2008 with the decline of the hegemonic dominance of the US-led world order. The rise of emerging powers has successfully penetrated into some power areas in terms of economic competition, capital accumulation, political and economic influence, as well as technical and material capacities. China, in particular, is performing outstandingly in terms of its global share of high-tech manufacturing products, financial competitiveness, as well as international aid and overseas investment. Based on the phenomenon of the rise of new or emerging powers, coupled with the situation of the financial crisis that has been weakening the traditional powers, global research and academic communities are observing a multifaceted and intertwined situation: on the one hand, the world order is experiencing a rebalancing of power due to the economic downturn in the US and Europe since 2008 and due to the survival of the crisis by emerging powers on the whole; on the other hand, while the emerging powers argue for increasing their political position based on their economic clout, they are also concerned about the negative impact that the decline of the established powers will have on them. This is because emerging powers have much closer economic and trade relations with, ironically, the established economies, than with one another.

In many ways, BRICS is interpreted as a kind of "balancing coalition". Often it has been the main opposing force to Western powers in global negotiations. Particularly in the international financial arena, the world is witnessing movements toward new patterns of IPE in terms of the formation of new alliances, resulting from global responses to the new situations. The "BRICS Bank" (New Development Bank) and the Asian Infrastructure Investment Bank (AIIB) are now part of IR and IPE vocabularies, symbolizing a growing phenomenon of the changing world order in which the system is no longer ruled and governed by the US-led postwar treaties. This phenomenon is interpreted and termed by this author as an emerging world order characterized by "interdependent hegemony" (Li, 2014, 2016). The concept of "interdependent hegemony" implies a dialectic process of mutual challenge, mutual constraint, mutual need, and mutual accommodation. It symbolizes a dynamic situation in which the existing system's defenders and the new emerging powers are intertwined in a constant interactive process of shaping and reshaping the world order.

When taking into consideration the economic dimensions of power rebalancing, and when applying them in the current global political domains, some scholars draw a relatively darker picture in which they highlight this transformation from a realist perspective that the world is experiencing an interesting but "disturbing" moment, characterized by an imbalance between the order and the distribution of power which is becoming more diffused. The world is seen as entering into "the age of entropy", in which "international politics is transforming from a system anchored in predictable, and relatively constant, principles to a system that is, if not inherently unknowable, far more erratic, unsettled, and devoid of behavioral regularities" (Schweller, 2014).

Seen from the perspectives of the critics, BRICS have, since their birth, failed in articulating a coherent agenda of joint action. As highlighted by Martin Wolf in a 2012 interview to the Council on Foreign Relations:

> These countries have basically nothing in common whatsoever, except that they are called BRICS and they are quite important. But in all other respects, their interests and values, political systems, and objectives are substantially diverse. So there's no reason whatsoever to expect them to agree on anything substantive in the world, except that the existing dominating powers should cede some of their influence and power. That's the one thing they have in common.
>
> (Christopher Alessi, interview with Martin Wolf, March 30, 2012)

"BRICS" is indeed an exogenous invention that was intentionally institutionalized as a convenient geopolitical unit, which suits the interest of each of the five BRICS countries in different ways. It is a political group, but without strong cultural commonalities and without solid historical roots. In this connection, the future of BRICS as an emerging power actor or not, will be conditioned by internal and external political, economic, and security correlations and divergences.

After almost a decade since the birth of the "BRICS" acronym, what is the situation today? The situation in Brazil is not completely encouraging, if not discouraging. The Brazilian economy is heavily reliant on commodity exports, and it went into recession (South Africa has a similar situation). The Russian economy has, for many years, pulled back and suffered from collapsing oil prices. The Ukraine crisis turned Russia-West relations back to the Cold War. Due to a devaluation in currency and Western sanctions restricting its trade, Russia is experiencing its worst recession in six years. India's economic growth is far from robust, and the country still has a high level of unemployment, and suffers from comprehensive poverty and backward infrastructure. These situations led to some pessimistic claims that "the world's rising powers have fallen", that "there will be no bloc of 'emerging economies' rising up to challenge the Western order", and that "Brics' New World Order Is Now on Hold" (Nossel, 2016; Talley, 2016).

Seen as an "emerging superpower", China is apparently the only BRICS country that is globally recognized as "unambiguously the one realistic great power rival of the U.S. in the 21st century" (*Washington Post*, January 25, 2018). Despite the fact that China has also experienced its slowest pace of economic growth at a rate of 6–7% in recent years, the country is the world's second largest economy, and it is becoming the biggest challenge to BRICS' future. In many ways, China is seen as the only emerging power that matters, and it is seemingly dominating all the new institutions in which the BRICS' interest is claimed to be presented. The world is much divided with regard to how to perceive China's rising power.

Beijing seems to be identified both as a revisionist emerging power with respect to setting up an alternative global financial architecture, and as a status-quo power with regard to safeguarding the global free trade system and rejecting the enlargement of the Security Council in the United Nations system. Even though Beijing claims that the potential and strength of BRICS is "unchanged", there is an increasingly worldwide consensus, even amongst BRICS, that power relationships amongst BRICS are very asymmetrical (Christensen and Li, 2016). In other words, while China is seen as the "real engine of the BRICS" (*Financial Times*, July 10, 2015), consequently its global rise and leadership also generates intra-BRICS core-periphery asymmetrical power relations and economic dependency.

Much of the current debate on BRICS is centered around the question of whether this alliance is really a "historical bloc" that is based on not only benefits and opportunities, but also on shared beliefs, values and visions, or whether it is just a "marriage of convenience" that is based on cost-benefit calculations and issue-based alliance. Another research question regarding BRICS is whether the creation of such a coalition bloc simply represents power diffusion that is relocated from the world system's core (the North) to emerging powers from the South without challenging the fundamental substance that underpins the current world order. In other words, the issue to be investigated is whether the BRICS bloc is merely a functional re-arrangement of the existing fixed "social, political, and economic arrangements" (Strange, 1988), or whether it can generate any impact on IPE restructuring that will radically challenge the existing global structural arrangements.

The year 2018 is witnessing the phenomenon that the BRICS nations have been on the frontline of the Donald Trump's global trade wars. The US' move toward unilateral action has wounded traditional allies and rivals alike, including the five BRICS countries. In its 10th Summit in Johannesburg this year, BRICS have once again shown their awareness of the importance of voicing cohesive positions on politics and forging deeper trade ties. The leaders from the BRICS bloc are expected to band together in defense of the multilateralism the US once set up. It is expected that trade flows between BRICS member states are going to be fostered, and the New Development Bank is to increase its lending to the BRICS members as well as non-members. What deserves special attention, is that the 10th BRICS Summit Johannesburg Declaration of 2018 affirms that BRICS seek to project stability and predictability in a rules-based order threatened by US President Trump. Despite the serious challenges ahead, BRICS represents a spirt of emerging powers attempting to increase their political and economic integration in response to new global challenges.

The objective of the book and the chapter contributions

This volume takes its point of departure from the fact that emerging powers are changing the dynamics of power in the existing international system by seeking a greater voice and role in international institutions and by becoming important economic and political actors through new global financial organizations, shaping a new era of multilateral economic and development politics.

Since the book deals exclusively with BRICS, its main objective aims to examine if and to what extent the BRICS alliance is a significant global actor and if, and to what extent, the BRICS group is challenging the global order or aspects of it. While focusing on the debate on BRICS as an actor, this volume also explores the IPE of individual BRICS countries. As mentioned, these five BRICS countries have highly asymmetrical individual power capacities in connection with their foreign policy strategies and potential relevance as leaders in regional and global governance. The volume focuses on the degree and consequence of their emergence as important global powers, as well as contributes to an understanding of how important the cooperation in the BRICS group is to individual BRICS member's political and economic interest and their overall foreign policy strategies. These analytical discussions are heuristic, since the dynamics between BRICS themselves includes conflictual and competitive elements, in addition to their collective alignment and common purpose.

This volume intends to shed light on many ongoing scholarly discussions. The chapters included in this volume cover a variety of aspects and dimensions, which enrich the ongoing discussions. While some chapters take their point of departure from analyzing the historical evolution of BRICS, and the extent of BRICS' economic, political, and intellectual impacts on the current world order, others try to examine the knowledge-generating tendency it might bring about. While some authors emphasize the domestic constraints of some individual BRICS countries in fulfilling their "power expectation" as well as the extent to which domestic politics affect their foreign policy choices and shape the BRICS' sense of identity and common objectives, others see BRICS as a global stage/platform or an intermedium for each country to position itself in its region and in the world. A common feature of the book is that all contributions acknowledge the fact that individual BRICS countries experience different development challenges and outcomes in a changing world order, and different development outcomes affect the cohesion of BRICS in one way or another.

Chapter 1 by Li Xing plays the role of being the introduction of the book. The author guides readers through the book's theme by discussing the core concept "emerging power", which is the key concept for this book. The chapter argues that it is important to understand the connotations and differences underlining the concept of "emerging power" or other similar terms and notions such as "rising power", "emerging market", "middle power", "regional power", "semi-periphery", etc. The chapter introduces both the variety of studies on BRICS (attitude) and the current situation of BRICS (actuality). Both the attitude and actuality show that, under the present-day IPE context, BRICS – a collective international entity or as individual countries – are facing a complex situation in which a variety of factors, interplays, and dynamics are intertwined with challenges, constraints, and opportunities. Finally, the chapter introduces the other chapter contributions which are included in the book.

Chapter 2 by Peter Marcus Kristensen takes its departure not from the mainstream way of perceiving international relation discourses on emerging power as an outcome of political, economic, military, and institutional changes brought about by a power shift from the "West" to the "Rest", particularly BRICs, but from an inquiry on whether the world is witnessing the rise of BRICS as intellectual powers, or "theorizing powers". The chapter argues that, although it is commonly expected that rising powers will become "theorizing powers", i.e. powers who are able to develop their own indigenous theories about world politics and global order, it is often unclear what the relationship between rising material power and knowledge production is. The author outlines five arguments made in the existing literature about why rising powers will or should become theorizing powers: 1) the expanding foreign policy scope of rising powers; 2) their need for alternative ordering principles; 3) the opened space caused by a hegemonic order transition; 4) a general expansion of material resources; and finally, 5) discipline-internal developments.

Chapter 3 by Yang Xiao critically examines the question on whether BRICS are challenging or reinforcing the current world order. The author draws from different theoretical perspectives on the rise of China and extends the underlying arguments and logics to BRICS. The chapter heavily engages itself in theoretical discussions by focusing on some IR/IPE theories, such as power transition and hegemony, and investigating the relationship between them. The analysis goes beyond scrutinizing and illustrating the tensions between and amongst competing Western IR/IPE theories, such as offensive and defensive neorealist theory, neoliberal institutionalist theory, regionalization theory, critical theory, and cultural and civilizational theory, and involves discussions on Chinese IR theories, such as moral realist theory or the Tsinghua approach, relational theory, and social evolution theory. The author posits that a plural and multidimensional conceptualization of the current world order, rather than a singular understanding, more accurately reflects the complexities of the rise of BRICS and adds more explanatory power to it.

Chapter 4 by Laura C. Mahrenbach identifies cooperation between emerging and established powers as the center of debates about how to meet the political and economic challenges of the 21st century. This chapter explores conditions facilitating or hindering such cooperation in the crucial field of trade. By focusing empirically on Brazil, a BRICS country, and the United States, the author argues the inconsistent ability of the two governments to navigate conflicting domestic preferences related to ideas and interests results in inconsistently successful cooperation. This argument is briefly illustrated in two case studies: the negotiations for a Free Trade Area of the Americas, where Brazil and the United States were at loggerheads, and the World Trade Organization's 2008 mini-ministerial meeting, where they found common ground. The chapter concludes by applying the lessons of trade cooperation to emerging and established state cooperation in global economic governance more broadly.

Chapter 5 by Javier Vadell and Leonardo Ramos follows a historical evolution of the foundation of "BRIC" (Brazil, Russia, India, and China) and later "BRICS" with the inclusion of South Africa. This outreach is seen as a real geopolitical turn encouraged by China's broad strategic vision. The authors share the analytical position that the BRICS forum is the first sign of a coordinated challenge to Western supremacy in the world economy. The chapter aims to understand the institutional evolution of the BRICS forum and to examine to what extent BRICS have a common agenda of pushing international economic governance away from neoliberalism and Western dominance. The chapter's special attention is given to the role of Brazil and China in this process.

Chapter 6 by Li Xing sees the rise of China as a highly complex phenomenon in the capitalist world order. Based on the analysis that the Chinese economy is simultaneously occupying multiple positions and playing multiple roles in all three stratifications of the capitalist world economy – the core, semi-periphery, and periphery, the author argues that China's multiple positions are enabling the country to compete with the conventional core countries in high-tech sectors and financial institutions, while still enjoying a comparative advantage in competing or cooperating with the conventional semi-periphery and periphery countries (including BRICS) in manufacturing and commodity industries. The chapter intends to provide a framework for understanding the current China-rise complexities, i.e. China is playing multiple roles, occupying multiple positions, and generating multiple impacts in the existing world order. The chapter concludes that China's roles both as a counter-hegemon versus the existing core powers, and as an emerging hegemon versus the developing world is bringing about a new changing and complex situation in the world order in which countries and country blocs, such as BRICS, existing and emerging powers, and existing and new international institutions are engaged in a continuous process of mutual challenge, mutual constraint, mutual opportunity, mutual need, and mutual accommodation.

Chapter 7 by Raúl Bernal-Meza puts an emphasis on Brazil, a BRICS power in Latin America. The author points out that Brazil used the soft power of its regional leadership as a balancing factor against the hegemonic power, but this power is no longer present. The chapter critically posits that Brazil is actually weakening BRICS for three reasons: First, the country's political, economic, and social crises have devitalized its status as an emerging economic power and weakened its naturally perceived role as a regional leader. Second, since last year, Brazil's foreign policy has abandoned its commitment to link the country's wellbeing with that of the region of South America. Third, Brazil is in a peripheral position in the intra-BRICS economic structure whose core is China. This analysis postulates that, internally, BRICS reproduce the core-periphery structure, and Brazil has a mechanism of weakness that affects its status as a global emerging power. The chapter's critical analysis leads to the pessimistic conclusion that Brazil's external and internal problems manifested in its relationships with China and South America, and the country's internal socio-political and socio-economic deterioration especially weaken BRICS and threaten its eventual demise.

Chapter 8 by Danielly Silva Ramos Becard, Ana FláviaBarros-Platiau, and Antônio Carlos Lessa focuses on Brazil and it highlights that, in recent years, Brazil's policies and strategies for BRICS have evolved significantly. The chapter evaluates the main changes in the diplomatic strategy of Brazil in relation to

BRICS after ten years since its creation. It applies a pluralistic theoretical approach from the perspective of foreign policy to explain how BRICS have become a product of a competitive environment with dynamic interactions between governments, economic interest groups, and decision makers under social and political-economic structures. The analysis of the chapter sees "Presidential diplomacy" and "ministerial level" as central elements of Brazil's position to BRICS. The chapter concludes that Brazil has accepted participating in BRICS because of its strong relationship with Brazil's strategy of "active and autonomous diplomacy" to become a global actor. Despite the mitigated results, BRICS have become a growing priority for Brazil's diplomatic agenda and has progressively connected with its private sectors, especially in infrastructure, energy, and health.

Chapter 9 by Mette Skak presents Russia's claims to have masterminded the BRICS great power concert, a claim that can partly be substantiated via the Russia-India-China concept invented by Primakov in the 1990s. The study shows that the Russian approach to BRICS differs from the pragmatic geo-economics of the other BRICS countries – Russia always sees BRICS as a platform for geopolitical balancing against the United States and as an alliance that is becoming ever more radical and revisionist in its pursuit of this goal. The chapter highlights that Russia's policy to BRICS has become a hard test of their capacity for great power management partly due to its weak economic position, and partly due to China's rising global leadership role. The chapter concludes that, although Russia has been using its brief power transition window of opportunity to pull BRICS cooperation in the archaic direction of geopolitics, China may guarantee a future course correction for the benefit of more holistic climate change geo-economics.

Chapter 10 by Jørgen Dige Pedersen turns its attention to India. The author argues that India had clear political and strategic interests in joining the BRICS coalition. BRICS is seen as leverage for India to advance its own interests in shaping the international economic institutions as much as possible, forming new alternative institutions and, in general, securing for itself a role in global consultations on a variety of international political and economic issues. The study shows that in BRICS, India has formed a kind of bridge between the Eurasian continental powers of Russia and China on the one hand, and the traditional members of the coalition of developing countries, Brazil and South Africa, on the other. Although India has supported the many initiatives to increase mutual economic collaboration amongst the member countries, the outcome of this has been modest. Nevertheless, India still sees considerable political value and long-term economic potential in the BRICS group.

Chapter 11 by Justin van der Merwe claims, despite South Africa's membership in BRICS, its role in the Africa rising phenomenon has often been overlooked, and so has Africa's role within the broader rise of the South narrative. In this chapter, the author demonstrates the links between these spatio-temporal phenomena and indicates how these impulses are generated in the interests of financial capital. Although promoted as a triumphalist development for the non-West, a more accurate reading connects the key drivers back to crises in Western centers.

References

Alessi, Christopher (2012) "Does the BRICS Group Matter?" Interview by Martin Wolf on March 30, the Council on Foreign Relations. Available at www.cfr.org/interview/does-brics-group-matter.

Bartenstein, Ben (2018) "BRICs Inventor Says G-7 'Irrelevant' Because China and India Are Left Out." *Bloomberg*, June 12. Available at www.bloomberg.com/news/articles/2018-06-12/bric-inventor-says-g-7-irrelevant-as-china-and-india-left-out.

Buzan, Barry (2011) "A World without Superpowers: Decentered Globalism." *International Relations*, 25(1): 1–23.

Cai, Chunlin (2009) *Research on the Economic and Trade Cooperation Mechanism among BRICs*. Beijing: China Financial and Economic Press.

Christensen, Steen F., and Li Xing (2016) *Emerging Powers, Emerging Markets, Emerging Societies: Global Responses*. London: Palgrave Macmillan.

CNBC (2017) "Merkel Says Europe 'Must Take Our Fate into Our Own Hands' after Tough G-7, NATO Meetings." May 28. Available at www.cnbc.com/2017/05/28/merkel-says-europe-must-take-our-fate-into-our-own-hands-after-tough-g-7-nato-meetings.html.

Cooper, Andrew (2013) "Squeezed or Revitalized? Middle Powers, the G20 and the Evolution of Global Governance." *Third World Quarterly*, 34(6): 963–984.

Cristensen, Steen F., and Raúl Bernal-Meza (2014) "Theorizing the Rise of the Second World and the Changing International System." In Li Xing (ed.) *The BRICS and Beyond: The International Political Economy of the Emergence of a New World Order*. Farnham Surrey: Ashgate.

Duggan, Niall (2015) "BRICS and the Evolution of a New Agenda within Global Governance." In Marek Rewizorski (ed.) *The European Union and the BRICS*. Cham: Springer.

Elen, Maurits (2018) "Sino-US Trade: The Battle for the Future." *The Diplomat*, April 26. Available at https://thediplomat.com/2018/04/sino-us-trade-the-battle-for-the-future/.

Fan, Qimiao, Michael Jarvis, José Guilherme Reis, Andrew Beath, and Kathrin Frauscher (2007) *The Investment Climate in Brazil, India and South Africa: A Comparison of Approaches for Sustaining Economic Growth in Emerging Economies*. Washington: World Bank.

Financial Times (2015) "The Real Engine of the Brics Is China." July 10. Available at www.ft.com/content/b688d836-8402-33b4-84b5-8e3be642ea2b.

Fonseca, Pedro C.D., Lucas D.O. Paes, and André M. Cunha (2016) "The Concept of Emerging Power in International Politics and Economy." *Brazilian Journal of Political Economy*, 36(1): 46–69.

Giaccaglia, Clarisa (2016) "Poderes medios emergentes y orden internacional: hacia un manejo colectivo de los asuntos mundiales." In Gladys Lechini and Clarisa Giaccaglia (eds.) *Poderes emergentes y Cooperación Sur-Sur: perspectivas desde el Sur Global*. Rosario: UNR Editora. Editorial de la Universidad Nacional de Rosario.

Gu, Jing, Alex Shankland, and Anuradha Chenoy (eds.) (2016) *The BRICS in International Development*. London: Palgrave Macmillan IPE Series.

Guimarães, Samuel Pinheiro (2005) Cinco siglos de periferia. Buenos Aires: Prometeo.

The Guardian (2011) "South Africa Gains Entry to Bric Club." April 19. Available at www.theguardian.com/world/2011/apr/19/south-africa-joins-bric-club.

The Guardian (2018) "The Guardian View on Trump and the G7 Summit: A Watershed Moment." June 10. Available at www.theguardian.com/commentisfree/2018/jun/10/the-guardian-view-on-trump-and-the-g7-summit-a-watershed-moment.

Ikenberry, John G. (2008) "The Rise of China and the Future of the West." *Foreign Affairs*, 87(1): 23–37.

Ikenberry, John G. (2011) "The Future of the Liberal World Order: Internationalism After America." *Foreign Affairs*, 90(3): 56–68.

Khanna, Parag (2008) *The Second World: Empires and Influence in the New Global Order*. New York: Random House.

Khanna, Parag (2009) *The Second World: How Emerging Powers Are Redefining Global Competition in the Twenty-First Century*. New York: Random House.

Khanna, Parag (2012) "Surge of the 'Second World.'" *The National Interest*, 119: 62–69.

Layne, Christopher (2009) "The Waning of U.S. Hegemony: Myth or Reality." *International Security*, 34(1): 147–172.

Layne, Christopher (2012) "This Time It's Real: The End of Unipolarity and the 'Pax Americana.'" *International Studies Quarterly*, 56(1): 203–213.

Lechini, Gladys, and Clarissa Giaccaglia (2016) "Introducción." In Gladys Lechini and Clarisa Giaccaglia (eds.) *Poderes emergentes y Cooperación Sur-Sur: perspectivas desde el Sur Global*. Rosario: UNR Editora. Editorial de la Universidad Nacional de Rosario.

Li, Dan, and Yunhui Wang (2010) *Decline and Rise: BRIC Construct the New World*. Beijing: Enterprise Management Press.

Li, Xing (2014) "The Nexus of 'Interdependent Hegemony' between the Existing and the Emerging World Orders." *Fudan Journal of the Humanities and Social Sciences*, 7(3): 343–362.

Li, Xing (2016) "From 'Hegemony and World Order' to 'Interdependent Hegemony and World Reorder'." In Steen F. Christensen and Li Xing (eds.) *Emerging Powers, Emerging Markets, Emerging Societies: Global Responses*. London: Palgrave Macmillan.

Li, Yang (2011) *BRICs and the Global Transformation*. Beijing: Social Sciences Academic Press.

Lin, Yueqin, and Zhou Wen (eds.) (2011) *Blue Book of Emerging Economy: Annual Report on BRICS Social-Economic Development*. Beijing: Social Sciences Academic Press.

Marr, Julian, and Cherry Reynard (2010) *Investing in Emerging Markets: The BRIC Economies and Beyond*. London: Wiley.

Mearsheimer, John (2006) "China's Unpeaceful Rise." *Current History*, 105(690): 160–162.

Mearsheimer, John (2014) "Can China Rise Peacefully?" *The National Interest*, October 25. Available at http://nationalinterest.org/commentary/can-china-rise-peacefully-10204.

Milani, Carlos R.S., Leticia Pinheiro, and Maria R.S.D. Lima (2017) "Brazil's Foreign Policy and the 'Graduation Dilemma'." *International Affairs*, 93(3): 585–605.

Nossel, Suzanne (2016) "The World's Rising Powers Have Fallen." *Foreign Policy*, July 6. Availableathttp://foreignpolicy.com/2016/07/06/brics-brazil-india-russia-china-south-africa-economics-recession/.

O'Neill, Jim (2001) "Building Better Global Economic BRICs." *Global Paper No. 66*, Goldman Sachs' Economic Research Group, London.

Paes, Lucas de Oliveira et al. (2017) "Narratives of Change and Theorizations on Continuity: The Duality of the Concept of *Emerging Power* in International Relations." *Contexto Internacional*, 39(1): 75–95.

Schweller, Randall L. (2014) "The Age of Entropy: Why the New World Order Won't Be Order." *Foreign Policy*, June 16. Available at www.foreignaffairs.com/articles/united-states/2014-06-16/age-entropy.

Strange, Susan (1988) States and Markets. California: University of California.

Stuenkel, Oliver (2015) *The BRICS and the Future of Global Order*. Reprint ed. London: Lexington Books.

Sun, Xingjie (2010) *The Road of BRIC: Brazil: Samba Dancing*. Changchun: Changchun Press.

Talley, Ian (2016) "Brics' New World Order Is Now on Hold." *The Wall Street Journal*, January 19. Available at www.wsj.com/articles/brics-new-world-order-is-now-on-hold-1453240108.

Tank, Pinar (2012) *The Concept of "Rising Powers"*. NOREF Policy Brief, June. Norwegian Peacebuilding Resource Centre and the Peace Research Institute, Oslo.

Velloso, João Paulo dos Reis (2009) *A Crise Global e o novo papel mundial dos Brics (The Global Crisis and the New Role of the BRICs)*. São Paulo: José Olympio Editora.

Velloso, João Paulo dos Reis, and Roberto Cavalcanti de Albuquerque (eds.) (2009) *Na crise global, como ser o melhor dos Brics (In Global Crisis: How to Be the Best of BRICs)*. São Paulo: Editora Campus.

Waltz, Kenneth (1993) "The Emerging Structure of International Politics." *International Security*, 18(2): 44–79.

Wang, Wenqi (2010) *The Road of BRIC: China: Peaceful Rise of the Eastern Dragon*. Changchun: Changchun Press.

Washington Post (2018) "America Has Little to Fear from a China-Centered World." January 25. Available at www.washingtonpost.com/news/theworldpost/wp/2018/01/25/china-us-relations/?utm_term=.0b3fc962bba3.

Worth, Owen (2015) *Rethinking Hegemony*. London: Palgrave Macmillan.

2 The BRICs and knowledge production in international relations

Peter Marcus Kristensen

Introduction

There is a pervasive sense in both popular and academic discourse that world politics is currently in flux: the economic and political rise of what was once known as the Third World, now more often referred to as "rising" and "emerging" world, combined with a prolonged crisis and even relative decline of Western great powers, is changing the center of gravity from the "West" to the "Rest". Based largely on projections and expectations of future power, rising powers have been the subject of considerable policy and academic debate. It can be difficult to dissect exactly who and what is emerging from a discourse that comprises investment bankers, politicians, journalists, and researchers alike. China undoubtedly gets most of the spotlight, but there is also a sense that China is only part of a broader rise of the "rest", in particular the rise of the BRICs (Brazil, Russia, India, China).

The literature on rising powers is marked by substantial disagreement about whether these powers are rising at all, and, if so, whether they will eventually be "status quo"-oriented or not: Will they aim merely to free-ride, prosper, and thus integrate into what is commonly known as the American or Western-led liberal international order, will they set out to reform and revise it from within, or will they perhaps even overturn it and construct a radically "non-Western" world order? (Gray and Murphy, 2013; Kahler, 2013; Mansfield, 2014; Stuenkel, 2015; Paul, 2016; Lipton, 2017; Stephen, 2017). The discourse on emerging powers is diverse and multifaceted, but has primarily focused on economic, political, and institutional power shifts. Amitav Acharya has therefore recently called for a change in focus from "power shifts" to "idea-shifts" or "paradigm shifts"; that is, the potential intellectual dimension of power transitions whereby new concepts, theories, and approaches to international relations are being developed by "the rest" and not only by "the west" (Acharya, 2014, 2016).

The lack of attention to this potential "idea-shift" is all the more striking considering that the literature devoted to International Relations "beyond the west" has shown that attempts are actually being made to develop alternative IR theory in emerging powers. This trend is particularly notable in China, where scholars have long debated whether and how to construct "IR with Chinese characteristics"

(Liang, 1997; Chan, 1998; Callahan, 2001; Geeraerts and Men, 2001; Song, 2001) and more recently a "Chinese school of IR" (Qin, 2007, 2012; Wang, 2007, 2009; Wang, 2013a, 2013b; Ren, 2008; Zhang, 2012; Horesh and Kavalski, 2014; Zhang and Chang, 2016; Kristensen and Nielsen, 2014, 2013; Cunningham-Cross, 2014; Wang and Buzan, 2014; Noesselt, 2015; Kim, 2016: 20). Indian scholars have also called for the development of an "Indian grammar", "indigenous theorizing" and "post-Western" IR (Behera, 2007; Mattoo, 2012; Shahi, 2013; Shahi and Ascione, 2015). Brazilian scholars have promoted the development of "Brazilian concepts", mainly the so-called "Brasília School" of "international insertion", to counter US theories (Cervo, 2008; Pinheiro, 2008; Saraiva, 2009; Jatoba, 2013; Kristensen, 2017). Finally, surveys of Russian IR also note an ongoing debate on developing a "Russian school" or "Russian theory" (Lebedeva, 2004; Tsygankov and Tsygankov, 2004, 2010; Makarychev and Morozov, 2013).

The list is far from exhaustive, but it serves to illustrate that there are numerous studies of IR in Brazil, Russia, India, and China, and of their respective discussions about IR theory. However, most are single case studies and there are no comparative studies that take all the rising BRIC countries into account. By bringing together and critically examining the secondary literature on the development of IR in the four original BRIC countries (Brazil, Russia, India, and China), this chapter aims to shed light on the possible connection between their "rise" in international politics and the evolution of their IR disciplines, particularly the development of IR theory. Before delving into these arguments, it should be emphasized that my focus will be primarily on the arguments found in this literature *about the relationship between rising power and the evolution of IR, particularly IR theorizing*. The following will therefore primarily stress the macro-level factors driving theorizing in rising powers, although by no means argue that these are the only or necessarily most important factors driving theory construction. Nevertheless, the link between (rising) power and knowledge production is made so often in the literature and in such different ways that it is worth dedicating the chapter to examining this connection alone.

The paper proceeds by examining the evolution of IR country-by-country, starting in the order of the BRICs with Brazil, Russia, India, and finally China. The analysis of each country proceeds chronologically by tracing the historical evolution of IR in each country leading up to its "rise". Finally, the conclusion draws comparative lines of differences and similarities among the four BRICs.

Brazil

Most studies of IR in Brazil tend to start its history with the establishment of the first university courses and departments of IR in the 1970s, its consolidation with the expansion of courses in the 1990s, and thus often portray IR as a new discipline in Brazil (Miyamoto, 1999, 2003; Herz, 2002: 15; Lessa, 2005a, 2006; Faria, 2012: 99; for an exception see Jatoba, 2013). IR understood as "international thought" existed outside the university system before the 1970s, of course, but was the almost exclusive province of diplomats and parts of the armed forces (Vizentini,

2005: 18). An important step in the institutionalization of Brazilian IR was the establishment of the Rio Branco Institute, the diplomatic academy under the Ministry of External Relations (known as the Itamaraty) in 1945, although it only offered IR courses to diplomats (Fonseca, 1987: 273). It is an important characteristic feature of Brazilian IR that diplomats were, until very recently, part of the academic field when it comes to work on diplomatic history and Brazilian foreign policy (Miyamoto, 1999: 90; Santos and Fonseca, 2009: 361; Daudelin, 2013: 205; Vigevani et al., 2014: 7). Overall, Itamaraty and the Rio Branco Institute's monopolization of foreign policy thinking is seen as historically inhibiting for the development of IR in Brazil (Tickner, 2003: 333, 2009: 37; Jatoba, 2013: 38).

During the military dictatorship (1964–1985), which founded its exceptionalist rule on a doctrine of national security, foreign policy thinking remained monopolized by the state. A general neglect of IR among governmental funding agencies meant that academic work on foreign policy and national security was discouraged. Many academics were either exiled or held a low profile due to the political limits to academic freedom ranging from censorship to potential loss of job and even torture (Miyamoto, 1999: 85–88). Although some note that Brazilian academia suffered only a "relative modest repression" compared to other South American countries, there was self-censorship (Giacalone, 2012: 336, 339; Tickner, 2009: 36). The connection to European and American IR theory was also limited in these years, as Brazilian IR was somewhat introverted, focusing mostly on Brazilian foreign policy. Although the conventional story is that IR was at a standstill during authoritarian rule, it is worth noting that Brazil's military dictatorship did support the establishment of new academic institutions (including in IR), social science associations, international exchange programs and the meritocratic peer review were introduced in this period (Trindade, 2005: 313, 316; Jatoba, 2013: 37). However, academia largely "absorbed" policy discourse, and there was a low degree of autonomy from the state (Fonseca in Santos and Fonseca, 2009: 360; Julião, 2012: 17). For example, the implementation commission that led to the creation of the first IR course at University of Brasília envisioned IR as a discipline serving the government's developmentalist growth model (Julião, 2012: 19).

While downplaying that it was born under the military dictatorship, most historical accounts date the discipline to the mid-1970s when it first became institutionalized in the university, specifically with an undergraduate course in IR offered at University of Brasília in 1974 and the establishment of the Institute of International Relations at PUC-Rio in 1979 (Fonseca Jr., 1987: 273; Miyamoto, 2003: 105; Lessa, 2005a: 5, 2006: 15; Santos and Fonseca, 2009: 361; Julião, 2012: 16; Jatoba, 2013: 39; Ribeiro et al., 2013: 10). In terms of international politics, this period was marked by aspirations surrounding Brazil's "economic miracle", superpower détente and Third World calls for a new international economic order. These factors, some observers stress, increased the foreign policy space for peripheral countries like Brazil and explain why IR suddenly flourished in Brazil (Lessa, 2005b: 34; Pinheiro, 2008: 4; Jatoba, 2013: 37). Interest in Brazilian foreign policy is widely seen as the main impetus for developing IR in the 1970s and several studies therefore identify Brazilian IR with the study of

Brazilian foreign policy (Fonseca, 1987: 273; Pinheiro, 2008: 4–5; Hirst in Faria, 2012: 100). The "Brazilian Way" of doing IR, as Fonseca argued, is prescriptive and policy-focused: "The 'Brazilian way' to reflect on international relations is essentially characterized by a search for an understanding of the major Brazilian foreign policy trends and decisions" (Fonseca, 1987: 274). IR, as Pinheiro puts it, serves primarily to explain the foreign policy "formulated and implemented by the government in power" (Pinheiro, 2008: 4). Theory, by contrast, is seen as a useless luxury of little value for solving practical real world problems (Tickner, 2008: 744). The theoretical and epistemological debates that characterized IR in Europe and the U.S. made little impact in Brazilian IR in its first decades when most researchers conducted historical and prescriptive studies of Brazilian diplomacy and foreign policy (Herz, 2002: 8, 16).

Most scholars argue that the real "rise" of Brazilian IR scholarship started when Brazil democratized, opened up, and started its entry into world politics in the 1990s. The gradual transition from the military dictatorship toward democracy in the late 1980s and early 1990s opened up the space for academic debate, increased transparency and access to documentation (Vigevani et al., 2014: 10). The 1990s witnessed an immense growth in IR institutions, scholars and research. According to some recent figures, there are now 126 IR programs (Jatoba, 2013: 39). The most common explanation for the immense growth in IR programs in the 1990s is that it was a product of larger transformations in the post-Cold War world and Brazil's emergence on the global scene (Miyamoto, 2003: 103; Lessa, 2005b: 40; Daudelin, 2013: 206; Jatoba, 2013: 40). Brazil's growing international "insertion" through Mercosul, regionalization and globalization led to a growing demand for IR students from the public and private sectors due (Miyamoto, 1999: 90, 2003: 105; Herz, 2002: 22; Cruz, 2005: 116; Santos and Fonseca, 2009: 356; Ventura and Lins, 2014: 109). IR also exploded during this period because the neoliberal reforms of the Fernando Henrique Cardoso government (1995–2003) deregulated higher education to make it easier for private institutions to offer undergraduate degrees (Lessa, 2005b: 42–43; Vizentini, 2005: 18; Julião, 2012: 29–30). The result was an explosion and commodification of higher education. Of more than 100 undergraduate and graduate programs in 2010, around 80% were offered by private universities (Faria, 2012: 106; Julião, 2012: 29; Ribeiro et al., 2013: 10; Ventura and Lins, 2014: 110).

While earlier generations of scholars were trained in Europe, rather than America, and not in IR theory *per se*, but rather in foreign policy studies and the "history of IR" (Lessa, 2005a: 3; Santos and Fonseca, 2009: 354; Saraiva, 2009: 33–35), it is commonly argued that IR *theory* was imported in the 1990s. During the 1990s, postmodernism, constructivism, critical theory and other Euro-American approaches gained influence in Brazil, but the majority of research focused on the history of Brazilian foreign policy (Herz, 2002). More recently, however, Brazilian scholars have started to criticize earlier theorizing for its reliance on an "American social science" (Jatoba, 2013) and for lacking autochthonous Southern perspectives (Pinheiro, 2008: 7–8). Compared to the other BRIC countries, however, the "rise" of the discipline of International Relations in Brazil is not commonly portrayed as culminating in an "indigenous theory stage". One generally does not find a similar euphoria about the "rise" to global power in the case of Brazil, especially not in the post-Lula and post-Lava Jato era. There are, however, some foreign policy researchers and scholars associated with the so-called Brasília School that do advocate for the development of indigenous Brazilian concepts to support Brazil's rise to global power (Kristensen, 2017). According to a sympathizer of the project, the development of indigenous Brazilian concepts should support the foreign policy of Brazil as an "emerging nation" and "Brazilian concepts would replace the macro-theories of (supposed) universal scope, developed by the academic thinking of the 'centers', mainly the United States". (Bernal-Meza, 2010: 201). If American IR serves the needs of the American government, the argument goes, Brazilian IR should serve the Brazilian government. As one scholar associated with the Brasília School contends, American theories "are useful to the national strategic apparatus" of the US but "function to those outside the system, especially to peripheral capitalist countries, as hegemonic accommodation theories". (Saraiva, 2009: 20). These "old and arrogant" IR theories reflecting American "desires and wants" underwent a crisis in the, 21st century, and now Brazilian, Latin American, Asian, African, and European scholars seek to build new visions and concepts for IR (Saraiva, 2009: 22–24). The Brasilia School is criticized and hardly recognized by many other Brazilian centers for IR, however, and the debate on whether to construct a national concepts or theories of IR is more subdued than in China and Russia (Kristensen, 2017).

Russia

The conventional history of IR in Russia starts in the 1940s. As the Soviet Union emerged as a victor from World War II, its diplomatic relations and global influence expanded rapidly. The government was "was interested in developing analytical expertise on different parts of the world as a background to its expanded international role in world affairs". (Lebedeva, 2004: 264). It therefore established its first research centers in the post-WWII period in order to accommodate a growing need for well-trained diplomats and researchers with expertise on different regions and languages. A Faculty of International Relations was established at Moscow State University in 1943 and became a separate institution for the training of diplomats under the Ministry of Foreign Affairs in 1944. Moreover, the Soviet Union had a system of governmental research and training institutions as well as the Russian Academy of Science under which new institutes of International Studies were established during the 1950s and 1960s (Lebedeva, 2004: 263–264; Sergounin, 2009: 225–228).

The IR research conducted was multidisciplinary, area-oriented, empirical, historical, applied and policy-oriented, not theoretical (Lebedeva, 2004: 264; Sergounin, 2009: 225–226). To the extent that it was theoretically oriented, Soviet-Marxist theories emphasizing class struggles between capitalist and socialist, bourgeois and revolutionary forces remained dominant for most of the Cold war, although they often incorporated a number of, seemingly incompatible, state-centric and realist assumptions. Overall, however, Russian IR was isolated from engagement with the bourgeois and capitalist IR theories of the West, barring some sporadic scholarly exchanges during the 1970s détente period (Lebedeva, 2004: 266, 269–270; Sergounin, 2009: 223–225; Makarychev and Morozov, 2013: 332; Mäkinen, 2017: 291). Moreover, limits on freedom of expression, closeness to the state, and the dominance of Soviet-Marxist orthodoxy meant that there was little competition of ideas (Lebedeva, 2004: 270–271).

The main political event that affected the course of IR studies was, unsurprisingly, the end of the Cold War and the collapse of the Soviet Union, which led to "fierce debate" on foreign policy (Sergounin, 2009: 223). Domestically, Gorbachev's reforms, which eventually led to the fall of the Soviet Union and end of the Cold War, also had the effect of gradually liberalizing academia. Russia also experienced an increasing demand for IR expertise after the collapse of the Soviet Union and throughout the 1990s existing universities expanded their IR programs and a number of new programs were established (Lebedeva, 2004: 271; Sergounin, 2009: 226–227). There was a rapid increase in international interactions and exchange with foreign scholars from the late 1980s and early 1990s onwards (Lebedeva, 2004: 271). Paradoxically, instead of producing more academic and theoretical IR, the end of the Cold War led to a migration of scholars either to other countries or into think tanks, media, and policy. As a result, this period was actually marked by a scarcity of researchers and teachers (Sergunin, 2004: 20; Sergounin, 2009: 225–226).

In terms of theory, Russian IR experienced a "very quick and dramatic transformation" (Sergounin, 2009: 237). The demise of Soviet and Marxist approaches created a "theoretical vacuum" that facilitated the introduction of Western IR theories such as liberalism, realism, constructivism, and post-structuralism (Lebedeva, 2004: 271–278; Sergunin, 2004: 19; Tsygankov and Tsygankov, 2004: 8; Sergounin, 2009: 225, 230–236; Tsygankov and Tsygankov, 2010: 670–672). American foundations were also involved in this process (Sergounin, 2009: 226; Tsygankov and Tsygankov, 2010: 672). More recent surveys indicate a move away from "familiarizing" with Western theories and a growing sense that the time is "ripe" for the construction of indigenous theories (or even outright isolationism), even if they co-exist with "Westernization" (Lebedeva, 2004: 278; Tsygankov and Tsygankov, 2004: 10–11, 2010: 10; Makarychev and Morozov, 2013: 333). In Russian IR, one also finds arguments that IR is Western-centric, that it reflects the biases of Western, particularly American, civilization, and that it is nothing but a more or less sophisticated tool to produce, secure, defend, and propagandize Western hegemony (Tsygankov and Tsygankov, 2004: 2–3; Schouten and Dugin, 2014). Despite the Soviet and Russian penchant for national schools of science, Lebedeva argued in, 2004 that there was still no Russian school of IR (Lebedeva, 2004: 269).

This situation has arguably been changing over the past decade as Russian geopolitics, and "neo-Eurasianism" in particular, has risen in prominence. Geopolitical and spatial thinking has to some extent filled the worldview vacuum after the decline of Soviet orthodoxy, although it is important to stress that it comes in more than a neo-Eurasianist version (Mäkinen, 2017). Russian geopolitics is arguably the closest to a distinctly Russian school of IR today. As a prominent advocate of Eurasianism puts it, "To think spatially means to think 'Russian-ly'" (Schouten and Dugin, 2014). The neo-Eurasianist version of geopolitics has an anti-liberal, exceptionalist, and even expansionist bent. In an almost Huntingtonian manner, it stresses the civilizational and geographical exceptionalism of Russia, as a bridge between East and West, and as a pivotal civilizational balancing force (Lebedeva, 2004: 275; Sergounin, 2009: 231–233; Mäkinen, 2017).

However, this theoretical discourse is rarely coupled to an argument that it is Russia's *rise* that drives the construction of a Russian school of IR. Here it is important to note that Russia and Russian IR is clearly in a different category than the other BRICs. It "rose" during the Cold War and has long been a global power. In fact, the historical moment that bears some resemblance to the rise of the other BRICs is the trajectory of IR studies in the Soviet Union in the post-WWII era. As the Soviet Union rose to global power, it experienced a similar development in which growing diplomatic and multilateral engagement and an "expanded international role" spurred more research on various regions and global issues (Lebedeva, 2004: 263–264). But today there are few scholars who view Russian IR in the context of the country's geopolitical "rise" (although its political assertiveness is another issue). Indeed, Russia is arguably declining rather than rising at this point in history and it could actually be argued that it is fears of Russia's pending decline from great power status, not its rise, that has driven the assertive and anti-liberal geopolitics discourse.

India

Most studies of IR in India note its short history, starting "at best" from 1940 but only taking off after independence in 1947 (Appadorai, 1987: 134–135). The reason is that the British colonial power, in charge of India's foreign relations, had limited the intellectual space for thinking about foreign policy, foreign relations, and India's role in the world (Bajpai, 1997: 35). The postcolonial period therefore constitutes the major break in the history of Indian IR. As an independent country, India's relations to other countries changed dramatically and there was a dire need for "insight into the real nature of the world community" (Appadorai, 1987: 135). The field, which is usually called *International Studies*, therefore got off to "a promising start" and enjoyed a "favorable climate" in the 1950s (Mattoo, 2009: 38; Sahadevan, 2009: 1; Sahni, 2009: 51).

In postcolonial India, Jawaharlal Nehru loomed large in IR thinking, almost monopolizing it. Nehru stressed the importance of knowing the world beyond India's borders as well as the importance of training Indian experts in international affairs that could inform the foreign policymaking of the newly independent country (Biswas, 2007: 305). The legacy of Jawaharlal Nehru on Indian IR is contested, however. On the one hand, Nehru gave birth to the IR discipline in India and was instrumental in establishing the Indian Council of World Affairs and the Indian School of International Studies (today the School of International Studies at Jawaharlal Nehru University) to support the newly independent country's non-aligned foreign policy (Rajan, 1997: 2; Alagappa, 2009b: 9–10; Mallavarapu, 2009: 168; Mattoo, 2009: 38; Mohan, 2009: 153; Paul, 2009: 132). On the other hand, critics argue, Nehru's dominance stifled Indian IR thinking because most of the research conducted within these new institutions was devoted to area studies, not to grand theoretical thinking which remained monopolized by Nehru who was largely unresponsive to academia (Dixit, 1997: 55; Alagappa, 2009b: 11; Paul, 2009: 132). Non-alignment was the "master narrative" until the 1970s (Alagappa, 2011: 217–218) and critics argue that IR scholars became conformist and "good as cheer leaders for their preferred political leaders, but not as generators of new ideas or new stratagems for the conduct of foreign policy". (Mohan, 2009: 153). Non-alignment has been likened to a Kuhnian paradigm under which a lot of normal science, but less creative and revolutionary work, was carried out (Bajpai, 1997: 36). Not only was non-alignment the dominant "paradigm" but other theoretical paradigms, especially American ones, were also excluded (Paul, 2009: 132–133; Alagappa, 2011: 217–218).

In terms of international connectivity, Indian IR actually started out with more extensive interaction with Euro-American IR scholars and institutions in the 1940s and 1950s (Rajan, 1994: 208, 2005: 199; Bajpai, 2009: 111; Mohan, 2009: 152). However, the influence of Western IR began to dissolve in the 1960s as Nehruvian India non-aligned itself and sought to reduce outside interference, and this gradual process continued under Indira Gandhi's Emergency and Third Worldist foreign policy (Bajpai, 2009: 110; Mohan, 2009: 152; Paul, 2009: 132–133). While the idea was to produce non-aligned knowledge, observers have subsequently characterized this period as stifling to intellectual progress (Bajpai and Mallavarapu, 2005; Alagappa, 2009b: 11; Mohan, 2009: 157; Paul, 2009: 132). This isolation gradually dissolved during the 1990s with the neoliberal reforms and the process of opening up. Like in both Brazil and Russia, India also witnessed an immense institutional expansion in the post-Cold War era (Rajan, 2005: 195, 200). Although Indian IR remains centered on the massive School of International Studies at JNU, one estimate is that "International Studies" courses, broadly defined, are taught at more than 150 Indian universities, although there are fewer degree-granting institutions (Alagappa, 2009b: 10).

In terms of IR theory, despite "opening up" to the West, Indian IR scholars never imported the "American Social Science". American foundations, exchange, and translation programs never entered to the same extent as in other BRICs. There has also long been a fundamental dissatisfaction with the reliance on Western theoretical frameworks and the lack of indigenous theories in India (Rajan, 1997, 1994; Harshe, 1997; Paul, 2009). This resistance is mounting in a period when India is increasingly seen as an emerging power in world politics but much less so in IR (Alagappa, 2009b; Mattoo, 2009). For example, the 2014 Teaching, Research and International Policy (TRIP) survey found that a staggering 85% of Indian IR scholars agree or strongly agree that IR is a Western dominated discipline (compared to a global average of 77%) and that 86% also believe that it is important to counter Western dominance in IR (global average: 62%). Moves toward constructing "indigenous theories" rather than mimicking the West are also growing, with some scholars calling for the development of an “Indian grammar” or “indigenous theorizing” (Behera, 2007; Mattoo, 2012; Shahi, 2013; Shahi and Ascione, 2015). Scholars have argued that India as a rising power *should* also be a leading center of knowledge production and that Indian academics *should* meet the needs of a modernizing and rising power (Alagappa, 2009a: 4–6). A scholar like T.V. Paul, for example, argues that the lack of an IR theoretical discourse that can help India develop its grand strategic vision might end up constituting a potential impediment to the rise of India:

> The neglect of IR, especially IR theory, in India has generated serious problems as India’s power and position at the global level grows and it is called upon to make substantive decisions at the global level . . . a country with India’s stature in the international system could be adversely affected if it does not develop a proper “grand strategy” based on theoretical foundations to face different challenges. A country, especially a rising power, without a grand strategy is somewhat like a multinational corporation without a business plan.
> (Paul, 2009: 137)

As India rises, Indian policymakers should understand causes and effects so that they can pursue active rather than reactive policies.

Some expect it to be simply a matter of time; the increasing status and influence of countries rising in the wake of China will also be conducive to innovative IR theorizing. One Indian scholar sees its rise in world politics as gradually opening up a space for redefining the world, not only in terms of strategy and policy, but also in terms of IR theorizing: “The rise of India as an emerging power in the post-recession world grants it a significant position in theoretically defining as well as strategically designing the evolving form of multilateralism, thereby indicating the uplifting status of IR theorizing in India”. (Shahi, 2013: 56). Overall, however, there is still much disappointment with the state of Indian IR in the literature, especially compared to China, and less of a sense that it has entered a stage of theory construction. Instead, several scholars have asked why India is rising politically and economically, but not intellectually? (Alagappa, 2009a: 3; Mattoo, 2009: 37; Paul, 2009: 129; Shahi, 2013: 50).

China

In China, IR was also born in an intimate relationship to the state. The discipline was institutionalized already during the 1950s with the Department of Diplomatic Studies at Renmin University (later Foreign Affairs College). However, the origins of IR studies is often traced specifically to Premier Zhou Enlai’s (Mao-endorsed) proposal to strengthen institutions for training diplomats in 1963–4 (Shambaugh, 2011: 341), specifically a December 1963 directive issued by the Central Committee of the Chinese Communist Party “Decision on Strengthening the Research on Foreign Affairs in China”, which called for strengthening research on international relations. Subsequently, the Department of Politics at Peking, Fudan, and Renmin

Universities were renamed Department of International Politics – a process personally supported by Zhou Enlai and former Foreign Minister Chen Yi. The establishment of these three first departments was intended to provide area and language expertise as well as diplomatic training to meet the needs of the newly established People's Republic (Geeraerts and Men, 2001: 253; Shambaugh, 2011: 341). In terms of the wider (geo)political context, some observers have argued that the political condition of Sino-Soviet split in the early 1960s increased the interest in IR and contributed to its institutionalization (Song, 1997: 40, 2001: 62; Geeraerts and Men, 2001: 253)

Domestically, however, the Maoist period was dominated by Maoist-Marxist orthodoxy and is seen as a pre-theoretical "starting-Marxism" phase, during which "theory" (in scare-quotes) served ideological policy needs and sometimes more pragmatic ends (Song, 1997; Geeraerts and Men, 2001; Qin, 2007: 318; Wang, 2009: 104). IR was a "policy science", and theories were produced by political leaders and analyzed by academics (Zhang, 2002: 102–103). The major political event that affected the trajectory of the field was the Cultural Revolution, which resulted in the repression and dismantling of the field, thus leaving what almost amounted to a tabula rasa for the coming generations (Song, 1997: 40; Shambaugh, 2011: 341). Deng Xiaoping's "Reform and Opening Up" policy initiated a break from ideological research and Chinese scholars started importing and learning IR theory from the West. Numerous Chinese scholars were trained in the United States, and American theories started traveling to China with aid from American foundations (Zhang, 2003: 99–103). During what is called the "theory catching up", Westernization or "learning-copying" stage, American theories like realism, liberalism, and constructivism were imported to China, with the aid of American foundations, and for a while structured debates among Chinese IR scholars (Qin, 2007: 316, 2009: 188; Ren, 2008: 296; Wang, 2009: 105–106).

With the rise of China in the 2000s, IR has become a *xianxue* (hot discipline) at Chinese universities. Before the 1980s, only three universities offered IR courses, but, by the late 1990s, more than 100 institutions and 60 IR departments had been established (Song, 1997: 57; Wang, 2002: 72, 2009: 107). It now boasts one of the world's largest IR communities in terms of students, faculties and research centers, second only to the United States (Zhang, 2002: 101; Qin, 2007: 316; Wang, 2009: 107). In terms of theory, the rise of China, a common argument goes, means that Chinese IR has arrived at the "theory construction", "theory creation" or "Chinese school" stage (Qin, 2007: 321). In the most deterministic versions of the argument, it is not posed as a question about *whether* but *when* China's rising power will led to the construction of its own IR theory, simply due to its growing global footprint. Rising powers have expanding global interests and economic, political, and diplomatic interactions with different parts of world, and these developments encourage more IR theorizing. Qin Yaqing, the main proponent of a Chinese School, argues, "Since the beginning of the twenty-first century, China has dramatically increased its interaction with the rest of the world which has encouraged the development and promotion of a Chinese school of IRT". (Qin, 2009: 195, 2011b: 250). Elsewhere, Qin contends that China's rise will "inevitably" lead to a Chinese School of IR theory: "The emergence of the Chinese School is not only possible but is also inevitable. China is experiencing rapid development, huge social transformations, and deep conceptual change. These changes can lead China to address the problem of its integration with international society, and the process of negotiating its relationship with the world will inevitably lead to the emergence of the Chinese School of IR theory". (Qin, 2012: 50). The logic, to put it differently, is that rising powers with expanding global engagements need to re-negotiate their role in the world and need their own IR theory for that purpose.

China is clearly the BRIC country where this type of argument is most prevalent. This leads Zhang to ask, "Will the rise of China as a great power afford Chinese scholars greater influence in the theorization of world politics? How much will that erode the predominant position of Western IR theory in the discipline?" (Zhang, 2002: 106). Similarly, Wang asks whether "China's rise bring the rise of Chinese IR theory?" and goes on to answer it by arguing that "non-western schools, including a Chinese School, will come into being along with the rise of countries like the BRICs" (Wang, 2009: 115). In one of the most counter-hegemonic calls for a Chinese School, Wang argues that the rise of former colonies and developing countries will result in "censuring" of the status-quo Western IR and the construction of revolutionary indigenous IR theories:

> Once these undeveloped countries rise, their wills should be expressed in the international system, making it possible to deconstruct the western system. This will be the real revolution of international relations. This is the theoretical and temporal background for censuring western IRT and approaching the possibility of a future *Chinese School.*
>
> (Wang, 2007: 194)

The argument that China as a rising power needs theory takes various forms, but often centers on the needs of the state. Ren Xiao, a proponent of a Chinese School, directly advocates a theory serving the needs of China's rising power: "By and large there is a consensus that such a 'Chinese-style exploration' has to be based upon the significant issues that are facing China as a rising power in the world, and to seek solutions through Chinese independent research". (Ren, 2008: 306). The Coxian maxim that "theory is always for someone and for some purpose" is commonly invoked (Qin, 2007: 328, 2011a: 474). The logic is clear, according to Qin Yaqing: if the theory is always for someone and for a specific purpose, particularly the United States and the preservation of American hegemony, then China must develop its own "big idea" serving the national purposes of a rising power. This deployment of Cox's maxim means that existing theories must necessarily support the interests of status-quo countries and therefore cannot serve China's purposes as a rising power. Even the leading *opponent* of the label "Chinese School", Yan Xuetong, who is nonetheless working on theorizing ancient Chinese philosophy in IR, argues that "If we can rediscover more interstate political ideas of ancient Chinese philosophers and use them to enrich contemporary international relations theory, this will provide the guideline for a strategy for China's rise". (Yan, 2011: 106).

The Chinese School was initially centered on the problematique of the "Peaceful Rise of China". Chinese scholars tried to articulate alternative visions of world order, peace and change to counter the dire predictions about rising powers that dominate the Western discipline of International Relations. Critical observers also read theorizations of China's traditional philosophy as directly motivated by a rising China's need to create a Pax Sinica as a new hegemonic vision for the world after Pax Americana. William Callahan, for example, argues that material power is not sufficient; according to Callahan, "World leadership demands an ideology to order the globe symbolically", and he reads Chinese IR theorizing through this lens, specifically the notion of "Tianxia" (All-Under-Heaven) as resonating with the Chinese government's "Harmonious World" policy (Callahan, 2008). In this line of argument, it is unsurprising or even expected that a rising power such as China will try to develop a theory about a peaceful ascent to power and try to formulate a *Pax Sinica*. Theorizing becomes intrinsically related to foreign policy needs. With China's more assertive foreign policy under Xi Jinping, however, there has been a gradual shift also in IR from the reassuring and defensive *Peaceful Rise* toward theorizations of Chinese global leadership and the *China Dream* (Yan, 2014, 2016; Callahan, 2015; Chen et al., 2018).

Conclusion

This chapter set out to examine how the IR disciplines in the BRICs countries have responded to their so-called "rise". In reviewing the existing literature on IR in the four original BRICs, the chapter identifies a clear expansion of research and teaching. The literature shows that rising powers generally have experienced improved material *conditions* for theorizing because the growth of the BRIC economies has led to increased funding and expansion of their research and higher education sectors. Some of this funding is allocated to IR and, therefore, all four countries have experienced an immense growth in the number of IR scholars, institutions, and journals, and in funding and international travel since the 1990s. This institutional growth has been accompanied by an increase in the volume and theoretical sophistication of the scholarship produced.

In a comparative perspective, Alagappa argues that the

> continued rise of Asian powers is likely to sustain and further energize interest in IRS in Asia and the West. The net effect of this trend would be to enrich existing concepts, theories, and paradigms, provide fresh perspectives and new impetus for the study of IR, and diversify sources of growth making the discipline more international.
>
> (Alagappa, 2011: 197)

Moreover, the growth in material funding has supported theorizing through international travel and connectivity. As commonly narrated, the history of IR in all four countries began with an initially multidisciplinary field consisting of scholars trained in different disciplines, but with a common focus on foreign areas and foreign policy. It was only during the 1990s that IR theory became more central in the discipline when a "new" generation of scholars started traveling abroad to conferences and for research stays and training, and returned home with IR theory (Herz, 2002; Bajpai and Mallavarapu, 2005; Lessa, 2005b; Qin, 2007, 2009, 2011b; Mallavarapu, 2009; Jatoba, 2013; Makarychev and Morozov, 2013). In histories of the discipline, the import and application of Western IR theories from the 1990s onwards is seen as consolidating the field and eventually leading to contemporary theory construction efforts.

This institutional expansion and international "opening up" has been accompanied by a general trend toward debating theory construction rather than only consuming theory. In that sense, rising powers do seem to claim to be studying the world theoretically. While the externalist story of rising powers tending to theorize about world politics may identify a very general common denominator, it also paints a very crude and simplistic picture. While all countries provide examples of the move against IR as an "American social science" that serves American foreign policy and unipolar/hegemonic maintenance, not all scholars use it in support of a more nationalist move to create a national school of IR. These debates are not always couched in terms of national "theories" or "schools"; they are also portrayed as indigenous concepts or as post-Western theorization. The argument for national schools is made most forcefully by scholars associated with the "Chinese School" and the "Brasília School".

By tracing the narrative of IR's evolution in each case, we find that the trend toward theory construction is often seen as connected to their political and economic "rise". It is a common story that the IR discipline was launched by an exogenous political shock that catalyzed their geopolitical rise and launched the country's IR community on a trajectory toward increasing theoretical sophistication (post-Mao in China and post-Cold War in Russia, India, and Brazil). But in the way the history of the IR discipline is narrated, scholars in rising powers are turning to theorizing not only as a product of their material "rise", but also due to an inherent logic of maturation in the historical evolution of the IR discipline in each country. The specific disciplinary trajectories of the BRIC countries exhibit more diversity than uniformity. The history of IR in China, and partly Russia, is conventionally told as a narrative running through consecutive stages of isolation, opening up, learning, applying, and culminating in theory construction. Meanwhile, IR in India and Brazil is commonly portrayed as having more extensive contacts with Western IR earlier on and their "rise" not as culminating in theory production. In that sense, the countries' "rise" figures only as a background condition, albeit one that opened the local IR disciplines to global-Western scholarship, in most cases allowing more freedom of research and more resources, even though the former is being rolled back in some cases. In all four BRICs, IR was first born in an intimate relationship to the state and IR communities have actually been gradually distancing themselves from the policy community. The first IR programs were established in their capital cities with the purpose of training skilled labor for the country's growing international role. Compared to the early years, IR scholars in all the BRICs arguably enjoy *more* autonomy and distance from power today, despite the rising demand for expertise.

Overall, their geopolitical "rise" seems to provide a meta-narrative for the development of IR in rising powers, but it does so only at the most generic macro-political and externalist level. It over-simplifies in that the "rising powers" examined here differ immensely. The conversation about "indigenous theory" is not the same in Brazil, Russia, India, and China, and even the meaning of the term may vary. We do not even see a uniform movement *within* each country, but rather internal debate and a variety of different moves in these debates. Not all IR in China, India or Brazil is anti-hegemonic and that not all scholars in the BRICs set out to reject or overturn Western IR theories. There are debates and disagreements, even in China, where the construction of a "Chinese School" has been a theoretical *leitmotif* for many. Yet, at a general level, the very fact that rising powers are engaged in debate about indigenous IR theorizing and how to theorize world politics at all may be the similarity that unites them (cf. Miller, 2016).

Bibliography

Acharya, Amitav (2014) "Power Shift or Paradigm Shift? China's Rise and Asia's Emerging Security Order." *International Studies Quarterly*, 58(1): 158–173.

Acharya, Amitav (2016) "'Idea-Shift': How Ideas from the Rest Are Reshaping Global Order." *Third World Quarterly*, 37(7): 1156–1170.

Alagappa, Muthiah (2009a) "Guest Editor's Note." *International Studies*, 46(1–2): 3–6.

Alagappa, Muthiah (2009b) "Strengthening International Studies in India: Vision and Recommendations." *International Studies*, 46(1–2): 7–35.

Alagappa, Muthiah (2011) "International Relations Studies in Asia: Distinctive Trajectories." *International Relations of the Asia-Pacific*, 11(2): 193–230.

Appadorai, A. (1987) "International and Area Studies in India." *International Studies*, 24(2): 133–143.

Bajpai, Kanti (1997) "International Studies in India: Bringing Theory (Back) Home." In M.S. Rajan (eds.) *International and Area Studies in India*. New Delhi: Lancers Books.

Bajpai, Kanti (2009) "Obstacles to Good Work in Indian International Relations." *International Studies*, 46(1–2): 109–128.

Bajpai, Kanti, and Siddharth Mallavarapu (2005) *International Relations in India: Bringing Theory Back Home*. New Delhi: Orient Blackswan.

Behera, Navnita Chadha (2007) "Re-Imagining IR in India." *International Relations of the Asia-Pacific*, 7(3): 341–368.

Bernal-Meza, Raúl (2010) "International Thought in the Lula Era." *Revista Brasileira de Política Internacional*, 53(Special Issue): 193–213.

Biswas, Aparajita (2007) "African Studies in India." In P.T. Zeleza (ed.) *The Study of Africa: Global and Transnational Engagements*. Oxford: African Books Collective.

Callahan, William (2001) "China and the Globalisation of IR Theory: Discussion of 'Building International Relations Theory with Chinese Characteristics'." *Journal of Contemporary China*, 10(26): 75–88.

Callahan, William (2008) "Chinese Visions of World Order." *International Studies Review*, 10(4): 749–761.

Callahan, William (2015) "Identity and Security in China: The Negative Soft Power of the China Dream." *Politics*, 35(3–4): 216–229.

Cervo, Amado (2008) "Conceitos Em Relações Internacionais." *Revista Brasileira de Política, Internacional*, 51(2): 8–25.

Chan, Gerald (1998) "Toward an International Relations Theory with Chinese Characteristics?" *Issues & Studies*, 34(6): 1–28.

Chen, Zhimin, Guorong Zhou, and Shichen Wang (2018) "Facilitative Leadership and China's New Role in the World." *Chinese Political Science Review*, 3(1): 10–27.

Cruz, Jose da (2005) "Brazil's International Relations at the Dawn of the Twenty-First Century." *Latin American Politics & Society*, 47(1): 115–122.

Cunningham-Cross, Linsay (2014) "Narrating a Discipline: The Search for Innovation in Chinese International Relations." In Nicola Horsburgh, Astrid Nordin, and Shaun Breslin (eds.) *Chinese Politics and International Relations: Innovation and Invention*. London: Routledge.

Daudelin, Jean (2013) "Coming of Age?: Recent Scholarship on Brazilian Foreign Policy." *Latin American Research Review*, 48(2): 204–217.

Dixit, J.N. (1997) "Inadequacies in the Study of International Relations and Area Specialization in India's Policy and Relations." In M.S. Rajan (eds.) *International and Area Studies in India*. New Delhi: Lancers Books.

Faria, Carlos Aurélio Pimenta de (2012) "Teaching and Research on Foreign Policy in the Field of International Relations in Brazil." *Austral*, 1(2): 95–128.

Fonseca, Gelson, Jr. (1987) "Studies on International Relations in Brazil." *Millennium*, 16(2): 273–280.

Geeraerts, Gustaaf, and Jing Men (2001) "International Relations Theory in China." *Global Society*, 15(3): 251–276.

Giacalone, Rita (2012) "Latin American Foreign Policy Analysis: External Influences and Internal Circumstances." *Foreign Policy Analysis*, 8(4): 335–354.

Gray, Kevin, and Craig N. Murphy (2013) "Introduction: Rising Powers and the Future of Global Governance." *Third World Quarterly*, 34(2): 183–193.

Harshe, Rajan (1997) "The Status of International Relations Studies: An Agenda for the Future." In M.S. Rajan (ed.) *International and Area Studies in India*. New Delhi: Lancers Books.

Herz, Mônica (2002) "O Crescimento Da Área de Relações Internacionais No Brasil." *Contexto Internacional*, 24(1): 7–40.

Horesh, Niv, and Emilian Kavalski (2014) *Asian Thought on China's Changing International Relations*. London: Palgrave Macmillan.

Jatoba, Daniel (2013) "Los Desarrollos Académicos de Las Relaciones Internacionales En Brasil: Elementos Sociológicos, Institucionales y Epistemológicos." *Relaciones Internacionales*, 22: 27–46.

Julião, Taís Sandrim (2012) "A Graduação Em Relações Internacionais No Brasil." *Revista Monções*, 1(1): 13–48.

Kahler, Miles (2013) "Rising Powers and Global Governance: Negotiating Change in a Resilient Status Quo." *International Affairs*, 89(3): 711–729.

Kim, Hun Joon (2016) "Will IR Theory with Chinese Characteristics Be a Powerful Alternative?" *The Chinese Journal of International Politics*, 9(1): 1–26.

Kristensen, Peter Marcus (2017) "Southern Sensibilities: Advancing Third Wave Sociology of International Relations in the Case of Brazil." *Journal of International Relations and Development*, onlinefirst, 1–27.

Kristensen, Peter Marcus, and Ras Tind Nielsen (2013) "Constructing a Chinese International Relations Theory." *International Political Sociology*, 7(1): 19–40.

Kristensen, Peter Marcus, and Ras Tind Nielsen (2014) "You Need to Do Something That the Westerners Cannot Understand': The Innovation of a Chinese School of IR." In Nicola Horsburgh, Astrid Nordin, and Shaun Breslin (eds.) *Chinese Politics and International Relations: Innovation and Invention*. London: Routledge.

Lebedeva, Marina (2004) "International Relations Studies in the USSR/Russia: Is There a Russian National School of IR Studies?" *Global Society*, 18(3): 263–278.

Lessa, Antônio Carlos (2005a) "Instituições, Atores e Dinâmicas Do Ensino e Da Pesquisa Em Relações Internacionais No Brasil." *Revista Brasileira de Política Internacional*, 48(2): 169–184.

Lessa, Antônio Carlos (2005b) "O Ensino de Relações Internacionais No Brasil." In Amado Luiz Cervo and José Flávio Sombra Saraiva (eds.) *O Crescimento Das Relações Internacionais No Brasil*. Brasília: Instituto Brasileiro de Relçacões Internacionais.

Lessa, Antônio Carlos (2006) "A Evolução Recente Dos Estudos e Dos Programas de Pós-Graduação Em Relações Internacionais No Brasil." *Meridiano*, 47, 7(68): 14–16.

Liang, Shoude (1997) "Constructing an International Relations Theory with Chinese Characteristics." *Political Science*, 49(1): 23–39.

Lipton, Merle (2017) "Are the BRICS Reformers, Revolutionaries, or Counter-Revolutionaries?" *South African Journal of International Affairs*, 24(1): 41–59.

Makarychev, Andrey, and Viatcheslav Morozov (2013) "Is 'Non-Western Theory' Possible? The Idea of Multipolarity and the Trap of Epistemological Relativism in Russian IR." *International Studies Review*, 15(3): 328–350.

Mäkinen, Sirke (2017) Professional Geopolitics as an Ideal: Roles of Geopolitics in Russia. *International Studies Perspectives*, 18(3): 288–303.

Mallavarapu, Siddharth (2009) "Development of International Relations Theory in India: Traditions, Contemporary Perspectives and Trajectories." *International Studies*, 46(1–2): 165–183.

Mansfield, Edward (2014) "Rising Powers in the Global Economy: Issues and Questions." *International Studies Review*, 16(3): 437–442.

Mattoo, Amitabh (2009) "The State of International Studies in India." *International Studies*, 46(1–2): 37–48.

Mattoo, Amitabh (2012) "An Indian Grammar for International Studies." *The Hindu*. December 11. Available at www.thehindu.com/opinion/op-ed/An-Indian-grammar-for-International-Studies/article12442433.ece. (Accessed August 31, 2018).

Miller, Manjari Chatterjee (2016) "The Role of Beliefs in Identifying Rising Powers." *The Chinese Journal of International Politics*, 9(2): 211–238.

Miyamoto, Shiguenoli (1999) "O Estudo das Relações Internacionais no Brasil." *Revista de Sociologia e Política*, 12: 83–98.

Miyamoto, Shiguenoli (2003) "O Ensino Das Relações Internacionais No Brasil." *Revista de Sociologia e Política*, 20: 103–114.

Mohan, C. Raja (2009) "The Re-Making of Indian Foreign Policy: Ending the Marginalization of International Relations Community." *International Studies*, 46(1–2): 147–163.

Noesselt, Nele (2015) "Revisiting the Debate on Constructing a Theory of International Relations with Chinese Characteristics." *The China Quarterly*, 222: 430–448.

Paul, T.V. (2009) "Integrating International Relations Studies in India to Global Scholarship." *International Studies*, 46(1–2): 129–145.

Paul, T.V. (ed.) (2016) *Accommodating Rising Powers: Past, Present, and Future*. Cambridge: Cambridge University Press.

Pinheiro, Leticia (2008) "International Relations Studies in Brazil: Epistemological and Institutional Characteristics." Paper presented at the IPSA Conference, Concordia University, Montreal, Canada, April 30–May 2.

Qin, Yaqing (2007) "Why Is There No Chinese International Relations Theory?" *International Relations of the Asia-Pacific*, 7(3): 313–340.
Qin, Yaqing (2009) "Development of International Relations Theory in China." *International Studies*, 46(1–2): 185–201.
Qin, Yaqing (2011a) "Development of International Relations Theory in China: Progress and Problems." In Yizhou Wang (ed.) *Transformation of Foreign Affairs and International Relations in China, 1978–2008*. Leiden: Brill ebooks.
Qin, Yaqing (2011b) "Development of International Relations Theory in China: Progress through Debates." *International Relations of the Asia-Pacific*, 11(2): 231–257.
Qin, Yaqing (2012) "The Possibility and Inevitability of a Chinese School of International Relations Theory." In William A. Callahan and Elena Barabantseva (eds.) *China Orders the World: Normative Soft Power and Foreign Policy*. Baltimore: Johns Hopkins University Press.
Rajan, M.S. (1994) "International and Area Studies in India." *International Studies*, 31(2): 207–214.
Rajan, M.S. (1997) *International and Area Studies in India*. New Delhi: Lancers Books.
Rajan, M.S. (2005) "Golden Jubilee of the School of International Studies: An Assessment." *International Studies*, 42(3–4): 195–204.
Ren, Xiao (2008) "Toward a Chinese School of International Relations." In Gungwu Wang and Yongnian Zheng (eds.) *China and the New International Order*. London and New York: Routledge.
Ribeiro, Pedro Feliú, Mariana Kato, and Gary Rainer (2013) "Mercado de Trabalho e Relações Internacionais No Brasil." *Meridiano*, 47, 14(135): 10–18.
Sahadevan, P. (2009) "Editor-in-Chief's Note." *International Studies*, 46(1–2): 1–1.
Sahni, Varun (2009) "The Fallacies and Flaws of Area Studies in India." *International Studies*, 46(1–2): 49–68.
Santos, Norma Breda dos, and Fúlvio Eduardo Fonseca (2009) "A Pós-Graduação Em Relações Internacionais No Brasil." *Contexto Internacional*, 31(2): 353–380.
Saraiva, José Flávio Sombra (ed.) (2009) *Concepts, Histories and Theories of International Relations for the 21th Century*. Brasilia: IBRI.
Schouten, Peer, and Alexander Dugin (2014) "Theory Talk #66: Alexander Dugin." Available at www.theory-talks.org/2014/12/theory-talk-66.html. (Accessed August 31, 2018).
Sergounin, Alexander (2009) "Russia: IR at a Crossroads." In Arlene Tickner and Ole Wæver (eds.) *International Relations Scholarship around the World*. London and New York: Routledge.
Sergunin, Andrei (2004) "Discussions of International Relations in Post-Communism Russia." *Communist and Post-Communist Studies*, 37(1): 19–35.
Shahi, Deepshikha (2013) "Indian Scholarship on International Relations and Multilateralism." *Economic and Political Weekly*, 48(5): 50–58.
Shahi, Deepshikha, and Gennaro Ascione (2015) "Rethinking the Absence of Post-Western International Relations Theory in India." *European Journal of International Relations*, 22(2): 313–334.
Shambaugh, David (2011) "International Relations Studies in China: History, Trends, and Prospects." *International Relations of the Asia-Pacific*, 11(3): 339–372.
Song, Xinning (1997) "International Relations Theory-Building in China." *Political Science*, 49(1): 40–61.
Song, Xinning (2001) "Building International Relations Theory with Chinese Characteristics." *Journal of Contemporary China*, 10(26): 61–74.

Stephen, Matthew (2017) "Emerging Powers and Emerging Trends in Global Governance." *Global Governance*, 23(3): 483–502.

Stuenkel, Oliver (2015) *The BRICS and the Future of Global Order*. Lanham: Lexington Books.

Tickner, Arlene (2003) "Hearing Latin American Voices in International Relations Studies." *International Studies Perspectives*, 4(4): 325–350.

Tickner, Arlene (2008) "Latin American IR and the Primacy of Lo Practico." *International Studies Review*, 10(4): 735–748.

Tickner, Arlene (2009) "Latin America: Still Policy Dependent after All These Years?" In Arlene Tickner and Ole Wæver (eds.) *International Relations Scholarship around the World*. London and New York: Routledge.

Trindade, Hélgio (2005) "Social Sciences in Brazil in Perspective: Foundation, Consolidation and Diversification." *Social Science Information*, 44(2–3): 283–357.

Tsygankov, Andrei, and Pavel Tsygankov (2004) "New Directions in Russian International Studies: Pluralization, Westernization, and Isolationism." *Communist and Post-Communist Studies*, 37(1): 1–17.

Tsygankov, Andrei, and Pavel Tsygankov (2010) "National Ideology and IR Theory: Three Incarnations of the 'Russian Idea'." *European Journal of International Relations*, 16(4): 569–601.

Ventura, Deisy de Freitas Lima, and Maria Antonieta del Tedesco Lins (2014) "Educação Superior e Complexidade: Integração Entre Disciplinas No Campo Das Relações Internacionais." *Cadernos de Pesquisa*, 44(151): 104–131.

Vigevani, Tullo, Laís Forti Thomáz, and Lucas Batista Leite (2014) "As Relações Internacionais No Brasil: Notas Sobre o Início de Sua Institucionalização." *Interrelações*, 14(40): 5–11.

Vizentini, Paulo (2005) "A Evolução Da Produção Intelectual e Dos Estudos Acadêmicos de Relações Internacionais No Brasil." In Amado Cervo and José Flávio Sombra Saraiva (eds.) *O Crescimento Das Relações Internacionais No Brasil*. Brasília: IBRI.

Wang, Hung-Jen (2013a) "Being Uniquely Universal: Building Chinese International Relations Theory." *Journal of Contemporary China*, 22(81): 518–534.

Wang, Hung-Jen (2013b) *The Rise of China and Chinese International Relations Scholarship*. Lanham: Lexington Books.

Wang, Jiangli, and Barry Buzan (2014) "The English and Chinese Schools of International Relations: Comparisons and Lessons." *The Chinese Journal of International Politics*, 7(1): 1–46.

Wang, Jianwei (2002) "International Relations Studies in China." *Journal of East Asian Studies*, 2(1): 69–88.

Wang, Yiwei (2007) "Between Science and Art: Questionable International Relations Theories." *Japanese Journal of Political Science*, 8(2): 191–208.

Wang, Yiwei (2009) "China: Between Copying and Constructing." In Arlene Tickner and Ole Wæver (eds.) *International Relations Scholarship around the World*. London and New York: Routledge.

Yan, Xuetong (2011) *Ancient Chinese Thought, Modern Chinese Power*. Princeton: Princeton University Press.

Yan, Xuetong (2014) "From Keeping a Low Profile to Striving for Achievement." *The Chinese Journal of International Politics*, 7(2): 153–184.

Yan, Xuetong (2016) "Political Leadership and Power Redistribution." *The Chinese Journal of International Politics*, 9(1): 1–26.

Zhang, Feng (2012) "Debating the 'Chinese Theory of International Relations'." In Fred Reinhard Dallmayr and Tingyang Zhao (eds.) *Contemporary Chinese Political Thought: Debates and Perspectives*. Lexington: University Press of Kentucky.
Zhang, Yongjin (2002) "Review: International Relations Theory in China Today: The State of the Field." *The China Journal*, 47: 101–108.
Zhang, Yongjin (2003) "The 'English School' in China: A Travelogue of Ideas and Their Diffusion." *European Journal of International Relations*, 9(1): 87–114.
Zhang, Yongjin, and Teng-Chi Chang (2016) *Constructing a Chinese School(s) of International Relations*. London: Routledge.

3 Theorizing the BRICS

Does the BRICS challenge the current global order?

Xiao Alvin Yang

Introduction

Does the rise of BRICS challenge the current global order? If so, will these countries form a coalition to contest the established order collectively or will they challenge it individually? Will the power transition lead to conflicts or will a peaceful transition be possible? If BRICS, particularly China, does not challenge the current global order, how will global order evolve? This chapter aims to theorize BRICS by focusing on competing theoretical understandings of power transition and hegemony centering around these questions. Particularly, it examines theories that are related to the rise of China and the current global order because China is the most powerful player in BRICS. I will try to relate and extend these theories and their underlying logics to BRICS.

This chapter illustrates the tensions between and among competing international relations (IR) theories and international political economy (IPE) theories in describing, conceptualizing, and theorizing the current global order. It focuses on the aspects of power transition and hegemony because these two aspects are interrelated and interconnected. Power transition may or may not lead to the change of hegemony, at least in a Gramscian understanding of hegemony, i.e. the underlying values and logic embedded in a system. For instance, one scenario in power transition could be that when actor A (e.g. China) surpasses actor B (e.g. the US) materially, but the underlying values and logic that govern the current global system remain. This scenario shows the change of an actor's position in a system but not the change of the system itself. An alternative scenario could be that both power transition and the change of hegemony happen simultaneously. This means that actor A surpasses actor B, and in the process actor A establishes a new system with new values. *Therefore, it is important to distinguish power transition which includes the change of military capability and the change of economic position from the fundamental change of hegemonic values or weltanschauung.*

This chapter links together the political, economic, and cultural dimensions of potential implications of the rise of China on the current global order as opposed to conventional approaches, which study these dimensions separately. Moreover, it not only shows the tensions between rising powers and established powers, namely between China and the US, but also the tensions between the rising powers, such as between China and India.

This chapter goes beyond Western IR theories by introducing several emerging Chinese IR theories, such as Yan's (2016) moral realism, Qin's (2016) relational theory, and Tang's (2013) social evolution theory, in order to shed some light upon the rise of BRICS from Chinese IR perspectives. Western IR and Chinese IR are chosen because they actively engage with each other on theoretical discourses of power transition, hegemony and global order. For example, Yan Xuetong engages with John Mearsheimer, Qin Yaqing with Alexander Wendt, and Tang Shiping with Robert Jervis and the great debates in IR.

Although the theoretical perspectives on the rise of China and the (changing) global order are diverse and highly contested, the main discourse revolves around the question of whether the rise of China will fundamentally challenge and/or reshape the current global order. I begin with both offensive and defensive neorealist theories because the variants of their logics dominate both the academic and public discourses on the rise of China and the global order. I then bring in Yan's moral realism or the *Tsinghua* approach comparing this to Western neorealist theories. Subsequently, I discuss neoliberal institutionalist theory, linking this with regionalization and regional order. Afterwards, I introduce Qin's relational theory focusing on relational epistemology and ontology. To broaden the theoretical horizon, various critical theories are discussed because they deepen the understanding of hegemony in addition to mainstream America IR by illuminating the values and logic of the current global system. Furthermore, a number of cultural and civilizational theories are briefly discussed because IR and IPE are experiencing a cultural turn. Finally, a brief introduction is given to Tang's social evolution theory, which may potentially connect all these aforementioned theories together. To better understand the complexity and multidimensionality of BRICS, this chapter aims to bring out the central ideas of each competing theory on power transition and hegemony as clearly and as precisely as possible by critically examining the interactions of their key dependent variables, intervening variables and independent variables.

On power transition

Will China and the US have conflicts during the power transitioning period? What will be the effects of the rise of China on American hegemony? These questions tend to dominate the mainstream theoretical discourses of power transition. However, as illustrated, these discourses tend to be American-centric because they fixate on Sino-American relations, concentrating on the potential conflicts between China and the US while neglecting the potential conflicts between China and other rising powers, such as between China and India. Even prominent Chinese IR scholars, such as Wang Jisi and Yan Xuetong, fixate on the Sino-American relations, such as in the aspects of stability and instability of Sino-American relations (Wang, 2005; Yan, 2010).

Moreover, various power transition theories inexplicitly assume that the change of an actor's position in the power distribution of a system will lead to the change of the order of that system. For example, the change of economic strength will lead to the change of economic order. This logic also applies to other dimensions, such as security and culture. We should keep in mind that a change in economic strength does not necessarily lead to a change in the underlying economic, political, or cultural order. Moreover, IR theories that focus on the security aspects tend to have a more pessimistic outlook on power transition than theories that concentrate on economics.

Neorealist theory on the rise of China

Although the dominance of neorealist theory has faded in IR, its underlying logic has been re-invented and is still present in various forms in theoretical and public discourses and foreign policy debates. Thus, it is important to understand the fundamental logic of neorealist theory.

From an offensive neorealist perspective, the rapid rise of China will inevitably lead to military conflict with the US because historically, rising powers and established powers went to war with each other, as exemplified by the rise of Germany and Japan in the 20th century, which led to the disastrous World War II (Mearsheimer, 2001, 2006). The key explanatory variable for Mearsheimer is the distribution of power in the anarchical international system which determines the outcome of power transition. However, Graham Allison (2017) contends that even though most rising powers and established powers were caught in the "Thucydides' Trap" and clashed, a Sino-American conflict is not inevitable if both sides can build mutual understanding and learn to adapt.

It is important to reveal the assumptions and logic of Mearsheimer, which often drive many neorealist theorists and analysists of power transition who do not explicitly spell them out. Mearsheimer (2001: 30–31) constructs his offensive neorealist theory based on the following five assumptions: 1) "the international system is anarchic", 2) "great powers inherently possess some offensive military capability", 3) "states can never be certain about other states' intentions", 4) "survival is the primary goal of great powers", and 5) "great powers are rational actors".

In short, since great powers want to survive in the anarchical international system and they cannot be certain as to how other powers will behave, their rational actions will be based on the power distribution. In other words, all the factors in the assumptions remain constant except power distribution in the international system, which is an independent variable.

Mearsheimer's five assumptions, and particularly assumptions 1), 4), and 5), have been challenged by a number of competing theories, such as the neoliberal institutionalist theory, the social evolutionary theory, variants of critical theory and constructivist theory, and Chinese IR theories. For example, Wendt (1992) points out that the anarchical and self-help nature of international systems and states is often treated as an independent variable, but in fact, it is constituted as a state identity (dependent variable) via interaction and practice (independent variable). Put differently, the practice of a state and the interactions among states are what create the anarchical and self-help international system.

Moreover, Mearsheimer's notion that conflict simply equals war neglects that conflict can also manifest in other forms. For instance, conflicts nowadays can manifest in the forms of currency, trade and cyberspace. From a critical perspective, various forms of socio-economic conflicts may be seen as global civil wars taking place within a singular global imperialist system (Hardt and Negri, 2005). This perspective offers a systemic explanation in which the global system is treated as an explanatory variable.

It is important to distinguish structural explanation from systemic explanation. For example, Tang (2013) distinguishes social structure and social system, seeing the former as a subset of the latter. Mearsheimer's explanation leans more toward a structural explanation, which is in line with Waltz' structural neorealism, although Waltz is not an offensive neorealist. In *Man, the State and War*, Waltz (2001[1959]) advocates that the level of analysis in international relations should shift from the first image (the individual) and the second image (the state) to the third image of structural analysis. Waltz defines structure by three criteria: 1) "according to the principle by which a system is ordered. Systems are transformed if one ordering principle replaces another", 2) "the specification of functions of differentiated units", and 3) "the distribution of capability across units" (Waltz, 1979). In this understanding, structure is somehow conflated with system.

Seen from Waltz's structural perspective, China is currently expanding its capabilities rapidly, which may soon ravel those of the US. If this development continues, the change of the distribution of capabilities may potentially lead to a change from the current anarchical international system to a hierarchical system dominated by China. Essentially, Waltz holds a materialist notion of structure and system, similar to that of Mearsheimer's. The problem of Waltz's materialist notion is that it contradicts his own definition of structure and system. For example, the keyword in his first criterion of a structure is "the principle" which governs a system. But principles are not tangible and visible. Rather, they are normative values, which constantly evolve and vary across different times and spaces. Even if China's capabilities may surpass those of the US one day, this does not mean that China will inevitably replace the US by implementing its current operating principles because by then, China's current principles may have already changed and evolved.

Although both offensive and defensive neorealist theories are state-centric, their underlying logics can be extended to other units of analysis, such as transnational organizations and institutions led by a particular state. For instance, the BRICS Development Bank or the China-initiated Asian Investment Infrastructure Bank (AIIB) can be seen as BRICS countries' strategies to challenge the established global order. Moreover, the Shanghai Cooperation Organization (SCO) may also be perceived as a state-led security bloc that competes with NATO. The BRICS Development Bank or the AIIB or the SCO may or may not challenge the current global financial order, but it is the underlying neorealist logic that emphasizes the competitive side rather than the complimentary side.

Recently, the neoclassical realist theory has linked Waltz's structural independent variable with domestic intervening variables such as leader images, strategic culture, domestic institution and state-society relations in order to explain the outcomes in the international system (Ripsman et al., 2016). In other words, the theory incorporates the domestic dimension, which was neglected by traditional structural neorealist theories. Considered from a neoclassical realist perspective, variables in the domestic dimension may change and modify how each BRICS member acts and behaves in the international system, particularly the state-society relations variable in an era of rising income, wealth inequality and ideological polarization but also the resurgence of nationalism.

Perception matters

During power transition, perception is a crucial intervening variable between the outcome of conflict or cooperation and the actual power distribution. Robert Jervis has pointed out how perception can influence decision makers in choosing whether to cooperate or defect based on their rational calculations (Jervis, 1978). Similarly, Stephen Van Evera shows that the perception of offense-defense advantages has a greater effect than the actual offense-defense advantages in determining the outcome of conflict or cooperation (van Evera, 1998). Furthermore, Walt (1990) argues against the classical balance of power theory by proposing a balance of threat theory in which he posits that the perceived threat by a state has greater influence than the actual threat it is facing.

Seen from these defensive neorealist perspectives, perception explains why China is often perceived as a threat to the US even though its military power still lags behind that of the US, as exemplified in a variety of China threat theories. In contrast, perception also explains why Canada does not see its superpower neighbor, the US, as a threat, even though Canada's military capabilities are far inferior to those of the US.

In the case of BRICS, perception may explain why India may perceive China as a greater security threat than the US, even though the US has a greater military capability than China. Economically, the China-Pakistan Economic Corridor is also seen as a threat to India. Seen through this theoretical lens, the success or failure of the future cooperation and solidarity within BRICS will depend on how these countries perceive each other rather than the actual power distribution among them.

The Tsinghua approach or moral realism

Chinese IR theories are heterogenous, not homogenous. In contrast to the opinions expressed in *Constructing a Chinese School of International Relations*, edited by Zhang and Chang (2016), I argue that there is no such thing as a Chinese school or the Chinese school; rather, there are diverse and competing Chinese IR schools or theories.

The Tsinghua Approach was named by Feng Zhang in 2012 as an emerging IR school centering around Tsinghua University. This approach combines ancient Chinese thoughts with a positivist research methodology and policy recommendations (Zhang, 2012a). The leading figure of this approach is Yan Xuetong, who is also known as a Chinese moral realist.

In contrast to Mearsheimer, Yan Xuetong argues that the rise of China will not only contribute significantly to economic growth and scientific progress in the world, it will also make the world a more peaceful and civilized place because China will play a positive role in reducing the current unequal global power distribution (Yan, 2001). Later on, he asserted in a New York Times' column that the competition between China and the US is inevitable and a zero-sum game in which China could defeat the US by exercising its more humane and moral leadership (Yan, 2011). Although his line of reasoning resembles the neorealist logic, Yan's reasoning differs from this in that it brings in the notion of a humane and moral leadership which draws from ancient Chinese philosophies of governance, such as the teaching of Mencius.

In Yan's theory, morality and human factors are placed at the center, and his understanding of a state's comprehensive power is different from that of American neorealists. To measure a state's comprehensive power, Yan (2013: 102) uses a key concept, political leadership as an operating variable, which is succinctly summarized in the following formula:

$$CP = (M + E + C) \times P$$

Where CP=Comprehensive Power, M=Military Power, E=Economic Power, C=Cultural Power, and P=Political Power. M, E, and C in the bracket are considered as resource power and P as operating power.

Yan's formula can be understood intuitively. According to Yan, even if a country has ample resource power but lacks the operating political power, i.e. political leadership, it will not be able to mobilize and turn this resource power into comprehensive power. Let us suppose that country A has tremendous resource power, but its political power is zero or negative; in this case, its comprehensive power (the dependent variable) will also be zero or negative. Therefore, Yan emphasizes the important role of great individuals (the first image) in his theory, which has long been abandoned by structural neorealists, such as Kenneth Waltz and John Mearsheimer. Yan Xuetong categorizes and defines political leadership in the following way:

> Political leadership could be categorized into four types: inactive, conservative, proactive, and aggressive. (i) Inactive leadership refers to policymakers with no ambitions to expand their national interests . . . (ii) Conservative leadership refers to the kind of policymakers that advocate maintaining the current status quo, and who are satisfied with the achievements of their predecessors . . . (iii) Proactive leadership refers to policymakers that devote themselves to the work of enhancing the status of their country . . . (iv) Aggressive leadership refers to policymakers who are disciples of military determinism, and who prefer to achieve strategic goals through military might, including aggressive wars.
>
> (Yan, 2016: 18)

According to Yan's concept of political leadership, the current Chinese approach to international relations may be perceived as proactive leadership. For example, President Xi has stated many times on different occasions that China is committed to globalization. Moreover, the Belt and Road Initiative (BRI) can be seen as a strategic preference for China to lead in the global economy. China has also taken the leadership in pushing the fourth industrial revolution by investing heavily in new and high-tech industries, such as artificial intelligence, 5G, renewable energy, quantum communication, and nanotechnology.

Another example is President Trump's proactive leadership. However, facing criticism both at home and abroad, his proactive leadership may be perceived as negative because he has withdrawn from several international agreements, such as the TPP and the Paris Agreement. He has also created tensions between the US and its traditional close allies such as NATO, G7, and the EU. Thus, if we apply Yan's formula, the US may have greater resource power than China, but if it has a negative political leadership, its comprehensive power will be lesser than that of China. As Yan argues, "there is thus a positive correlation between the leading state's strategic credibility and the durability of the international order it established" (Yan, 2016: 23). However, whether China or the US has a more positive or negative political leadership remains debatable; this is subject to different criteria and depends on whom we ask. Thus, it is crucial to understand power beyond hard power and soft power and critical IPE perspectives may offer some insights into this.

Expanding Yan's categorizations to the other BRICS members, we can observe diverse forms of leadership. For example, some may argue that the political leadership of Russia is an aggressive leadership, as demonstrated in the Crimea case. India may be seen as pursuing a proactive leadership and so may both Brazil and South Africa at a regional level. Whether Russia's aggressive leadership or the other BRICS members' proactive global or regional leadership will challenge the current global order, remains to be seen. The proactive leadership of BRICS members may not converge with each other, and at times, they may compete with each other, such as in the case of China and India as they are trying to exert their influence in South and Southeast Asia. Thus, it is not clear whether BRICS will act collectively with solidarity during power transition, and they may act differently at particular points of time and context and toward a specific actor.

Neoliberal institutionalist theory

In contrast to both American and Chinese neorealists, the neoliberal institutional theorists posit that the interdependence created when cooperating and interacting with China will make China a peaceful and responsible player on the world stage. Countering the pessimism in the variants of neorealist theory, Robert Keohane argues that international regimes or institutions, such as the General Agreement on Tariffs and Trade (GATT), make cooperation possible among states in the anarchic international system (Keohane, 2005[1984]). Furthermore, institutions are simultaneously conceptualized as independent and dependent variables because human actions can influence institutions, and vice versa (Keohane and Martin, 1995).

However, institutions can also be seen as an intervening variable between the anarchical international system and the outcome of conflict or cooperation, which mitigates the potential conflicts due to an imbalance in the distribution of power. Thus, institutions can be conceptualized as a dependent variable or an independent variable or an intervening variable, depending on the context in which they appear.

In contrast to both Mearsheimer and Yan, Ikenberry (2008) argues that it is easier for China to join the current Western liberal order that is "open, integrated, and rule-based" than it is to challenge it. Moreover, the rise of China can be accommodated by the Western liberal order precisely because it is an open and rule-based system. In addition, war has become obsolete in the age of nuclear weapon (Ikenberry, 2008). Therefore, the current liberal order can be conceptualized as an institution in the broadest sense of the word.

Drawing from the concept of "international society" in the English IR school, Buzan (2010) believes that the peaceful rise of China can happen via "a two-way process", which not only depends on China and its relations with the international society both globally and regionally, particularly with Japan, but also on how others respond to China. After surveying Chinese academic discourse on global order, Tang (2018) argues that the dominant view is that China has no need to transform the current global order but only to make some revisions to it.

Studies have also shown how the socialization of China since the 1970s via interactions with international institutions has changed China's international behavior from one of *realpolitik* to a more cooperative stance (Johnston, 2008). Taking Johnston's concept of socialization of the state as a point of departure, we might ask whether BRICS-led institutions, such as the BRICS Development Banks, will also be socialized into the current dominant international organizations that promote a liberal global order. If so, the extent of socialization process expands beyond state actors into institutional actors, which may further expand into other actors, such as civil society and individuals.

Surprisingly, the current challengers of the liberal order do not come from the emerging powers, but from within the West. For example, by scrapping the TPP, withdrawing from the Paris Agreement, and recently imposing heavy tariffs on steel and aluminum, the US seems to be diverting from the liberal order that it once established and defended. Moreover, a resurgence of nationalism is seen in both Europe and North America. Nevertheless, Ikenberry (2018) still insists that the liberal order is here to stay despite the recent resurgence of nationalism within the West, which is challenging the liberal order. In contrast, Henry Kissinger (2015) argues that China has reshaped the unipolar world into a multipolar world order. Contrary to both Ikenberry and Kissinger, Acharya (2017) contends that the future world order will not be the current liberal order nor will it return to the previous multipolar order; rather, it will be a "multiplex order" in which liberal values and institutions will coexist with other values and institutions, and globalization will be driven increasingly by the East and South-South linkages, particularly China and India.

Regional orders

If Acharya's prediction is accurate, will multiple regional orders emerge as opposed to a single global order? Some scholars have already voiced their arguments about the emerging regional orders. For example, Barry Buzan (2011) argues that the world is moving toward a "de-centered globalism" in which there is no longer a hegemonic global order maintained by a superpower, but rather, regionalized orders with great powers. Similarly, Peter Katzenstein (2005) points out the importance of region in theorizing world politics to fill the gap between the nation-state and globalization approaches.

Furthermore, if the regional argument as regards the global trend of various forms of regionalization, as illustrated by the EU and the ASEAN cases, is correct, is regionalization happening within a larger global framework? Is there a shared fundamental logic that drives both globalization and regionalization? Phrased differently, does the regionalization process of restructuring and integrating supply, production and distribution chains, as well as regional trade and investment, fit into the general logic of the current world economy? These questions are explored in the upcoming critical IPE theories section.

Furthermore, competing IR theories can easily apply their logics from the global level to the regional level. If the logic of neorealist theory is applied to regional order, the rise of India will lead to a conflict with the more or less established China as they are competing for dominance in Asia, particularly in South Asia. Conversely, if the neoliberal institutionalist theory is valid, then the potential conflicts between China and India may be mediated and mitigated by institutions, such as BRICS and the SCO. Yan's concept of political leadership is a crucial variable in determining the success or failure of regionalization and regional integration. Furthermore, Tang (2018) predicts that China is likely to push for regionalism in East Asia and Central Asia and to invest in interregional cooperation and coordination via the Belt and Road Initiative (BRI). Will BRICS create a new trans-regional order?

Constructing a Chinese relational theory

Returning to Chinese IR, Qin Yaqing is aiming to construct a Chinese IR School, in contrast to Yan (2013), who rejects the idea of constructing a Chinese IR school because he believes that IR theory should be universally applicable. Qin challenges Western IR theories on both epistemological and ontological levels. He posits that relationality is the theoretical hardcore of Chinese IR, and that the relation between and among actors is the most important independent variable in understanding China's approach to international relations (Qin, 2016).

Qin Yaqing proposed two key concepts as epistemological foundation: 1) a meta-relationship that is based on *Yin* and *Yang* (male and female) and 2) *Zhongyong* dialectics as a way to understand the meta-relationship as co-theses, i.e. one being within the other, rather than a thesis and an anti-thesis in a Hegelian sense (Qin, 2016: 39).

In other words, he is aiming to shift from the "either-or" paradigm to the "both-and" paradigm. This "both-and" paradigm may help us better understand China and, to a certain extent, BRICS' behavior in foreign policy and international relations where contradictory behaviors are observed.

Ontologically, Qin contends that the mainstream Western IR theories, be they neorealist, neoliberal institutionalist, constructivist, or even the English School, all metaphysically share individualistic rationality (Qin, 2016: 34). In contrast to the ontology of the autonomous and rational individual in mainstream Western IR, Qin argues that relationality is the metaphysical core in Confucian cultural communities. The concept of relationality is built on three assumptions which are: 1) inter-relatedness, i.e. people and events are interconnected by overlapping relational circles, 2) actor-in-relations, i.e. actor cannot exist independently but only in a social relation, and 3) process, i.e. everything is constantly in a state of becoming rather than static being (Qin, 2016: 35–37). These ideas have been more systematically developed and further elaborated in Qin's recent new book, *A Relational Theory of World Politics* (Qin, 2018).

Rational-choice theorists may still rationalize relations between and among actors as interests and utilities but in a different dimension. They may even integrate rational-choice theory with the relational theory by adding the relational dimension to their calculation of interests. This approach, however, still holds on to the ontology of rationalistic individualism, which Qin aims to overcome by using the ontology of relationality that posits actors can only exist in social relations. Ultimately, it is a philosophical battle on what constitutes a unit of analysis.

If we take Qin's ontology seriously, we will shift the unit of analysis from the actors themselves to the relations between and among actors. Rather than examining the rational calculation of utility functions by each BRICS member, we would investigate the relations between and among them. Taking China, India, and Russia as an example, neorealist theory would predict that Russia's behavior will be determined by regional power distribution. Thus, if China becomes too dominant in Asia, Russia and India will join together to contain China. Conversely, if we apply a relational logic, then the determinant will be the condition of bilateral relations among China, India, and Russia, which can change in various directions via the process of interaction between actors. For example, if China and Russia enjoy a close relationship, Russia will not join India to contain China even if China becomes dominant in Asia. The reason is that states behave differently to their friends, allies, rivals, and enemies. Similarly, if China enjoys good relationships with Brazil and South Africa, investments to these countries will be seen in a positive light. If their relationships deteriorate, investments will then be perceived as threats and even colonial. Thus, it is the relationship between actors that determines these actors' actions, and this is not fixed but open to different trajectories and constantly in the process of becoming. Considered power transition from this relational logic, it is the nature of relationship between a hegemonic power and a rising power that determines the outcome rather than power distribution or institutions.

Critical IPE theory

As in other theoretical perspectives, diversity is also found in critical IPE perspectives. Neo-Gramscian theorist, Stephen Gill, offers a counter perspective to both the emerging regionalized orders and the liberal order, arguing that the current world order can be conceptualized as new constitutionalism led by the US and influenced informally by the Trilateral Commission, to which even China is susceptible (Gill, 1991; Gill, 1998; Gill, 2008). Gill (2008: 139) defines new constitutionalism as "the political project of attempting to make transnational liberalism, and if possible liberal democratic capitalism, the sole model for future development".

New constitutionalism is defined as a politically driven project. In this case, a liberal democratic capitalism ideology and a monopolistic developmental mode constitute the only model which does not allow any alternative. Liberal democratic capitalism as the sole model is in line with Francis Fukuyama's idea of the end of history (Fukuyama, 1992). If this is true, there will no longer be power transition as in the previous eras in human history because we have reached the end point of history at which the world will be forever governed by variants of liberal democratic capitalism. This notion of history is teleological and somehow quasi-religious because the cold, harsh, and cruel world is saved by the gospel of liberal democratic capitalism. The conception of "Paradise" on earth differs among different theorists; to Fukuyama, the Paradise is liberal democracy, to Marx, it is communism. However, they both adhere to the teleological view of history that there is an end point toward which human history inevitably is progressing.

The world-systems theory is another important approach in critical IPE that may offer insights to understand and analyse BRICS. Immanuel Wallerstein divides the world into core, semi-periphery, and periphery, which represent the global division of labor in a global capitalist economy (Wallerstein, 2004). Although Wallerstein claims that his unit of analysis is a system, he still uses nation-state as a unit to categorize his core, semi-periphery, and periphery. Thus, his categorization is geographically bound by national territorialities, which is highly problematic and neglects the evolving complexities of the current global economy. For example, in his categorization, China would still be considered as a periphery or semi-periphery rather than as one of the cores. In reality, China simultaneously engages in both capital-intensive and labor-intensive economic activities, varying in different regions and sectors. In contrast to Wallerstein, in his book, *Adam Smith in Beijing*, Giovanni Arrighi argues that the core of global capitalist economy is shifting from the US to China in the 21st century (Arrighi, 2008). Applying a dialectical method, Minqi Li (2008) posits that the rise of China accelerates the historical processes of the demise of the current capitalist world economy. However, their arguments still operate within the nation-state framework.

Conceptualizing core, semi-periphery, and periphery as other units, such as industrial clusters and global cities may better capture the complex realities in the current globalized economy. There are cores within peripheries and peripheries within the cores that is no longer defined by national boundaries. Sassen's (2001) concept of the global city is useful to understand how the core and periphery have evolved over time. Nowadays, resources are increasingly concentrated in global cities, such as New York, London, Tokyo, and Shanghai. The gap is often bigger between global cities and the rest within a country than between countries.

Applying the concept of the global city to BRICS, Shanghai, Moscow, Mumbai, São Paulo, and Johannesburg could be considered as parts of the cores of the global capitalism because of the high concentrations of financial capital and capital-intensive economic activities there. However, there are peripheries within and surrounding these global cities as a considerable amount of the population still participates in labor-intensive economic activities. Therefore, the core-periphery distinction has become hybridized, i.e. it is no longer divided by national boundaries, but by specific locality, sector, and industry. In other words, a country could be part of the global cores but at the same time part of the global peripheries, depending on the regions and segments of the local population and industry. This new conceptualization of core-periphery helps us to think about BRICS beyond the constraints of nation-state thinking and pose novel questions. For example, instead of asking whether China or BRICS will challenge the West, one can ask whether Shanghai or Mumbai will replace New York or London as the top global financial capital. Moreover, one may ask more specific questions such as which segment of the population or industry in the BRICS supports or challenges the current global order.

Cultural or civilizational theory

Culture or civilization has become an important independent or explanatory variable in IR and IPE theorizing. Based on a civilizational perspective, Huntington (1997) claimed that China will clash with the West because its civilizational values are conflicting and incompatible with the West. Extending his logic to the BRICS, there will be clashes among BRICS countries because their cultures and civilizations are heterogenous.

Peter Katzenstein made a rebuttal to Huntington's thesis by arguing that civilization is not monolithic as assumed by Huntington, but pluralistic, and it does not tend to engage in clashes but rather to pursue "intercivilizational encounters and transcivilizational engagements" (Katzenstein, 2010). If we examine BRICS closely, they fit into Katzenstein's argument that civilization is pluralistic as there is great diversity within each of these countries.

In contrast to both Huntington and Katzenstein, Zhang Weiwei (2012b) posits that China is a rising civilizational state, which is peaceful and beneficial to the world precisely because of its traditional cultural values, such as the notion of *ren* or benevolence in dealing with foreign countries. Furthermore, Jacques (2012) contends that the rise of China will fundamentally reshape the world with Chinese characteristics which may lead to a Sino-centric world order that resembles the ancient tributary system. The *tianxia* or all-under-heaven system was proposed by Chinese philosopher Zhao Tingyang in replacement of the current Westphalia system. According to him, it is more peaceful and beneficial (Zhao, 2006). Callahan

(2008) critiques the *Tianxia* system as new hegemony that is aiming to revive the old Sino-centric order rather than create a post-hegemonic world order.

These authors all use culture or civilization as their explanatory variables. However, they neglect the evolutionary nature of culture and civilization. Can one really understand China's behaviors in the global arena in light of its ancient civilization/s?

Beyond national cultures, Bob Jessop advances a cultural turn in IPE by constructing a cultural political economy that links the constitutive role of semiosis with the political economy (Jessop, 2004). Furthermore, culture does not necessarily come in the form of a nation-state or civilization; it may also come in the form of a sector or an organization. For example, studies have been conducted on how financial cultures created and influenced the 2008 financial crisis (Jessop et al., 2014). This creates subtle nuances in the conceptualization of cultures in which the culture of a particular sector (e.g. the financial sector) is more similar across different countries than within their respective national cultures. In other words, similarities are shared more by industries and organizations rather than within a national community, which Anderson called an "imagined community" (Anderson, 2016[1983]). Furthermore, following the globalizing IR movement, there is now a movement of globalizing IPE in which the Western civilizational foundation of IPE is challenged by the examination of other non-Western civilizational foundations of IPE. This is reflected in the re-examination of the Haya-Mariátegui debate in Latin America and in Korean debates of IPE in the late 19th and early 20th centuries (Chey and Helleiner, 2018; Helleiner and Rosales, 2017). Therefore, the diverse cultures and civilizations of BRICS offer a tremendous potential to re-construct IPE from different civilizational foundations, which may create new perceptions and understandings of the global political economy.

Theories of hegemony

Hegemony is another crucial, relevant, and highly contested concept in theorizing the current global order in relation to power transition. As in power transition theories, there are numerous variants of political, economical, and cultural theories of hegemony.

From a defensive neorealist perspective, van Evera (1998) notes that states tend to favor balance of power, which means that they would join the weaker coalition in order to counter a regional hegemon, such as in the cases of the US and the UK who traditionally played the role of balancer to the regional hegemons in continental Europe. If this logic holds, as China becomes more powerful and dominant in Asia, more states (including neutral states) will form a coalition to counter China's hegemonic power. In this case, Japan, India, and perhaps Russia will join the coalition to balance China's regional hegemony. As a result, this will cause the geopolitical tension to be much greater within BRICS than between China and the US.

The hegemonic stability theory is another important hegemonic theory primarily based on economics, which often serves American interests. The key explanatory variable on war and peace in the hegemonic stability theory is presence or absence of a hegemonic power. Based on his study of the great depression, Charles Kindleberger (2013[1973]) argues that chaos happened during the great depression was due to the lack of a single hegemonic power who could shape and enforce a liberal global order. It is important to note that his theory mainly focuses on the stability and openness of the global economy in relation to the presence or absence of a hegemonic power who can set standards and enforce rules. Likewise, Robert Gilpin posits that a hegemonic power is indispensable in maintaining peace and openness in the international system (Gilpin, 1981).

By the logic of the hegemonic stability theory, the emergence of a multipolar global order will lead to chaos. Moreover, if this is the case, why can only the US play the hegemonic role? Why can China or other states not play the hegemonic role in the future?

Hegemony is understood too narrowly in the hegemonic stability theory. Li Xing (2014) contends that hegemony in the near future will not be an American hegemony but rather an "interdependent hegemony" in which the established powers and the emerging powers will constantly reshape the hegemony through consensus on competing interests. Many argue that the crisis of American hegemony may lead to chaos, but this is in fact normal in a capitalist system, which is prone to ongoing periodic crises (Li and Shaw, 2014).

Hegemony can also be understood as an ideology if drawing from Antonio Gramsci's understanding of hegemony in domestic Italian politics, which can subsequently be extended to the international level. In a Gramscian sense, hegemony is not achieved only via material forces, it is also achieved by the conformity to the ideology of the ruling class (Gramsci, 1995). Seeing hegemony from a Gramscian perspective, the US' material power may have declined greatly, but its cultural values are spreading rapidly via Hollywood, American media and popular culture, which has become influential and even dominant in many countries around the world. In a Gramscian sense, one may argue that American hegemony has not declined, it has actually increased.

Robert Cox argues that hegemony in the world is the manifestation of the externalization and expansion of the internal hegemony of a hegemonic state, dominated by a dominant social class and its mode of production (Cox, 1983). In line with Cox, Scherrer (2001) applies the concept of "double hegemony" to the current global order, in which, he argues there is a "nation-state hegemony" exercised by the American State on the one hand, and a "class-based" hegemony maintained by the global capitalist class on the other. To counter the narrative that the US is no longer a hegemonic power, Scherrer (2011) argues that a crisis, such as the financial crisis in 2008, is not enough to undermine American hegemony. He posits that the US has re-invented its hegemony from that which was based on its military internationally and productivity pacts domestically during the Fordist era to a new form of neoliberal hegemony achieved through globalization, financialization, and militarization.

Furthermore, David Harvey has argued that China has been developing into a neoliberal state ever since the country began to open its economy in 1978 (Harvey, 2005). If Harvey's argument holds, then Scherrer's nation-state hegemony needs to be revised and expanded from the American state so as to incorporate any powerful state that promotes a neoliberal agenda. Moreover, hegemony does not necessarily mean domination. Arrighi (2008) argues that China may achieve hegemony without domination. At this stage, this is still a speculative argument and time is needed for it to be verified.

Hegemony, however, is understood differently in China. When hegemonism was discussed in China during the cold war era, it referred to the Soviet Union and it implied the combined meaning of dominance of one state over another state and imperialism (Cox, 1983). The recent Chinese discourse of hegemony still centers around American hegemony, although changes in discourse have slowly begun (Wang and Pauly, 2013).

Drawing from ancient historical sources, such as Xunzi, Yan distinguishes the Chinese notion of hegemony from the Western notion of hegemony by differentiating *Wang*, *Ba*, and *Qiang* or humane authority, hegemon, and tyrant (Yan, 2013). While *Ba* shares many resemblances with Western notion of hegemony, *Wang* or humane authority is considered a higher form of power. Yan defines humane authority as:

> Humane authority is an inter-state leading power that practices moral principles and maintains high international strategic credibility, normally maintaining the international order in three ways: (i) making itself a good example to other states of moral practice according to international norms; (ii) promoting the internalization of particular international norms by rewarding the states that obey these norms; (iii) punishing the states that violate international norms.
>
> (Yan, 2016: 23)

The quote shows the central roles of morality and norms in humane authority. Yan advocates that China should change its traditional foreign policy approach of "keeping a low profile" to a new approach of "striving for achievement" on the global stage by pursuing the political leadership of humane authority rather than acting as a hegemon (Yan, 2014). Moreover, he recognizes the importance of comprehensive power if a state is aiming to become a humane authority. To him, it is impossible for a state to achieve humane authority without a solid foundation of comprehensive power. For example, if one state violates the international norms, but a more powerful state that can punish and hold the former accountable does not exist, it is impossible to maintain humane authority. Recently, Yan (2018: 19) argues that China can reshape the current global order and achieve modernized humane authority by combining traditional Chinese values, such as benevolence, righteousness, and rites with liberal Western values, such as equality, democracy, and freedom. A fusion of these values will create fairness, justice, and civility respectively as new global norms.

Tang's social evolution theory

Why did IR and IPE theorists arrive at competing understandings of the current global order when they were examining the same phenomenon? To solve this puzzle, Tang (2013) applies the social evolution theory to explain the changes of global order and the international system endogenously using an artificial variation-selection-inheritance mechanism. He has conducted empirical studies on various historical periods across different times and spaces, such as periods in ancient China from 1045 BC to 1759 AD and in the Post-Roman Europe periods from 1450 AD to 1995 AD, based on five key variables: 1) number of states at the beginning and end of each period, 2) years of the period, 3) number of states eliminated in the period, 4) rate of state death per century, and 5) average time needed to eliminate a state (Tang, 2013). He found the trend of these five variables, observing that 1), 2), 3), and 4) increased while 5) decreased over time. Based on these observations, Tang concluded that different grand theories are suitable to explain a particular period in history, arguing that international system has evolved from Mearsheimer's offensive realist world to a defensive realist world, and it will likely to evolve into a rule-based world in the near future (Tang, 2013, 2010).

It is important to note that social evolution is not a direct transfer of the biological evolution theory (e.g. Neo-Darwinism) to the social world; it combines both physical and ideational dimension. The mechanisms and forces working in the ideational dimension are different from mechanisms and forces working in the physical dimension. For instance, the most important force in the selection mechanism in the ideational dimension is social power, which is *artificially* achieved rather than takes place *naturally* in the biological world (Tang, 2013). Moreover, the mechanism of inheritance is "Darwinian nested within super-Lamarckian" in the ideational dimension, implying that genotype (e.g. ideas) and phenotype (e.g. institutions) can be directly inherited, whereas in the biological world, only phenotype can be inherited (Tang, 2013).

Tang's social evolutionary theory may or may not solve all the puzzles of these competing IR/IPE theories concerning power transition and hegemony, in which further observation, discussion, exploration, and examination are needed.

Conclusion

This chapter argues that a plural and multidimensional rather than a singular and one-dimensional conceptualization of the current global order, power transition, and hegemony as well as going beyond American-centric IR/IPE theories may help to better understand the rise of BRICS. Cooperation and contestation can happen simultaneously, varying in different dimensions, between and among rising powers, as well as between and among rising powers and established powers. Conflicts are more likely to happen between two rising powers who are geographically located close to each other than between a rising power and an established power.

Some BRICS members are caught up in complex relations. On the one hand, China, India, and Russia are members of the trans-regional organization BRICS and the regional security organization SCO. On the other hand, they are competing for leadership in Asia: China and India in South and Southeast Asia and China and Russia in central Asia. For instance, the China-Pakistan Economic Corridor (as a part of the BRI) may be perceived by India as evoking both economic competition and security concerns. Economically, this economic corridor may undermine the economic leadership of India in South Asia. In terms of security, the construction of rail tracks from China to Pakistan running through the contested Kashmir area can potentially lead to disruptions and conflicts. Despite these concerns, China and India still cooperate on a number of areas, such as within the frameworks of BRICS and the SCO. Thus, Qin's (2018) relational theory based on the "both-and" logic may shed more light upon these complex relations in Asia than American-centric IR/IPE theories. Moreover, human relationships play a central role in determining actions and behavior of individuals in Qin's theory.

Although BRICS is often considered as what Cooper (2016) calls "a state-centric project", theorizing BRICS should go beyond the unit of nation-state and explore other units of analysis, such as BRICS-led institutions and corporations that are based in these countries. For example, the BRICS Development Bank, the AIIB, and the SCO are important institutions which need in-depth studies. Multinational corporations based in the BRICS countries also need further examination in order to ascertain if they are similar or different from the multinational corporations that are based in the Global North. Moreover, the unit of analysis may expand from actor and structure to the relations between and among actors, as proposed by Qin Yaqing.

Theories of power transition and hegemony both in the US and China tend to fixate on Sino-American relations. To better understand the current (changing) global order, these theories need to not only address issues on Sino-American relations, but more importantly on China's relations with other rising and emerging powers, particularly with China's neighbors. American-centric IR/IPE theories tend to lead to partial and misleading questions, which are often formulated in the interests of the US. Unfortunately, Chinese IR/IPE theories may sometimes fall into the trap of American-centrism. Therefore, research questions are often framed in the ways that are unrelated to China's own interests and urgent issues in particular.

Furthermore, this chapter shows how the current global order can be conceptualized, described, and understood differently by various theorists. For example, neoliberal institutionalist theorists see it as the liberal order, whereas critical theorists call it the neoliberal order. It is important to note that variation is also seen within a particular IR/IPE school. We should not be constrained by the IR/IPE school label but should understand the specificity of a particular IR/IPE theorist.

Future research may further explore the tensions between and among the rising powers rather than the conventional approaches that are mostly focusing on rising powers and established powers. Moreover, theories that come from BRICS should be incorporated, such as the emerging Chinese IR theories, in order to better theorize global order, power transition, and hegemony and develop a global IR/IPE. Furthermore, if the BRI is successful in integrating Asia and Europe together, a new global order may emerge as power shifts from the Western Hemisphere to EurAsia. Therefore, Tang's social evolutionary perspective is crucial in explaining the fundamental changes and variations in power transition, hegemony, and global order.

Last but not least, a critical IPE perspective based on a social evolutionary understanding and drawing from other non-American IR/IPE perspectives, such as the emerging Chinese IR theories, may better understand and explain the changes and dynamics of the current rapidly changing global order, redistribution of power and the emergence of new hegemonies.

References

Acharya, Amitav (2017) "After Liberal Hegemony: The Advent of a Multiplex World Order." *Ethics & International Affairs*, 31(3): 271–285.

Allison, Graham (2017) *Destined for War: Can America and China Escape Thucydides's Trap?* Boston: Houghton Mifflin Harcourt.

Anderson, Benedict (2016[1983]) *Imagined Communities: Reflections on the Origin and Spread of Nationalism*. London: Verso.

Arrighi, Giovanni (2008) *Adam Smith in Beijing: Lineages of the Twenty-First Century*. London: Verso.

Buzan, Barry (2010) "China in International Society: Is 'Peaceful Rise' Possible?" *The Chinese Journal of International Politics*, 3(1): 5–36.

Buzan, Barry (2011) "The Inaugural Kenneth N. Waltz Annual Lecture a World Order without Superpowers." *International Relations*, 25(1): 3–25.

Callahan, William (2008) "Chinese Visions of World Order: Post-Hegemonic or a New Hegemony?" *International Studies Review*, 10(4): 749–761.

Chey, Hyoung-kyu, and Eric Helleiner (2018) "Civilisational Values and Political Economy beyond the West: The Significance of Korean Debates at the Time of Its Economic Opening." *Contemporary Politics*, 24(2): 191–209.

Cooper, Andrew (2016) *The BRICS: A Very Short Introduction*. Oxford: Oxford University Press.

Cox, Robert (1983) "Gramsci, Hegemony and International Relations: An Essay in Method." *Millennium*, 12(2): 162–175.

Fukuyama, Francis (1992) *The End of History and the Last Man*. New York: Free Press.

Gill, Stephen (1991) *American Hegemony and the Trilateral Commission*. Cambridge: Cambridge University Press.

Gill, Stephen (1998) "New Constitutionalism, Democratisation and Global Political Economy." *Pacifica Review: Peace, Security & Global Change*, 10(1): 23–38.

Gill, Stephen (2008) *Power and Resistance in the New World Order*. 2nd ed. Basingstoke and New York: Palgrave Macmillan.

Gilpin, Robert (1981) *War and Change in World Politics*. Cambridge: Cambridge University Press.

Gramsci, Antonio (1995) *Further Selections from the Prison Notebooks*. Minneapolis: University of Minnesota Press.

Hardt, Michael, and Antonio Negri (2005) *Multitude: War and Democracy in the Age of Empire*. New York: Penguin Books.

Harvey, David (2005) *A Brief History of Neoliberalism*. Oxford: Oxford University Press.

Helleiner, Eric, and Antulio Rosales (2017) "Toward Global IPE: The Overlooked Significance of the Haya-Mariátegui Debate." *International Studies Review*, 19(4): 667–691.

Huntington, Samuel (1997) *The Clash of Civilizations and the Remaking of World Order*. New Delhi: Penguin Books India.

Ikenberry, John (2008) "The Rise of China and the Future of the West: Can the Liberal System Survive?" *Foreign Affairs*, 87(1): 23–37.

Ikenberry, John (2018) "The End of Liberal International Order?" *International Affairs*, 94(1): 7–23.

Jacques, Martin (2012) *When China Rules the World: The End of the Western World and the Birth of a New Global Order*. 2nd ed. London: Penguin Books.

Jervis, Robert (1978) "Cooperation under the Security Dilemma." *World Politics*, 30(2): 167–214.

Jessop, Bob (2004) "Critical Semiotic Analysis and Cultural Political Economy." *Critical Discourse Studies*, 1(2): 159–174.

Jessop, Bob, Brigitte Young, and Christoph Scherrer (2014) *Financial Cultures and Crisis Dynamics*. 1st ed. London: Routledge.

Johnston, Alastair (2008) *Social States: China in International Institutions, 1980–2000*. Princeton: Princeton University Press.

Katzenstein, Peter (2005) *A World of Regions: Asia and Europe in the American Imperium*. Ithaca: Cornell University Press.

Katzenstein, Peter (2010) "A World of Plural and Pluralistic Civilizations: Multiple Actors, Traditions and Practices." In Peter J. Katzenstein (ed.) *Civilizations in World Politics: Plural and Pluralist Perspectives*. London: Routledge, 1–40.

Keohane, Robert (2005[1984]) *After Hegemony: Cooperation and Discord in the World Political Economy*. 1st ed. Princeton: Princeton University Press.

Keohane, Robert, and Lisa Martin (1995) "The Promise of Institutionalist Theory." *International Security*, 20(1): 39–51.

Kindleberger, Charles (2013[1973]) *The World in Depression 1929–1939: 40th Anniversary of a Classic in Economic History*. 40th ed. Berkeley: University of California Press.

Kissinger, Henry (2015) *World Order*. London: Penguin Books.

Li, Minqi (2008) *The Rise of China and the Demise of the Capitalist World-Economy*. New York: Monthly Review Press.

Li, Xing (2014) "Conceptualizing the Nexus of 'Interdependent Hegemony' between the Existing and the Emerging World Orders." *Fudan Journal of the Humanities and Social Sciences*, 7(3): 343–362.

Li, Xing and Timothy Shaw (2014) "'Same Bed, Different Dreams' and 'Riding Tiger' Dilemmas: China's Rise and International Relations/Political Economy." *Journal of Chinese Political Science*, 19(1): 69–93.

Mearsheimer, John (2001) *The Tragedy of Great Power Politics*. New York: W.W. Norton.

Mearsheimer, John (2006) "China's Unpeaceful Rise." *Current History*, 105(690): 160–162.

Qin, Yaqing (2016) "A Relational Theory of World Politics." *International Studies Review*, 18(1): 33–47.

Qin, Yaqing (2018) *A Relational Theory of World Politics*. Cambridge: Cambridge University Press.

Ripsman, Norrin, Jeffrey Taliaferro, and Steven Lobell (2016) *Neoclassical Realist Theory of International Politics*. Oxford: Oxford University Press.

Sassen, Saskia (2001) *The Global City: New York, London, Tokyo*. 2nd ed. Princeton: Princeton University Press.

Scherrer, Christoph (2001) "'Double Hegemony'? State and Class in American Foreign Economic Policymaking." *Amerikastudien/American Studies*: 573–591.

Scherrer, Christoph (2011) "Reproducing Hegemony: US Finance Capital and the 2008 Crisis." *Critical Policy Studies*, 5(3): 219–246.

Tang, Shiping (2010) "Social Evolution of International Politics: From Mearsheimer to Jervis." *European Journal of International Relations*, 16(1): 31–55.

Tang, Shiping (2013) *The Social Evolution of International Politics*. Oxford: Oxford University Press.

Tang, Shiping (2018) "China and the Future International Order(s)." *Ethics & International Affairs*, 32(1): 31–43.

van Evera, Stephen (1998) "Offense, Defense, and the Causes of War." *International Security*, 22(4): 5–43.

Wallerstein, Immanuel (2004) *World-Systems Analysis: An Introduction*. Durham: Duke University Press.

Walt, Stephen (1990) *The Origins of Alliance*. Ithaca: Cornell University Press.

Waltz, Kenneth (1979) *Theory of International Politics*. London: Addison-Wesley.

Waltz, Kenneth (2001[1959]) *Man, the State and War: A Theoretical Analysis*. New York: Columbia University Press.

Wang, Jisi (2005) "China's Search for Stability with America." *Foreign Affairs*, 84(5): 39–48.

Wang, Yong, and Louis Pauly (2013) "Chinese IPE Debates on (American) Hegemony." *Review of International Political Economy*, 20(6): 1165–1188.

Wendt, Alexander (1992) "Anarchy Is What States Make of It: The Social Construction of Power Politics." *International Organization*, 46(02): 391–425.

Yan, Xuetong (2001) "The Rise of China in Chinese Eyes." *Journal of Contemporary China*, 10(26): 33–39.

Yan, Xuetong (2010) "The Instability of China: US Relations." *Chinese Journal of International Politics*, 3(3): 263–292.

Yan, Xuetong (2011) *How China Can Defeat America* [online]. Available at www.nytimes.com/2011/11/21/opinion/how-china-can-defeat-america.html. (Accessed September 26, 2017).

Yan, Xuetong (2013) *Ancient Chinese Thought, Modern Chinese Power*. Princeton: Princeton University Press.

Yan, Xuetong (2014) "From Keeping a Low Profile to Striving for Achievement." *The Chinese Journal of International Politics*, 7(2): 153–184.

Yan, Xuetong (2016) "Political Leadership and Power Redistribution." *The Chinese Journal of International Politics*, 9(1): 1–26.

Yan, Xuetong (2018) "Chinese Values vs. Liberalism: What Ideology Will Shape the International Normative Order?" *Chinese Journal of International Politics*, 11(1): 1–22.

Zhang, Feng (2012a) "The Tsinghua Approach and the Inception of Chinese Theories of International Relations." *Chinese Journal of International Politics*, 5(1): 73–102.

Zhang, WeiWei (2012b) *The China Wave: Rise of a Civilizational State*. Hackensack: World Century Pub. Co.

Zhang, Yongjin, and Teng-Chi Chang (2016) *Constructing a Chinese School of International Relations: Ongoing Debates and Sociological Realities*. London: Routledge.

Zhao, Tingyang (2006) "Rethinking Empire from a Chinese Concept 'All-under-Heaven' (Tian-xia)." *Social Identities*, 12(1): 29–41.

4 The domestic foundations of emerging and established state trade cooperation

Laura C. Mahrenbach

Introduction

Much has been made much of the difficulties Northern and Southern states[1] face when cooperating in global economic governance (GEG). This is particularly true for cooperation between established states, such as the United States (US) or larger members of the European Union (EU), and emerging economies, including but not limited to the BRICS (Brazil, Russia, India, China, and South Africa). Such cooperation is oft depicted as mired in conflict. For example, scholars have highlighted disagreements between the US and EU on one side and the BRICS on the other in relation to the 2010 quota reforms of the International Monetary Fund (Lesage et al., 2013). Likewise, the US was at loggerheads with India and China at the World Trade Organization's (WTO) Geneva ministerial in 2008, leading to a breakdown of the negotiations (Ismail, 2009). Nonetheless, there have also been instances of successful emerging-established state cooperation in GEG. Examples include Chinese, German, and US willingness to sacrifice a portion of their entitled quota shares to ensure the World Bank quota reform process proceeded (Vestergaard and Wade, 2015) as well as cooperation between emerging and established states in the G20, which has led to positive policy outcomes and enhanced trust between these governments (Lin and Li, 2014). What determines whether emerging-established state cooperation will be successful in any given situation?

Nowhere are patterns of cooperation and conflict more apparent than in trade cooperation. On one hand, the WTO's Doha Round negotiations have featured some spectacular blow-ups and name-calling between emerging states, such as Brazil and India, and established giants, including the US and the EU, most notably in Cancún in 2003 and Potsdam in 2007. Conflictual relations have extended to the WTO's Dispute Settlement Body (DSB) as well, where Brazil, India, the US, and the EU number among the most frequent complainants overall and where China has reserved its use for targeting established states' policies (Kennedy, 2012). On the other hand, emerging-established state trade cooperation has concurrently flourished. Positive examples include US-Brazilian cooperation at the Geneva mini-ministerial in 2008 and a bilateral deal between India and the US that enabled implementation of the 2013 Bali Agreement. As such, understanding the challenges of trade cooperation can shed light on emerging-established state cooperation in GEG in general.

I will argue that the hiccups in US-Brazilian trade cooperation stem from governments' inability to navigate conflicting domestic ideas and interests. This is demonstrated in two case studies – the negotiations for a Free Trade Area of the Americas (FTAA) and the WTO mini-ministerial in 2008 – which demonstrate variation on the success of US-Brazilian trade cooperation. I conclude by discussing the future challenges for enhanced trade cooperation, and making suggestions for how to enhance such cooperation in the future.

Trade cooperation to date

Trade has long been central to bilateral cooperation between the US and Brazil. Traditionally dominated by trade in manufactured goods (Schott, 2003), the scope of bilateral trade has expanded in recent years, with US exports to Brazil in services, for example, more than doubling between 2002 and 2009 (Ward, 2011). This has been accompanied by an absolute increase in trade volume. As is evident in Figure 4.1, between 2001 and 2014, US exports to Brazil and imports from Brazil increased consistently, reaching US$ 44 billion and US$ 27 billion respectively (US Census Bureau, 2017). Renewed engagement between economic officials since March 2016 aims to "expand commercial ties and address non-tariff barriers to trade" (Bureau of Western Hemisphere Affairs, 2017), and figures for 2017 indicate trade levels which, if not on par with 2014, are at least consistently higher than corresponding months in the previous two years (US Census Bureau, 2017). The compatibility of the two markets further attests to the potential for future bilateral trade growth. Moreira (2009) notes that the production structures and size of Northern markets like the US are economically much more attractive to Brazil than the market gains available in preferential trade agreements with Southern countries. Similarly, markets like Brazil have been described as the "best prospects for US export growth" and Brazil itself as "a vital market for US companies" by both business representatives and economists alike (Marques, 2013; Schott, 2006).

The potential for trade cooperation is additionally enhanced by similar approaches in the two countries. First, both are "global rather than regional traders" (Phillips, 2003: 336). Consequently, they have both traditionally been strong proponents of multilateral trade governance. US engagement drove the first eight rounds of trade liberalization under the WTO's precursor, the General Agreement on Trade and Tariffs, and helped establish principles which remain fundamental to global trade governance today (Feinberg, 2003). Likewise, the Brazilian government's successful use of the WTO's DSB and its leadership of the trade G20 coalition have reinforced the continued relevance of the WTO and its principles (Hopewell, 2016). Second, both states support pursuing trade preferences in diverse fora. While President Trump's prioritization of bilateral negotiations has been much commented upon in the media, the basis for the US trade diversification in fact stretches back at least to the George W. Bush administration, whose officials viewed bilateral trade agreements as models for and building blocks to a successful WTO deal (Evenett and Meier, 2008). Similarly, Brazilian president Luiz Inácio

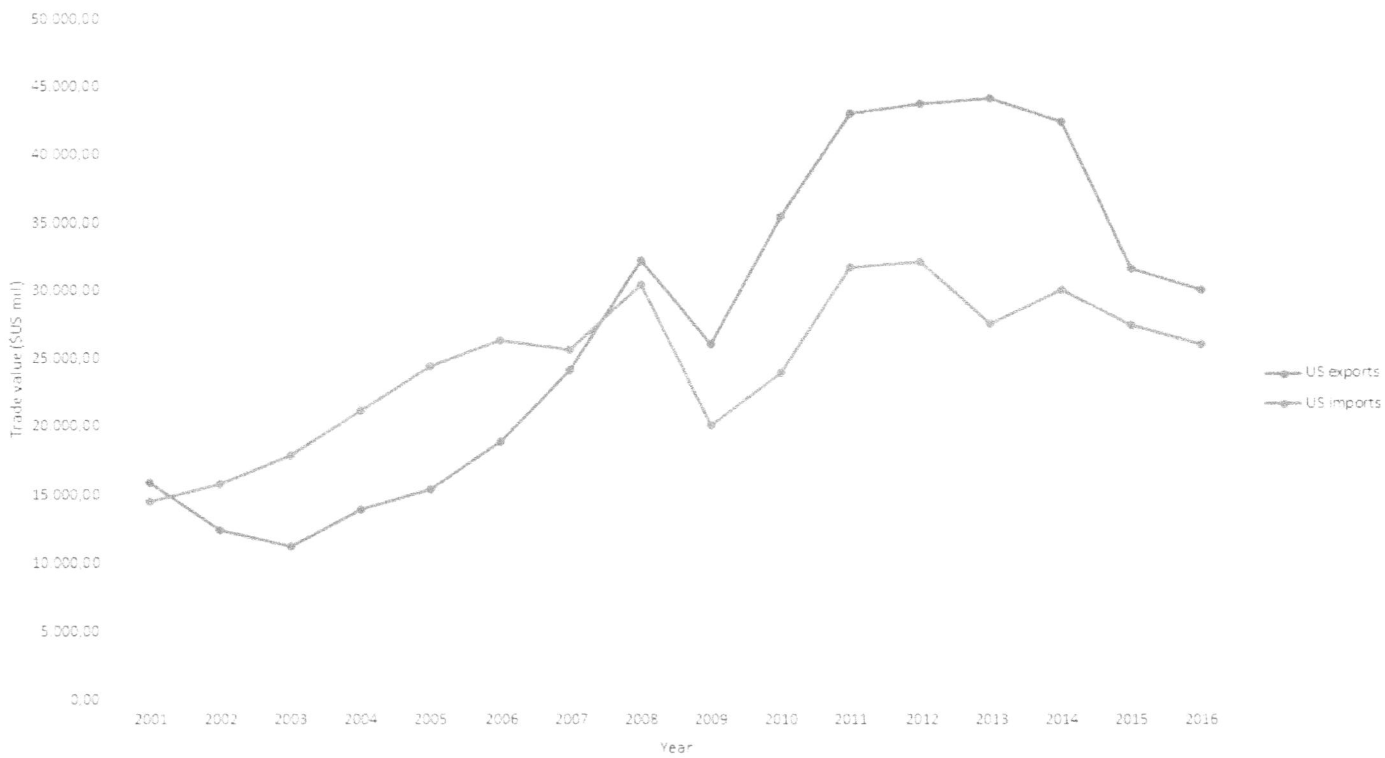

Figure 4.1 Brazilian-US bilateral trade in goods

Source: data from US Census Bureau

Lula da Silva (henceforth: Lula) stepped up South-South trade cooperation both within and outside the WTO, signing nine South-South trade agreements during his administration (OAS, 2017). Finally, the rhetoric of the two governments has underlined their desire to cooperate more closely on trade. A joint statement issued by US President Barack Obama and Brazilian President Dilma Rousseff in 2011 "emphasized the importance of building on, deepening, and broadening" their trade relationship (Obama and Rousseff, 2011). The Trade and Economic Cooperation Agreement signed at the same time reflected these intentions: five of the TECA's seven tasks related to expanding trade levels and cooperation.

Yet, despite these auspicious signs, bilateral trade cooperation remains below its potential. The prominence of South-South cooperation during the Lula administration has allowed Asian countries, especially China, to gain Brazilian market share largely at the cost of the US exporters (WTO, 2013), and this trend looks continued under Michel Temer's administration (Leahy, 2017). Similarly, the US' decision to negotiate mega-regional agreements with Europe and Asia implicitly reaffirmed the relative unimportance of Latin America within US trade policy (Hakim, 2014), while the Trump administration's decision to withdraw from the Trans-Pacific Partnership and its intractability in renegotiating the North American Free Trade Agreement raise questions about the importance of the trade portfolio in general in an "America First" foreign policy. Even when Brazil and the US do trade, their relationship has been characterized by persistent bilateral conflict over specific trade issues, including agricultural subsidies and intellectual property protection, creating "open and potentially damaging friction between the two countries" (Hakim, 2004). For instance, the decision in March 2018 to impose tariffs on steel and aluminum imports had the potential to strongly and negatively impact the Brazilians in particular, as Brazil is the US' second largest source of steel imports (CNBC, 2018). That Brazil was ultimately exempted from the tariffs after ruling out neither retaliation nor a legal challenge at the WTO (Reeves, 2018; BBC News, 2018) speaks both to the potential for bilateral cooperation and to the changeability of this evolving trade relationship.

The domestic foundations of US and Brazilian trade policy

Why this disjunction between economic potential and political commitment on one hand, and conflict and unfulfilled ambition on the other? The liberal theory of international relations (Moravcsik, 1997) and associated societal approach (Schirm, 2016) point to domestic factors as crucial for explaining a variety of outcomes in GEG. These approaches assume government preferences are formed at home before being transmitted to potential partners in international cooperative situations and that elected officials respond to domestic preferences because they are electorally dependent on voters. As Putnam's (1988) two-level games approach elaborates, successful cooperation requires negotiators at the international level to reach agreements which are simultaneously acceptable to fellow governments and fall within their own constitutents' "win-set". Such cooperation among democratic governments requires accommodation of partners' domestic preferences, for example, via incorporation of socially popular ideas or sectoral economic interests (Schirm, 2010). In relation to Brazilian-US trade cooperation, this implies the two governments' varying ability to accommodate the domestic ideas and interests of the other results alternately in more or less successful bilateral trade cooperation.

Although Brazilian domestic actors have traditionally had little influence over Brazilian trade policy decisions (Marconini, 2005; Hurrell and Narlikar, 2006), the impact of domestic groups on trade policy is growing. The FTAA negotiations marked a significant change in domestic-government relations as Brazilian domestic actors successfully institutionalized their role in preparing Brazilian negotiating positions for the first time (Veiga, 2005). By creating organizations like the Brazilian Business Coalition, domestic actors were able to better synthesize and communicate diverse domestic preferences to the government. In addition, they assisted the government by providing sector-relevant information which enabled the government to better assess the impact its proposed trade policy positions would have at home (Shaffer et al., 2008). Nowadays, the future of Brazilian trade integration "depends centrally on the country's domestic politics" (Martinez-Diaz and Brainard, 2009).

US domestic actors have long been a pivotal force in trade policymaking, for instance, providing government actors with technical advice to help them estimate the impact of potential trade policies on the US economy. This has granted domestic actors "great leverage on what the US government can and cannot agree to in trade negotiations" (Cohen, 2000). For example, lobbying expenditures have been shown to be effective in convincing elected and non-elected government officials to reach policy decisions favorable to domestic interests (Gawande and Hoekman, 2006; Drope and Hansen, 2004). Furthermore, domestic actors affect US government trade policy decisions indirectly through their ideas. Research shows US legislators' trade votes correlate strongly with their ideological positioning precisely because gaining voter support for trade initiatives depends on aligning voters' and legislators' ideological orientations (Baldwin and Magee, 2000). Although the impact of domestic preferences on both countries' trade policy may be moderated by the impact of foreign policy considerations (Evenett and Meier, 2008; Veiga, 2005), domestic preferences remain a crucial factor for understanding their trade policy decisions.

I will focus on two types of domestic preferences in this chapter. *Ideas* are defined as "path-dependent and value-based collective expectations about appropriate governmental policies" (Schirm, 2016). The collective nature of popular ideas is what gives them power in domestic politics. Therefore, while acknowledging the valuable contributions of non-governmental organizations to domestic political debates and framing in these countries (see Baiocchi et al., 2008, and Kim, 2017), the domestic reference group for ideas is voters in general. *Economic interests* are defined as economic actions which generate benefits and costs for private actors as a result of government decisions (Mahrenbach, 2013). Actors are assumed to band together in interest groups and lobby for their preferences, offering government actors both contributions and blocs of votes in exchange for adopting sectoral preferences (Grossman and Helpman, 1994). Consequently, sectoral and apex interest groups will be the domestic reference group for economic interest preferences.[2]

Ideational preferences

Two ideas appear especially relevant to US-Brazilian trade cooperation. The first is influence, defined here as the desire to exert control over outcomes in international trade negotiations. From the US perspective, influence is relevant since maintaining the US' unique position in global economic affairs has long been a foreign policy goal of the US government (Mastanduno, 2009). Furthermore, the US sees trade activities as a means of increasing US influence (Altieri, 2003), leveraging access to the US market for desired trade outcomes. US voters show clear and consistent support for this idea: 83% of US respondents considered US leadership in world affairs "very" or "somewhat desirable" in 2002 and 84% in 2010 (CCGA, 2012). Additionally, US respondents accept the link between trade and foreign policy which allows the US to leverage its market size for influence over partners' trade policies, with 67% of respondents finding FTAs "very" or "somewhat effective" in achieving US foreign policy goals (CCGA, 2012).

From a Brazilian perspective, influence should matter because, despite Brazil's elevation to emerging power status, US-Brazil bilateral relations remain asymmetrical. Brazilian opposition to US foreign policy initiatives in Latin America is at least partially motivated by Brazil's desire to realize its own self-perception as "one of the world's most important nations" (Hakim, 2004). Consequently, Brazilian domestic actors should be interested not only in avoiding exploitation but should also seek US acknowledgement that the bilateral relationship must adjust to Brazil's new status in global economic affairs. The logic of this argument is validated by Brazilian public opinion data. On one hand, Brazilians remain pragmatic regarding their country's relationship with the US. 55% of Brazilian respondents agreed the US "did not consider others" when making foreign policy decisions (Pew, 2002), and 76% indicated "rich countries" do not "play fair" in trade negotiations (GlobeScan, 2004). On the other hand, 73% expected Brazil to have "more importance" in the future, and 87% indicated they had "more pride than shame" in their country (Datafolha, 2000; Pew, 2010). Thus, while recognizing influence gains vis-à-vis the US will be hard-won, Brazilians nonetheless consistently expect Brazil's influence in the world to increase.

The second idea likely to be relevant to US-Brazilian trade cooperation is development. Development refers to efforts to create a stable and prosperous macroeconomic environment while simultaneously minimizing social inequalities. For Brazil, development should matter because of the development possibilities US-Brazilian trade cooperation offers. The US market is hugely attractive to Latin America because of its size (Wrobel, 1998), and the rapid growth in business ties between the US and Brazil suggests this is especially the case for Brazil (Bodman and Wolfensohn, 2011). Furthermore, Brazilian policymakers expect higher levels of trade to facilitate domestic development efforts, and have shown themselves willing to use Brazil's veto power within trade negotiations when outcomes veer away from this goal (Bahadian, 2008). US policymakers see a similar link between trade and development. Regional trade initiatives have long been considered a means of solidifying the economic foundations of Latin American democracy and creating a stable, prosperous neighborhood for the US and its businesses (Schott, 2003). Furthermore, scholars note that the success of US foreign policy initiatives in the region is largely dependent on the Brazilian government's success in achieving development goals within Brazil (Hakim, 2004).

Voters in both countries agree on the importance of development. 96% of Brazilians find social inequality either a "very big" or a "moderately big" problem in Brazil (Stokes, 2014), and 80% of respondents agree that the "Brazilian economic system generally favors the wealthy" (Pew, 2013). Other development issues requiring attention in Brazil included expansion of education, expansion of social programs, and economic development (IBOPE, 2007). Like policymakers, Brazilian voters consider trade a potential solution for some of these problems: 44% of respondents expected more trade to increase wages, and 56% thought more trade would mean more jobs in Brazil (Pew, 2014). In contrast, US voters focus their attention on development efforts abroad. Respondents identified the "growing gap between the rich and poor" as the third "greatest threat to the world" in 2007 (Pew, 2007). Further, 62% and 74%, respectively, support development aid to help developing countries "develop their economies" and "become more productive" (CCGA, 2010). Finally, like Brazilian respondents, US respondents see trade as an important means of addressing development problems (CCGA, 2010). In sum, while domestic support for development appears complementary and consequently conducive to trade cooperation, the strength of voter support for influence in both countries could make it hard for governments to compromise in relation to their influence in world affairs. This suggests ideational conflict over influence could complicate US-Brazilian trade cooperation.

Interest preferences

Two interests appear relevant to US-Brazilian trade cooperation. These represent opposing policy approaches vis-à-vis the purpose of trade cooperation, namely regulating market access opportunities and trade flows. The first interest, liberalization, is defined as gaining access to new markets or expanding access to existing markets. The second, protection, refers to maintaining or decreasing given levels of market access.

As US business "became globalized" and increasingly dependent on global markets in the late 1990s, domestic support for protection began to decline (Destler, 2012). This is evident in the mandates of the US' three apex interest groups, considered the "most politically influential" of US interest groups (Chorev, 2007). The Business Roundtable considers free markets for trade and investment "essential" to US economic health, identifies reaping the "benefits of trade and US trade agreements" as a priority, and actively urges Congress to pass legislation to facilitate the implementation of successful trade initiatives (Business Roundtable, 2014). Similar sentiments are expressed by the US Chamber of Commerce, which sees freer markets as the key to a "brighter future", and by the National Association of Manufacturers (US Chamber of Commerce, 2014; NAM, 2014). Beyond the apex level, however, interest preference appears less coherent. Some sectors, such as agriculture, continue to be wary of trade. For instance, the National Farmers Organization released press releases entitled "No to Fast Track" and "Brazilian Beef Imports a Bad Idea" (National Farmers Organization, 2014). While the former indicates support for increasing institutional obstacles to liberalization, the latter explicitly opposes improved market access for Brazilian exports to the US. Other sectors, including the US services sectors, actively lobby for liberalization (Chorev, 2007). The Telecommunications Industry Association, for example, explicitly supported extending President Obama's Trade Promotion Authority in 2014, claiming trade agreements lead to increased communication technology exports and should therefore be facilitated (TIA, 2014). Clearly, US domestic preferences toward trade are diverse.

Turning to Brazil, protectionist interest groups have traditionally been more successful than their liberal counterparts in gaining the government's ear (Veiga, 2009). During the Lula administration, however, some of these groups began to reconsider their positions toward market access (Marconini, 2010), and liberalization supporters concurrently gained some influence over trade policy. As such, Brazil is now characterized by "enormous ambivalence on the question of openness" (Martinez-Diaz and Brainard, 2009). On one hand, some sectors call for government intervention to ensure Brazilian competitiveness in global markets. The Brazilian Association of Machinery & Equipment, for example, says domestic competitiveness should be "encouraged by the state" and that the government should "ensure [competitive] equality with respect to trade competitors" (ABIMAQ, 2014). Such measures would bias market competition in favor of Brazilian producers and protect Brazilian companies from foreign competition. On the other hand, the highly competitive agriculture sector lobbies strongly for liberalization, establishing research institutions like the Institute for International Trade Negotiations to support trade officials and promote their own interests (Hopewell, 2013). This ambivalence between liberalization and protection is additionally reflected in the statements and missions of apex interest groups, such as the Federation of Industries of São Paulo and the National Confederation of Agriculture and Livestock (see CNA, 2014; or FIESP, 2014).

In sum, significant and powerful business groups are working to advance both interests in both countries. Interest-based conflicts which complicate bilateral cooperation should center on sectors where interest groups' preferences in the two countries conflict, such as agriculture or, given recent political developments, steel and coal.

Failed cooperation: Free Trade Area of the Americas negotiations, 2001–2005

The FTAA was first proposed at the Miami Summit of the Americas in 1994. Negotiations began in 1998, setting January 2005 as the target date for completion.[3] From the beginning, the process was characterized by conflict between co-chairmen Brazil and the US, both regarding the scope and the format of the negotiations (Kennedy, 2003–2004). By 2005, negotiations had fizzled out, with neither the US nor Brazil demonstrating the "political commitment" necessary to make concessions and reach a deal (Carranza, 2004). How did domestic ideas and interests contribute to this failure of US-Brazilian cooperation?

Starting with ideas, as expected, development played little role in the failure of US-Brazilian cooperation. In line with domestic preferences, Brazilian government actors spoke often during the negotiations of the FTAA's usefulness in "redressing the inequalities that affect us" (Seixas Corrêa, 2001). US officials likewise underlined the need to help FTAA partners promote "sustainable development" as one of the US' objectives in the negotiations (Zoellick, 2002). Influence, in contrast, appeared more obstructionist. On the Brazilian side, the literature highlights the Brazilian government's desire to balance US power in the region via the FTAA negotiations (Mera, 2005). Officials worried the negotiations would damage Mercosur, in which the Brazilian government had invested significant political capital (Veiga, 2005). They consequently sought a negotiation outcome which simultaneously ensured Brazil's future regional influence and avoided US regional dominance (Phillips, 2003). As then-presidential candidate Lula noted, "The FTAA, as proposed, is not a policy of integration, but of annexation. We will not be annexed" (Agence France Presse, 2002). On the US side, the FTAA negotiations were seen as a good opportunity to reinforce "the structural and ideological foundations of [US] hegemony" (Phillips, 2003). Specifically, the US government sought to promote the maintenance of domestic economic reforms in Latin America which supported US preferences, as well as to solicit FTAA partners' support for US foreign policy initiatives (Schott, 2003). Put differently, the US sought to exert influence over the economic and foreign policies of its FTAA trade partners. As such, the US refused to yield significant influence gains to either Brazil or its Mercosur partners during the FTAA negotiations (Grugel, 2004). These circumstances put the positions of the two governments at odds when it came to influence in the negotiations.

Turning to economic interests, both governments were intent on achieving liberalization. While the US focused on opening markets for its agricultural and manufacturing sectors, it also saw the FTAA as an opportunity to gain entrance to highly protected, Southern services markets (Phillips, 2003; Schott, 2006). Increasing trade with Brazil was an especially attractive goal for US government officials (Feinberg, 2003). Likewise, Brazil sought to increase access for its manufacturing and services sectors, both to the US market and to other regional markets (Barbosa, 2004; Schott, 2006). Officials also hoped to discuss the removal of existing protectionist structures with the US during the negotiations (Rios, 2006). However, domestic actors' ambivalence toward liberalization and protection in both countries meant the devil was in the details when it came to increasing market access via an FTAA. For both countries, the liberalization goals prioritized by officials corresponded to their partner's most protectionist sectors. The US government, for example, sought to "eliminate government practices [. . .] that adversely affect US exports" in agriculture, but simultaneously maintained its right to "improve US import relief mechanisms as appropriate" (Zoellick, 2002). Elimination of these protectionist "relief mechanisms" stood at the center of the Brazilian negotiating position in the FTAA negotiations. As Brazilian Minister Sergio Amaral noted, there were "no conditions for coming to an agreement (with agricultural subsidies in place) because most of our competitiveness is in agricultural products" (Brooks, 2002). Thus, the peculiar combination of who supported which interest in each country, and the failure of opposing governments to acknowledge these sensitivities, hindered progress in the negotiations.

The FTAA negotiations represent a clear failure of US-Brazilian trade cooperation. The conflicting goals arising from the idea of influence in the two countries delayed negotiations and resulted in constant competition over who would decide fundamental issues. Furthermore, both governments showed an unwillingness to compromise on issues, such as agriculture, where domestic interest preferences clashed.

Successful cooperation: WTO mini-ministerial meeting, Geneva, 2008

The WTO mini-ministerial meeting brought together ministers from roughly 40 countries in July 2008 in Geneva to start resolving the remaining issues of the Doha Round and to outline the next steps for the trade negotiations. The negotiations were primarily conducted within a small group, the G7, which contained both Brazil and the US. Unlike the FTAA negotiations, emerging-established state conflict within the G7 was largely between the US and India, not Brazil. In fact, US-Brazilian trade cooperation in Geneva almost led to a breakthrough: both governments' acceptance of the so-called Lamy Package, a compromise in which the US agreed to lower its agricultural subsidy cap in exchange for Brazil deepening industrial tariff cuts, extended the negotiations for several days (Miller, 2008). What role did domestic ideas and interests play in the success of US-Brazilian trade cooperation in this situation?

The name of the negotiations – Doha Development Agenda – points to the importance of development for the Round and suggests participants should, at least rhetorically, support positions in line with this idea. This supposition is confirmed by US and Brazilian government statements. USTR Susan Schwab noted "a successful Doha Round of trade negotiations will contribute to development and lift millions out of poverty around the world" (Schwab, 2008c). Likewise, Brazilian Foreign Minister Celso Amorim underlined the "inestimable" importance of the Round for "promoting development" (Amorim, 2008a).

In contrast, given the clashes between Northern and Southern states throughout the Doha Round and the US and Brazil's leadership roles, respectively, in each of these groups, influence seemed a likely point of conflict between the US and Brazil. Surprisingly, this was not the case. US government statements made clear that the US was aware it could not dictate the terms of the final deal but, rather, was dependent on cooperation and compromise with other governments. Similar content appears in Brazilian government statements (compare Amorim,

2008b, and Schwab, 2008a). Additionally, US officials went out of their way to praise Brazil's leadership in the Round, thus acknowledging Brazil's changing weight in the world. For example, USTR Schwab noted "Brazil was one of the countries that really exhibited leadership", showing itself "able to endorse and willing to endorse the Friday Lamy package even though it caused some pain and discomfort" (Schwab, 2008b). Brazilian officials returned the favor, declaring US "leadership in the multilateral process of agriculture reform" helpful in reaching a deal (Engeler, 2008) and minimizing, if not eliminating, verbal provocation. For instance, Amorim highlighted how, in participating in the "new Quad" (Brazil, EU, India, and US) of major players at the WTO, Brazil was not seeking to eliminate the US' influence in negotiations but, rather, simply adding Brazil's voice to the mix.

Economic interest preferences were similarly unproblematic for US-Brazilian cooperation. This is evident in the terms accepted by Brazil and the US in the Lamy Package. The US government's acceptance meant agreeing not to raise total US agricultural subsidies above US$ 14.5 billion in the future (Ismail, 2009). This was not as low as liberal agriculture exporters in Brazil wanted, but it was "a lower ceiling than US negotiators had ever accepted" (Blustein, 2008). It also marked a huge change from previous Doha negotiations, where disagreements over agricultural subsidies had resulted in much-publicized failures (Bhagwati, 2004). US acceptance thereby represented a symbolic concession on an issue that had become central to Brazilian trade policy given the strength of the Brazilian agriculture sector.

Brazilian acceptance of the Lamy Package, in turn, meant agreeing to the conditions the US set for its own acceptance. First, the US' agricultural subsidies would be exempt from litigation at the WTO for a designated period of time. This was unlikely to please Brazil's liberal agriculture sector, which had gained significant market access via disputes with the US and Europe. However, the market access potential arising from the US' subsidies offer must have been seen as an adequate trade-off, or at least one substantial enough to continue negotiating. As the president of the Association of Brazilian Pork Exporters noted, "If there is a chance, we should do it. But it is too low. [. . .] We are far from the promise of Doha" (Zanatta, 2008). Second, the Brazilian government had to offer WTO members "significant market access" in services and manufactured goods (Kaushik et al., 2008). The vagueness of the US' demand here made Brazilian compliance easier: not defining what qualified as "significant" enabled protectionist sectors in Brazil to accept their government's positions during the negotiations. As the president of the National Association of Automobile Manufacturers noted, the government assumed "a strong position respecting the limits of the industry" (Landim, 2008).

In this case, successful cooperation was characterized by a willingness on both sides to publicly acknowledge ideas valued by their trade partner in their communications. In addition, both governments showed their willingness to navigate ambivalent domestic interest preferences by agreeing to strategic and/or symbolic compromises which recognized the other's vulnerabilities.

Conclusion

I have argued that understanding the complementarity of domestic ideas and interests in Brazil and the US is crucial to understanding the successes and failures of US-Brazilian trade cooperation since the start of the Doha Round in 2001. In addition, I have claimed that this exercise will yield useful insights into emerging-established state cooperation within GEG more broadly. So what have we learned?

First, the forum of trade cooperation may matter for success. Domestic ideational differences were easier to navigate at the multilateral level than at the regional one. This is because the larger institutional context of the WTO – where questions of influence are negotiated among many countries rather than just two – made it easier to recognize *both* countries' leadership in international affairs. Likewise, the broader agenda of the multilateral institution facilitated cross-issue compromises in regard to domestic interests. This was evident in the Lamy Package, for example, where the US exchanged capping agricultural subsidies for increased market access in services and manufacturing.

Second, foreign and trade policy continue to be closely related in both countries and successful bilateral cooperation cannot happen in a vacuum. Foreign policy scandals, such as the 2013 discovery that the US National Security Agency had been spying on the Brazilian president, have strong negative repercussions on each government's ability to frame negotiations in a way compatible with trade progress. At the same time, however, trade cooperation can also moderate, if not eliminate, the impact foreign policy conflicts on the broader bilateral relationship. Resolution of the 11-year-old trade dispute over cotton in October 2014, for example, marked the first sign of easing the "strained" relationship between Brazil and the US evident since the spying scandal (BBC News Business, 2014).

Finally, concessions – symbolic or not – matter for the success of bilateral trade cooperation. Although the Lamy Package was unlikely to result in significant agricultural gains for Brazil, the US' concession had symbolic value in that it acknowledged both Brazil's influence aspirations as well as the interests of a significant sector within Brazil. Likewise, the Brazilian government's decision to minimize rhetorical provocation during the WTO negotiations, unlike in the FTAA negotiations, and even verbally support US leadership allowed negotiators to sidestep US domestic fears that emerging powers, among them Brazil, are seeking to replace the US in international affairs. The best case scenario in facilitating positive outcomes from US-Brazilian trade cooperation would be for both sides to agree to real market access concessions. Given that such concessions are by definition politically precarious, that both the Brazilian and American governments are embroiled in corruption scandals and that the current US administration has a penchant for a zero-sum view of trade relationships, this is unlikely to happen anytime soon. Hence, for now, the best that can be hoped for is symbolic concessions which ensure the governments continue talking.

These findings offer lessons for emerging-established state cooperation in GEG more broadly as well. Regarding forum choice, bilateral, regional, and multilateral fora have long been viewed as legitimate, if not equally optimal, contexts for trade cooperation between emerging and established states. Recent developments in other issue areas, such as the Asian Infrastructure Investment Bank, in contrast are often characterized as evidence of "hubris" or "aggression" on the part of emerging states and linked to pursuit of power-related goals (e.g., The Economist, 2016). Emerging-established state cooperation could be enhanced by acknowledging emerging states simply seek the same privileges – and forum flexibility – which established states have enjoyed for years. Doing so will expand and diversify the existing system of GEG, but it need not eliminate – and may even enhance – the benefits arising from that system. Assuming this attitude would also help embed new theoretical insights which highlight the link between foreign and foreign economic policy, such as Armijo and Katada's (2015) financial statecraft, into policymaker interpretations of partners' intentions. This could enhance the quality of emerging-established state discussions. As for concessions, the most transferrable lesson from trade cooperation regards the importance of symbolic concessions. Although these may not be sufficient to ensure GEG institutions' continued viability and effectiveness (Woods, 2010), US-Brazilian trade cooperation suggests acknowledging partners' sensitivities via such concessions can not only prolong cooperation by building (and repairing) relationships. In addition, doing so can blur the line between North and South by re-focusing discussions on domestically feasible policy options which are more likely to be implemented by, and therefore more likely to result in effective cooperation among, emerging and established states.

Acknowledgments

This research was funded by the Deutsche Forschungsgemeinschaft (DFG-German Research Foundation), project number 369896954. Thanks go to Steen Christensen, Erik Fritzsche, Li Xing, workshop participants at "The BRICS as an Emerging Power: Reality or Myth?" (Aalborg University), and an anonymous reviewer for comments on previous versions of this chapter.

Notes

1 "Northern states" refers to established states such as the US, Germany, or Japan, "Southern states" to emerging and developing countries.
2 Sectoral interest groups represent a single sector, such as sugar. Apex interest groups represent multiple sectors, such as all agricultural sectors.
3 This case study only considers the latter half of the negotiations, between 2001 and 2005.

References

ABIMAQ (2014) "Política Industrial." *Associação Brasileira da Indústria de Máquinas e Equipamentos*. Available at www.abimaq.org.br/site.aspx/Abimaq-Pauta-Reivindicatoria.

Agence France Presse (2002) "The FTAA Is a Proposed Annexation, Says Candidate Lula da Silva." September 28. Available at www.lexisnexis.com.

Altieri, Laura (2003) "NAFTA and the FTAA: Regional Alternatives to Multilateralism." *Berkeley Journal of International Law*, 21(3): 847–877.

Amorim, Celso (2008a) "Discurso do Ministro das Relações Exteriores, Embaixador Celso Amorim, na Reunião Informal do Comitê de Negociações Técnicas da OMC." *Itamaraty*, July 21. Available at www.mre.gov.br/portugues/politica_externa/discursos/discurso_detalhe3.asp?ID_DISCURSO=3346.

Amorim, Celso (2008b) "Palestra proferida pelo Ministro das Relações Exteriores, Embaixador Celso Amorim, aos alunos do Instituto Rio Branco." *Itamaraty*, August 6. Available at www.mre.gov.br/portugues/politica_externa/discursos/discurso_detalhe3.asp?ID_DISCURSO=3356.

Armijo, Leslie Elliot, and Saori N. Katada (2015) "Theorizing the Financial Statecraft of Emerging Powers." *New Political Economy*, 20(1): 42–62.

Associated Press (2018) "WTO Chief: If Not for Body, There Would Already Be Trade War." *CNBC*, March 15. Available at www.cnbc.com/2018/03/14/the-associated-press-wto-chief-if-not-for-body-there-would-already-be-trade-war.html.

Bahadian, Adhemar G. (2008) "FTAA Trade Negotiations: A View of the Brazilian Co-Chairmanship." *Journal of World Investment & Trade*, 9(3): 299–315.

Baiocchi, Gianpaolo, Patrick Heller, and Marcelo Kunrath Silva (2008) "Making Space for Civil Society: Institutional Reforms and Local Democracy in Brazil." *Social Forces*, 86(3): 911–935.

Baldwin, Robert E., and Christopher S. Magee (2000) "Is Trade Policy for Sale? Congressional Voting on Recent Trade Bills." *Public Choice*, 105(1/2): 79–101.

Barbosa, Rubens Antonio (2004) "The Free Trade Area of the Americas and Brazil." *Fordham International Law Journal*, 27(4): 1017–1028.

BBC News (2018) "EU and Six Other Countries Exempted from US Metals Tariffs." March 23. Available at http://www.bbc.com/news/business-43505804.

BBC News Business (2014) "US and Brazil Resolve Longstanding Cotton Dispute." October 1. Available at www.bbc.com/news/business-43505804.

Bhagwati, Jagdish (2004) "Don't Cry for Cancun." *Foreign Affairs*, 83(1): 52–63.

Blustein, Paul (2008) "The Nine-Day Misadventure of the Most Favored Nations: How the WTO's Doha Round Negotiations Went Awry in July 2008." Available at www.brookings.edu/research/articles/2008/12/05-trade-blustein.

Bodman, Samuel W., and James D. Wolfensohn (2011) "Global Brazil and US-Brazil Relations." *Council on Foreign Relations*. Available at www.cfr.org/report/global-brazil-and-us-brazil-relations.

Brooks, Bradley (2002) "Economic Storms Hit Brazil." *United Press International*, May 7. Available at www.lexisnexis.com.

Bureau of Western Hemisphere Affairs (2017) "US Relations with Brazil." *US Department of State*, January 27. Available at www.state.gov/r/pa/ei/bgn/35640.htm.

Business Roundtable (2014) "International Engagement Committee Priorities." Available at http://businessroundtable.org/.

Carranza, Mario E. (2004) "Mercosur and the End Game of the FTAA Negotiations: Challenges and Prospects after the Aregentine Crisis." *Third World Quarterly*, 25(2): 319–337.

CCGA (2010) "Global Views 2010: US Public Topline Report." *Chicago Council on Global Affairs*, September 22. Available at www.thechicagocouncil.org/publication/global-views-2010-us-public-opinion-topline-report.

CCGA (2012) "Global Views 2012: US Public Topline Report." *Chicago Council on Global Affairs*, July 27. Available at www.thechicagocouncil.org/publication/global-views-2012-us-public-opinion-topline-report.

Chorev, Nitsan (2007) *Remaking US Trade Policy*. Ithaca: Cornell University Press.

CNA (2014) "Sobre o Sistema CAN." *Confederação da Agricultura e Pecuária*. Available at www.canaldoprodutor.com.br/sobre-sistema-cna/missao-visao-objetivos.

Cohen, Stephen D. (2000) *The Making of United States International Economic Policy: Principles, Problems, and Proposals for Reform Degrees*. Westport: Praeger Publishers.

Datafolha (2000) "Utopia do brasileiro." *Datafolha Instituto de Pesquisas*, April 23. Available at http://datafolha.folha.uol.com.br/po/ver_po.php?session=97.

Destler, I.M. (Mac) (2012) "American Trade Policymaking: A Unique Process." In James M. McCormick (ed.) *The Domestic Sources of American Foreign Policy: Insights and Evidence*. 6th ed. Lanham: Rowman and Littlefield.

Drope, Jeffrey M., and Wendy L. Hansen (2004) "Purchasing Protection? The Effect of Political Spending on US Trade Policy." *Political Research Quarterly*, 57(1): 27–37.

The Economist (2016) "The Infrastructure of Power." July 2. Available at www.economist.com/finance-and-economics/2016/06/30/the-infrastructure-of-power.

Engeler, Eliane (2008) "WTO Countries Slam US Farm Bill." *Associated Press Financial Wire*, June 3. Available at www.lexisnexis.com.

Evenett, Simon J., and Michael Meier (2008) "An Interim Assessment of the US Trade Policy of 'Competitive Liberalization'." *The World Economy*, 31(1): 31–66.

Feinberg, Richard E. (2003) "The Political Economy of United States' Free Trade Arrangements." *World Economy*, 26(7): 1019–1040.

FIESP (2014) "Derex: Departamento de Relações Internacionais e Comércio Exterior." *Federation of Industries of São Paulo*. Available at www.fiesp.com.br/sobre-a-fiesp/departamentos/relacoes-internacionais-e-comercio-exterior/.

Gawande, Kishore, and Bernard Hoekman (2006) "Lobbying and Agricultural Trade Policy in the United States." *International Organization*, 60(3): 527–561.

GlobeScan (2004) "19 Nation Poll on Global Issues: Questionnaire." *GlobeScan Research Partners*. Available at www.pipa.org/OnlineReports/Other%20Studies/GlobalIss_Jun04/GlobalIss_Jun04_quaire.pdf.

Grossman, Gene M., and Elhanan Helpman (1994) "Protection for Sale." *The American Economic Review*, 84(4): 833–850.

Grugel, Jean B. (2004) "New Regionalism and Modes of Governance: Comparing US and EU Strategies in Latin America." *European Journal of International Relations*, 10(4): 603–626.

Hakim, Peter (2004) "The Reluctant Partner." *Foreign Affairs*, 83(1): 114–123.

Hakim, Peter (2014) "The Future of US-Brazil Relations: Confrontation, Cooperation or Detachment?" *International Affairs*, 90(5): 1161–1180.

Hopewell, Kristen (2013) "New Protagonists in Global Economic Governance: Brazilian Agribusiness at the WTO." *New Political Economy*, 18(4): 603–623.

Hopewell, Kristen (2016) *Breaking the WTO: How Emerging Powers Disrupted the Neoliberal Project*. Stanford: Stanford University Press.

Hurrell, Andrew, and Amrita Narlikar (2006) "A New Politics of Confrontation? Brazil and India in Multilateral Trade Negotiations." *Global Society*, 20(4): 415–433.

IBOPE (2007) "População aponta temas que exigem atenção especial da sociedade brasileira." *Instituto Brasileiro de Opinião Pública e Estatística*, December 13. Available at www.ibope.com.br/calandraWeb/servlet/CalandraRedirect?temp=6&proj=PortalIBOPE&pub=T&db=caldb&comp=pesquisa_leitura&nivel=null&docid=7CB6F016ABDB2DC5832573B000480B84.

Ismail, Faizel (2009) "An Assessment of the WTO Doha Round July–December 2008 Collapse." *World Trade Review*, 8(4): 579–605.

Kaushik, Atul, Rashid Kaukab, and Pranav Kumar (2008) "A Brief Analysis of the July 2008 Lamy Package." Available at www.cuts-citee.org/pdf/ADV08-11.pdf.
Kennedy, Kevin C. (2003–2004) "The FTAA Negotiations: A Melodrama in Five Acts." *International Law Review*, 1(2): 121–138.
Kennedy, Matthew (2012) "China's Role in WTO Dispute Settlement." *World Trade Review*, 11(4): 555–589.
Kim, Youngwan (2017) "How NGOs Influence US Foreign Aid Allocations." *Foreign Policy Analysis*, 13(1): 112–132.
Landim, Raquel (2008) "Setor privado lamenta colapso das negociações da Rodada Doha; Setor privado elogia governo e lamenta fracasso de Doha." *Valor Econômico*, July 30. Available at www.lexisnexis.com.
Leahy, Joe (2017) "Temer Stays Tough on Brazil Economic Reforms." *Financial Times*, February 2.
Lesage, Dries, Peter Debaere, Sacha Dierckx, and Mattias Vermeiren (2013) "IMF Reform after the Crisis." *International Politics*, 50(4): 553–578.
Lin, Hongyu, and Li Xing (2014) "G20 and C2: Sino-US Relations as an Institutional Cooperation Game?" In Li Xing (ed.) *The BRICS and Beyond: The International Political Economy of the Emergence of a New World Order*. Farnham: Ashgate.
Mahrenbach, Laura Carsten (2013) *The Trade Policy of Emerging Powers: Strategic Choices of Brazil and India*. Basingstoke: Palgrave Macmillan.
Marconini, Mario (2005) "Trade Policy-Making Process in Brazil." *London School of Economics*, London, England, May 25. Available at www6.miami.edu/hemispheric-policy/LSEWorkshopTradePolicy250505.pdf.
Marconini, Mario (2010) Interview with author. *ManattJones Global Strategies*, São Paulo, Brazil, May 26.
Marques, Roberto (2013) "Statement of Roberto Marques, Company Group Chairman, Johnson & Johnson Consumer Companies of North America." *CQ Congressional Testimony*, June 12, Washington, DC.
Martinez-Diaz, Leonardo, and Lael Brainard (2009) "Brazil: The 'B' Belongs in the BRICs." In Lael Brainard and Leonardo Martinez-Diaz (eds.) *Brazil as an Economic Superpower?: Understanding Brazil's Changing Role in the Global Economy*. Washington, DC: Brookings Institution Press.
Mastanduno, Michael (2009) "System Maker and Privilege Taker." *World Politics*, 61(1): 121–154.
Mera, Laura Gomez (2005) "Explaining Mercosur's Survival: Strategic Sources of Argentine-Brazilian Convergence." *Journal of Latin American Studies*, 37(1): 109–140.
Miller, John W. (2008) "Global Trade Talks Falter." *Wall Street Journal*, July 29. Available at http://online.wsj.com/article/SB121734618198593583.html?mod=hpp_us_whats_news.
Moravcsik, Andrew (1997) "Taking Preferences Seriously: A Liberal Theory of International Politics." *International Organization*, 51(4): 513–553.
Moreira, Mauricio Mesquita (2009) "Brazil's Trade Policy: Old and New Issues." In Lael Brainard and Leonardo Martinez-Diaz (eds.) *Brazil as an Economic Superpower?: Understanding Brazil's Changing Role in the Global Economy*. Washington, DC: Brookings Institution Press.
NAM (2014) "Manufacturing and Trade: Bilateral Trade." *National Association of Manufacturers*. Available at www.nam.org/Issues/Trade/Manufacturing-And-Trade-Bilateral-Trade.aspx.
National Farmers Organization (2014) "National Farmers Press Room." Available at www.nfo.org/About_Us/Press_Releases.aspx.

OAS (2017) "Information on Brazil." *Organization of American States*. Available at www.sice.oas.org/ctyindex/BRZ/BRZagreements_e.asp.

Obama, Barack, and Dilma Rousseff (2011) "Joint Statement by President Rousseff and President Obama." *Office of the Press Secretary*, March 19. Available at www.whitehouse.gov/the-press-office/2011/03/19/joint-statement-president-rousseff-and-president-obama.

Pew (2002) "What the World Thinks in 2002." *Pew Research Center*, December 4. Available at http://pewglobal.org/2002/12/04/what-the-world-thinks-in-2002/.

Pew (2007) "Final 2007 Comparative Topline." *Pew Research Center*, June 27. Available at www.pewglobal.org/files/2007/10/2007-Report-3-Comparative-Topline-REVISED-MAY-27-2014.pdf.

Pew (2010) "Brazilians Upbeat about Their Country, Despite Its Problems." *Pew Research Center*, September 22. Available at http://pewglobal.org/2010/09/22/brazilians-upbeat-about-their-country-despite-its-problems/.

Pew (2013) "2013 Spring Survey Topline Results." *Pew Research Center*, May 23. Available at http://assets.pewresearch.org/wp-content/uploads/sites/2/2013/05/Pew-Global-Attitudes-Economic-Report-Topline-May-23-2013.pdf.

Pew (2014) "Faith and Skepticism about Trade, Foreign Investment." *Pew Research Center*, September 16. Available at www.pewglobal.org/2014/09/16/faith-and-skepticism-about-trade-foreign-investment/.

Phillips, Nicola (2003) "Hemispheric Integration and Subregionalism in the Americas." *International Affairs*, 79(2): 327–349.

Putnam, Robert D. (1988) "Diplomacy and Domestic Politics: The Logic of Two-Level Games." *International Organization*, 42(3): 427–460.

Reeves, Philip (2018) "Brazil Reacts to Trump's Steel Tariffs." *Morning Edition*, March 9. Available at www.npr.org/2018/03/09/592196607/brazil-reacts-to-trumps-steel-tariffs.

Rios, Sandra Polónia (2006) "Integration in Latin America: Going Global or Becoming Fragmentary?" In Wonhyuk Lim and Ramon Torrent (eds.) *Multilateral and Regional Frameworks for Globalization: WTO and Free Trade Agreements*. Seoul: Korea Development Institute.

Shaffer, Gregory, Michelle Ratton Sanchez, and Barbara Rosenberg (2008) "The Trials of Winning at the WTO: What Lies Behind Brazil's Success." *Cornell International Law Journal*, 41(2): 381–501.

Schirm, Stefan A. (2010) "Leaders in Need of Followers: Emerging Powers in Global Governance." *European Journal of International Relations*, 16(2): 197–221.

Schirm, Stefan A. (2016) "Domestic Ideas, Institutions or Interests? Explaining Governmental Preferences towards Global Economic Governance." *International Political Science Review*, 37(1): 66–80.

Schott, Jeffrey J. (2003) "US-Brazil Trade Relations in a New Era." In Paulo Roberto de Almeida and Rubens Antonio Barbosa (eds.) *Brasil e os Estados Unidos num Mundo em Mutação*. Available at https://piie.com/commentary/speeches-papers/us-brazil-trade-relations-new-era.

Schott, Jeffrey J. (2006) "Free Trade Agreements and US Trade Policy: A Comparative Analysis of US Initiatives in Latin America, the Asia-Pacific Region, and the Middle East and North Africa." *International Trade Journal*, 20(2): 95–138.

Schwab, Susan C. (2008a) "Ambassador Susan C. Schwab, USTR Doha Media Roundtable." *Office of the United States Trade Representative*, July 17. Available at www.ustr.gov/sites/default/files/uploads/speeches/2008/asset_upload_file887_15028.pdf.

Schwab, Susan C. (2008b) "Press Briefing." *Office of the United States Trade Representative*, July 30. Available at www.ustr.gov/sites/default/files/uploads/speeches/2008/asset_upload_file786_15046.pdf.

Schwab, Susan C. (2008c) "Schwab Announces US Contribution to WTO Technical Assistance Efforts." *Office of the United States Trade Representative*, June 18. Available at www.ustr.gov/sites/default/files/uploads/pdfs/press_release/2008/asset_upload_file223_14945.pdf.

Seixas Corrêa, Luiz Felipe de (2001) Statement by the Secretary-General of External Relations, Ambassador Luiz Felipe de Seixas Corrêa. Americas Society, New York.

Stokes, Bruce (2014) "Global Public Downbeat about Economy." *Pew Research Center*, September 9, Washington, DC.

TIA (2014) "TIA Supports the Bipartisan Congressional Trade Priorities Act of 2014." *Telecommunications Industry Association Press Releases*, January 16. Available at www.tiaonline.org/news-media/press-releases/tia-supports-bipartisan-congressional-trade-priorities-act-2014.

US Census Bureau (2017) "Trade in Goods with Brazil." *US Census Bureau, Foreign Trade*. Available at www.census.gov/foreign-trade/balance/c3510.html.

US Chamber of Commerce (2014) "International Trade and Investment." Available at www.uschamber.com/international-trade-and-investment.

Veiga, Pedro da Motta (2005) "The Politics of Trade in Brazil." In Dominic Kelly and Wyn Grant (eds.) *The Politics of International Trade in the Twenty-First Century: Actors, Issues and Regional Dynamics*. New York: Palgrave Macmillan.

Veiga, Pedro da Motta (2009) "Brazil's Trade Policy: Moving Away from Old Paradigms?" In Lael Brainard and Leonardo Martinez-Diaz (eds.) *Brazil as an Economic Superpower? Understanding Brazil's Changing Role in the Global Economy*. Washington, DC: Brookings Institution Press.

Vestergaard, Jakob, and Robert H. Wade (2015) "Protecting Power: How Western States Retain Their Dominant Voice in the World Bank's Governance." In Dries Lesage and Thijs Van de Graaf (eds.) *Rising Powers and Multilateral Institutions*. Basingstoke: Palgrave Macmillan.

Ward, John (2011) "Brazil and the United States: Working to Advance Their Common Prosperity." *International Trade Update*. Available at http://trade.gov/publications/ita-newsletter/0411/brazil.asp.

Woods, Ngaire (2010) "Global Governance after the Financial Crisis: A New Multilateralism or the Last Gasp of the Great Powers?" *Global Policy*, 1(1): 51–63.

Wrobel, Paulo S. (1998) "A Free Trade Area of the Americas in 2005?" *International Affairs*, 74(3): 547–561.

WTO (2013) "Trade Policy Review: Brazil: Report by the Secretariat: Revision." *World Trade Organization*. Available at www.wto.org/english/tratop_e/tpr_e/tp383_e.htm.

Zanatta, Mauro (2008) "Agronegócio apoia acordo comercial global na Rodada Doha." *Noticias Financieras*, July 17. Available at www.lexisnexis.com.

Zoellick, Robert (2002) "USTR Outlines Objectives for Free Trade Area of the Americas." *Office of International Information Programs*, October 4. Available at www.lexisnexis.m.

5 The role of declining Brazil and ascending China in the BRICS initiative

Javier Vadell and Leonardo Ramos

Introduction

Radhica Desai (Desai, 2013) has claimed that the BRICS (Brazil, Russia, India, China, and South Africa) summit in Durban in 2013 constituted the first sign of a coordinated challenge to western supremacy in the world economy from developing countries since the Non-Aligned Movement and the demand for a new international economic order (NIEO) in the 1970s. The official summit declaration emphasized the importance of BRICS institutionalization through the New Development Bank. Nevertheless, this view is not shared by all. In fact, mainstream scholars and media from the United States were skeptical about this new bank. *The New York Times* for example, affirmed that the BRICS' members

> are deeply divided on some basic issues and are in many ways rivals, not allies, in the global economy. They have widely divergent economies, disparate foreign policy aims and different forms of government. India, Brazil and South Africa have strong democratic traditions, while Russia and China are autocratic. The bloc even struggles to agree on overhauling international institutions. India, Brazil and South Africa want permanent seats on the United Nations Security Council, for example, but China, which already has one, has shown little interest in shaking up the status quo.
>
> (Polgreen, 2013)

A year earlier, in 2012, Jim O'Neall, the Goldman Sachs executive who coined the acronym BRIC, criticized the inclusion of South Africa in this forum:

> It's just wrong. South Africa doesn't belong in BRICs (. . .) South Africa has too small an economy. There are not many similarities with the other four countries in terms of the numbers. In fact, South Africa's inclusion has somewhat weakened the group's power.
>
> (Naidoo, 2012)

O'Neall had failed to notice the geopolitical tectonic movement behind this decision: irreversibly, the BRIC created by O'Neall had become a BRICS which had moved beyond the "growth prospects" rationale. The relevance of South Africa as a middle power ensured its inclusion into the forum: geopolitically and geo-economically it was important as an "open door" for Chinese and Indian trade and investments in the African continent. In sum, from a creation representing the "emerging market" in accordance with the economic logic of Goldman Sachs, BRIC(S) had become a geopolitical bloc led by China and was evolving into a more institutionalized broader forum.

Other skeptics stated that Russia should not be considered part of the BRIC(S) because Russia did not share the interests and objectives of the other members (Macfarlane, 2006; Cooper, 2006; Khalid, 2014). Nevertheless, and especially since 2014, Russian commitment to supporting the bloc has increased: the Crimea crisis and the increasing tension between Russia and the West culminated in Russia's suspension from the G8 and contributed crucially to this new turn in foreign orientation as Russia sought to maintain its regional sphere of influence. In this context, it is also important to highlight Russia's growing economic links with China, embodied in cooperation and energy agreements (Ambrosio, 2017; Wu, 2017). More recently, from a broader perspective addressing the decline of the United States, Kiely (2016) has presented a skeptical account of the rise of BRICS, arguing that

> there are good reasons why this supposed rise was based on a one-sided discourse, and even more, that we are now moving into a new period where we can talk less about the rise of emerging powers, and more about an emerging market crisis.
>
> (Kiely, 2016: 3)

Georgy Toloraya is a former Russian diplomat and Executive Director of the Russian National Committee on BRICS. In 2016, after the Goa summit, Toloraya said:

> BRICS is still in the age of adolescence: it has been 15 years since the term was invented and 10 since the virtual reality became a physical reality. BRICS meeting its semi-anniversary not in the best shape. It is true that economically only India can boast more or less dynamic growth; however it is still mired in poverty with many social problems and economic regulations far from ideal. China has not overcome the basic structural problems of its economy and growth is slowing; Russia is in the midst of a prolonged economic slowdown. Brazil due to the unnatural change of government became an "odd man out" in BRICS: its' will and ability to pursue an independent policy agenda became doubtful in the wake of the impeachment of previous president Dilma Rousseff.
>
> (Toloraya, 2016)

In light of this long-lasting debate, this chapter sets out to address six questions. Allowing for the "normal" cyclical crises in the capitalist system, what can we say about the performance of the BRICS countries? How might we interpret the evolution of BRICS and its institutionalization? What is the role of China and Brazil in the evolving transformation process affecting BRICS? How might Brazil and its domestic political and economic crisis affect the forum? Could the Brazilian right-wing government affect BRICS priorities regarding the protagonist role of the emerging bloc? And finally, with the growing asymmetries between BRICS members, how might the ascent of China and the decline of Brazil affect the consolidation of the BRICS forum?

To answer these questions, this chapter focuses not only on uneven economic performance but also on two dimensions of the evolving BRICS forum. The first dimension is the gradual and persistent institutionalization of the bloc. The second dimension is the outreach process and its regional and global dilemmas. Our study suggests a conclusion that differs from the position taken by the skeptical scholars and analysts. Despite we agree in some sense with them concerning the consequences of economic crisis to BRICS, we strongly disagree with their analysis about the evolution and prospects for the BRICS as an institution. As will become evident from later onward, we see the evolving BRICS institutionalization process as strengthening a new single institutional economic governance in a multipolar world (Desai, 2015) under China's economic leadership; in other words, the forum is gradually becoming an institutionalized economic bloc anchored in the New Development Bank-Contingency Reserve Agreement (NDB-CRA), and recognition of this process provides an interesting and elucidative insight into the roles of Brazil and China in the development of the bloc.

Emerging countries and margins of opportunities in the multipolar world

The debate about emerging countries and emerging blocs entails a theoretical and methodological challenge which has not been sufficiently explored in mainstream International Relations and International Political Economy scholarship. Intending to overcome the antinomy of traditional middle powers and emerging middle powers, Eduard Jordaan (2017) has contributed to an interesting debate about the relevance of the "emerging middle power concept". This debate incorporates earlier discussions of middle powers and the rise of China (Gilley and O'Neil, 2014), the niche diplomacy of traditional middle powers (Cooper, 1997), the role taken by the middle powers into the institutions of Western "liberal governance" and its foreign policies (Cooper, 2013; Alexandroff and Cooper, 2010; Hurrell, 2000), and the concept of "middlepowermanship" (Cox, 1989).

Inquiring into the concept of middle powers and questioning its usefulness in the contemporary world, Jordaan turns to the classification of "middle powers" in terms of behavior and hegemony (or declining hegemony). The middle power concept is "too elusive" as a category (Jordaan, 2017: 2), and is better to categorize it as referring to international actors related mainly to "mid-range levels of power". Nevertheless, there is no clear answer about what factors (gross national product, regional significance, leadership, internal cohesion, diplomatic skills, or moral behavioral-based activities) should be measured and how to weight the various components of the state powers (Cooper, 1997; Jordaan, 2017).

In terms of hegemony, the concept brings up the debate about middle powers as stabilizer or destabilizers. Jordaan's perspective emphasizes agent-oriented positions and behavior in international politics, thus differentiating between three kinds of middle powers.

The first type is middle powers as stabilizer. In fact, they are "supporters of the hegemony" (Jordaan, 2017: 5) with a pro status-quo position. In the Cold War era, Robert Cox had pointed out that the task of the middle power – Japan in this case – was to support and to legitimize the prevailing international order (Cox, 1989: 826). Nevertheless, the context of the Cold War, the defeat of Japan in the Second World War, and the hegemonic position of the United States in the capitalist system were the main factors that determined the behavior of middle powers in this period.

The second type of middle power has an ambivalent position toward U.S. hegemony or primacy in global capitalism and international institutional governance. The preference for adherence to status-quo rules and institutions has varied from country to country since the Cold War ended, and especially in the new millennium. Some contemporary emerging middle powers, for example, are dissatisfied with certain norms and rules of the current institutional governance system, but not necessarily with the existing international organizations that embody these norms and rules. A good example is the IMF and World Bank reform debate (Ramos et al., 2012a), that is a persistent demand of BRICS countries in all annual meetings.

The third modality of middle power highlighted by Jordaan sees middle power behavior "as countering great power hegemony" (Jordaan, 2017: 6). The problem with this fixed model is the impossibility of using it to comprehend the current complex dynamics of the global economy and the ascendance of China in the Trump era. In the present era of "switching roles", when "following the United States" does not necessarily mean following a "liberal international order", the scenario becomes more complex. In other words, we must pay attention to the changing structural economic and geopolitical order and incorporate it into the analysis in order to understand the processes of emergence and hegemony constitution in the capitalist system.

As Li (2017) has pointed out, world system theory provides a historical perspective for understanding emerging countries and the possibilities (or impossibility) of "upward mobility". Changes in the capitalist economy and in the geopolitical game played by the great powers could alter the incentives for a "semiperipheral forum", individually or collectively, trying to change the rules. Nonetheless, as noted earlier, emerging countries may want to change the rules without wanting to change the organizations. Emerging countries can perceive the system and its rules as unfair, once it does not reflect the new multipolar political equation. Thus, as Wallerstein states, the role of the semi-periphery as the realm of "middle powers" is crucial to an understanding of the possibility of changing the global power balance. The semi-peripheral countries:

> must choose their alliances and their economic opportunities carefully and swiftly. For semiperipheral states are primarily in competition with each other. If, for example, during a Kondratieff B-phase there is significant relocation of an erstwhile leading industry, it will usually go to semiperipheral countries. But not, however, to all of them; perhaps only to one or two of them. There is not enough space in the production structure of the whole system to permit this kind of relocation (called "development") simultaneously in too many countries. Which one of perhaps fifteen countries will be the locus of such relocation is not easy to determine in advance or even to explain in retrospect. What is easy to grasp is that not every country can be so favoured, or profits would plummet downward too rapidly and too steeply. The competition between strong states and the efforts of semiperipheral states to increase their status and their power result in an ongoing interstate rivalry which normally takes the form of a so-called balance of power, by which one means a situation in which no single state can automatically get its way in the interstate arena.
>
> (Wallerstein, 2004: 57)

Hence, for our purposes, Jordaan's and Xing's arguments could be understood as complementary rather than competing positions: their approaches help us to cope with conjunctural role as well as structural position of emerging countries, which will be very important in looking at BRICS and the engagement of Brazil and China. A favorable conjuncture could offer some opportunities to the agents in a critical interstate rivalry scenario. In fact, in this context, promotion by invitation is possible. In the words of Li Xing:

> "Promotion by invitation" refers to the upward mobility path enjoyed by a semi-periphery or periphery country, whose geopolitical position is vital during the period of global power struggles, or whose internal condition is favorable to global capital mobility and production relocation. This upward mobility is stimulated by the favorable external environment created by the promotion and invitation of the existing hegemon, or by a group of core nations, for the sake of their own geopolitical and geo-economic interests.
>
> (Li, 2017: 4)

Li (2017) highlights the example of China entering the capitalist system in the 1970s and 1980s through the consolidation of Deng Xiaoping's system of "socialism with Chinese characteristics" and benefiting from the geopolitical anti-USSR scenario as well as the possibility of "promotion by invitation" in this historically critical period. After the Cold War, and particularly in the 21st century, emerging powers acquired a strong international identity "based on a clear view of world order and an understanding of the country's actual and potential position within this order" (Huelsz, 2009: 210). Furthermore, unlike traditional middle powers, emerging countries are also regional powers and tend to influence some issue areas of the global agenda. In this context, the economic crisis of the 1990s helped to catalyze and advance the demands of emerging countries for a "reforming" agenda in global governance institutions.

BRICS as an institutional creature of emergence

The national economic crises that have occurred since the mid-1990s – Mexico (1995), Asia (1997), Russia (1998), Brazil (1999), Argentina (2001), and Turkey (2001), for example – have made it clear that management of the world order cannot continue to ignore the presence of emerging countries and the ascendance of the semi-periphery (Wallerstein, 1974; Wallerstein, 2004; Li, 2017). The emerging middle powers did not participate in the G8 (G7 + Russia) until the late 1990s, when the G20 was created to accommodate more countries after the Asian crisis. But it was not until 2008 that it included a meeting of heads of state (Ramos et al., 2012b). In the early 2000s, Brazil, India, China South Africa and Mexico were gradually invited to act as G8 observers (G8 + 5); nevertheless, the five emerging countries did not take part in the debates on the direction of the world economy. In 2003, IBAS (India, Brazil, and South Africa) (Giaccaglia, 2013) was created, and in 2006 the first meeting of Brazil, Russia, India, and China's foreign ministers took place. This concatenation of events fertilized the ground for the first BRIC Summit in June 2009 in Yekaterinburg, Russia (BRICS, 2009).

The first Summit was marked by the outcomes of the G20 summit, reflecting the group's commitment to earlier decisions and indicating the nature of the group's cooperation at the coming G20 summit. In addition, BRIC emphasized the importance of reforming financial institutions to increase the participation of emerging middle powers in the international order. Finally, there were advances in cooperation among BRIC members in the areas of science and education (BRICS, 2009). The second BRIC summit took place in Brasília in 2010 and dealt with several issues, particularly those related to global governance and to international trade and finance. Particularly noteworthy was BRIC's support for UN reform and its emphasis on the stability of the international monetary system – both of which were related to the crisis of legitimacy of international organizations (BRICS, 2010). The third BRICS summit took place in Sanya in 2011. Two highlights of this summit were (i) the inclusion of South Africa in the bloc and (ii) the fact that, at the time, all countries participating in the BRICS were also on the UN Security Council, which made the summit especially important for security issues, such as, for instance, events following the Arab Spring. For the first time, there was an explicit reference to the UN reform in the final declaration resulting from the summit (BRICS, 2011: §8). It also reaffirmed the importance of the G20 in the international financial architecture and the need to complete the Doha Round (BRICS, 2011).

The fourth BRICS summit was held in New Delhi, in 2012. For the first time, the possibility of creating a new BRICS multilateral development bank was discussed. The resulting compromise committed the finance ministers of each BRICS country to an examination of the feasibility of such a bank. Moreover, the final declaration reiterated the importance of international cooperation while stressing the need for reform of the international financial institutions to ensure that the systemic importance of the BRICS countries would be institutionally recognized (BRICS, 2012a).

The fifth BRICS summit in Durban in 2013 closed the first cycle of summits. It was also a milestone in the South African quest for greater international presence, and it highlighted BRICS' relations with African countries.[1] As in previous summits, BRICS reaffirmed its commitment to multilateralism and to the quest for more democratic global governance through reform of the international financial institutions in general and more specifically of the IMF quota system, as had been agreed in 2010 (BRICS, 2013: §13). Moreover, BRICS re-emphasized its commitment to the conclusion of the Doha Round: it would support attempts to give Brazil, India, and South Africa a more prominent role in the UN. Finally, the BRICS countries expressed their support for Brazilian Roberto Azevedo as WTO General Director.

Subsequently, a US$ 100 billion reserve fund was also created to "help the BRICS countries to avoid short-term liquidity pressures" (BRICS, 2013: §10). This followed up on previous agreements between BRICS countries signed in 2012, namely: (i) the framework agreement for the extension of local currency credit facilitation under the BRICS Interbank Cooperation Mechanism, and (ii) the agreement to facilitate the confirmation of multilateral credit letters (BRICS, 2012b). Finally, BRICS announced the creation of a BRICS development bank, which was to seek "resources for infrastructure and sustainable development projects in BRICS and other emerging economies and developing countries to complement the existing efforts of multilateral financial institutions and regional partnerships for global growth and development" (BRICS, 2013: §9).

The sixth BRICS summit in Fortaleza in 2014 started the second cycle of summits. The theme was "Inclusive Growth: Sustainable Solutions", and it was one of the most important moments in the BRICS process of institutional consolidation. The "Agreement establishing the New Development Bank (NDB) was signed, with the purpose of mobilizing resources for infrastructure projects and sustainable development in BRICS and other emerging and developing economies" (BRICS, 2014: §11). The NDB authorized an initial capital of US$ 100 billion with a subscribed initial capital of $50 billion, "divided equally among founding members" (BRICS, 2014: §12). Furthermore, participants signed the BRICS-CRA (with capital of $100 billion), the Memorandum of Understanding for Technical Cooperation between Credit Agencies, and a number of export guarantees. The first would "have a positive effect in terms of precaution" and would "help countries counteract short-term liquidity pressures", while the second would "improve the enabling environment for increased trade opportunities" among the BRICS countries (BRICS, 2014: §13, §14).

There were high expectations concerning the seventh BRICS summit, held in Ufa, 2015 and some progress was made on intra-BRICS trade and on financial and investment cooperation by deepening the dialogue between the "BRICS Export Credit Agencies" and by increasing the role of the "BRICS Interbank implementation of the BRICS Framework for Trade and Investment Cooperation". A study on the feasibility of "wider use of national currencies in mutual trade" (BRICS, 2015: §13, §14, §23, and §24) also had a major impact.

However, in a critical context for the BRICS countries, the top priorities of the summit were the NDB and the CRA. The participants discussed the details of these new institutional arrangements, and there are already indications of how the NDB would function. In particular, it emerged that NDB resources were to be primarily focused on infrastructure investment in the BRICS countries – as was emphasized by the Russian finance minister, Anton Siluanov. However, this was directly related to negative economic growth in both Brazil and Russia at the time: Brazil wanted the NDB to favor investments in energy and infrastructure; Russia already saw the NDB as a major opportunity to attract Chinese capitals.[2] In addition, the summit saw the presentation of a proposal for cooperation between the NDB and the recently created Asian Infrastructure Investment Bank (AIIB),[3] which would be important in financing the infrastructure projects linked to the New Silk Road (BRICS, 2015: §15).

As usual in informal forums like BRICS, it was expected that the host country would drive the agenda of the summit. On this occasion, due to Russia's international interests since the Crimean crisis (2014), a convergence was expected between BRICS, the Shanghai Cooperation Organization (SCO), and the Eurasian Economic Union. Thus, two security issues stood out in the discussion: (i) the importance of respect for sovereignty and non-intervention in a number of cases (especially in Afghanistan, Iraq, and Syria); and (ii) the increasing emphasis on the security problems affecting the African continent as well as the stability of the region (Ramos et al., 2012b). Despite criticism of the current order and the actions of the traditional powers, the non-confrontational strategy was retained, and the existing multilateral arrangements were reaffirmed (BRICS, 2015: §11, §18, §19, and §26) .[4] To some extent, it was retained the following year in Goa.

A year later, the Goa Final Declaration (2016) reiterated that sustainable peace requires the construction of an "equitable and democratic multipolar international order" with a "concerted and determined global approach" based on mutual trust, equity, and cooperation. The BRICS countries reaffirmed a "strong commitment to international law and the central role of the United Nations as the universal multilateral organization entrusted with the mandate of maintaining international peace and security". While emphasizing the role of the UN, the document called for reform of the UN Security Council to make it more representative and efficient (BRICS, 2016: §6–8). It is important to notice that whereas this demand is repeatedly emphasized by India and South Africa, Russia, and China present a softer position, unclear about what they really understand – and defend – as a reform. Brazil has historically taken up a position closer to India and South Africa ones, but since the coup, the new government has made little effort in that direction.

Other important outcomes from Goa were (i) support for the recent decision of the working group of the UN Committee on the Peaceful Uses of Outer Space

(COPUOS) to create a long-term sustainability plan in space by 2018 (BRICS, 2016: §55–56); and (ii) support for the Russian initiative to develop an international convention banning chemical and biological terrorism on the basis of bilateral and international cooperation (BRICS, 2016: §58). Particularly evident is the preoccupation of Russian diplomacy with the fight against terrorism, specifically the problem of Chechen and such as those fighting in Syria against the Assad government.

As the main BRICS member involved in the Syrian conflict, Russia noted its position in the document: it was committed to building peace through an inclusive national dialogue and a political process led by the Syrian government and based on the Geneva Communiqué of June 30th, 2012, pursuant to UN Security Council resolution 2254 and 2268. Russia was also committed to the fight against terrorist groups such as ISIS and Jabhat al-Nusra (BRICS, 2016: §14). Russia's growing assertiveness in the Syrian conflict and its belief in the stability and integrity of Assad's government had been and continues to be at odds with the policy of the USA and its allies, whose aim is to dismantle the Assad government, even if this means supporting "rebel" Islamic jihadists (Pautasso et al., 2015).

Two other security themes were highlighted at the summit. The first was the need to implement the two-state solution to the Israel-Palestinian conflict on the basis of UNSC resolutions, the Madrid Principles, and the Arab Peace Initiative. Second, concerns were raised about security challenges in Afghanistan and support was expressed for the efforts of the Afghan government to build national reconciliation while combating terrorism and drug trafficking (BRICS, 2016: §15–16).

In addition to these security issues, the summit also focused on the progress of the BRICS process of institutionalization. Important developments included the signing of the Memorandum of Understanding for the Establishment of a BRICS Agricultural Research Platform (BRICS, 2016: §86); the first meeting of the BRICS Counter-Terrorism Working Group (BRICS, 2016: §60); the NDB's operational advances; and the start of negotiations on the proposal to create a BRICS rating agency (BRICS, 2016: §44). Of equal importance were (i) the creation of a joint discussion platform for the BRICS Export Credit Agencies to work on trade cooperation among the BRICS countries, following up on an "inaugural meeting" in Ufa (BRICS, 2016: §13), and (ii) the establishment of the BRICS Customs Cooperation Committee within the framework of the BRICS Strategy for Economic Partnership, previously established at the seventh summit in Ufa (BRICS, 2015: §17, §48).

Under the banner "BRICS: Stronger Partnership for a Brighter Future", the ninth BRICS summit was held in Xiamen, China. Three relevant documents signed at the summit were (i) the action plan for innovation and cooperation (2017–2020); (ii) the strategic framework for BRICS customs cooperation; and (iii) the MOU between the BRICS Business Council and the NDB on strategic cooperation. Initiatives were agreed for the development of BRICS Local Currency Bond Markets and to establish a future BRICS Local Currency Bond Fund (BRICS, 2017: §10), highlighting "the progress in concluding the MOU among national development banks of BRICS countries on interbank local currency credit line and on interbank cooperation in relation to credit rating" (BRICS, 2017: §11). In this meeting, the discussion of developments regarding NDBs was mentioned, and it was agreed that the NDB African Regional Center in South Africa would become the first NDB regional office (BRICS, 2017: §31). Moreover, the CRA System of Exchange in Macro-Economic Information was established (BRICS, 2017: §31).

In addressing security issues, the BRICS condemned "unilateral military interventions", referring to some of the declarations and behavior of the US president Donald Trump. Topics such as terrorism, Syria, and other international conflicts were mentioned, and the Financial Action Task Force against Money Laundering and Financing (FATF) discussed the implementation of international standards on combating money laundering and the financing of terrorism and proliferation (BRICS, 2017: §38, §11) For the first time, China recognized the presence of the Pakistan-based terrorist groups Lashkar-e-Taiba, Jaish-e-Mohammad, and the Haqqani network. This was important for Indian diplomacy (Pandey, 2017). Another important initiative was the 7th Meeting of the BRICS High Representatives for Security Issues, held on July 27–28 2017 in Beijing; here progress was made on security issues already discussed by BRICS. It is important to note that security issues in general constituted a significant portion of the Xiamen declaration (BRICS, 2017: §41–§51).

Certain tendencies are evident when it comes to institutional densification (summarized in Table 5.1). First, issues of international security have increasingly occupied a prominent place at the summits. BRICS has been tested by the geopolitical transformations associated with recent developments in US-Russian relations and, to a lesser extent, in relations between the US and China. In particular, the crisis in Ukraine and subsequent developments – for example in the

Table 5.1 BRICS: institutional densification and outreach process

	IPE/development	*Security (main topics)*	*Outreach*
3rd BRICS summit 14 April 2011 Sanya (BRICS, 2011)		Explicit mention: UNSC reform Arab Spring	South Africa inclusion as a member
4th BRICS summit 29 March 2012 New Delhi (BRICS, 2012a)	First discussion about NDB		
5th BRICS summit 26–27 March 2013 Durban (BRICS, 2013)	First proposal: BRICS institutionalization through a New Development Bank (NDB) and Contingent Reserve Arrangement (CRA)	Syria and Africa	Meeting with African leaders after this summit

	IPE/development	Security (main topics)	Outreach
6th BRICS summit 14–16 July 2014 Fortaleza (BRICS, 2014)	Accord signed – NDB-CRA	Syria, Iraq, Ukraine, Afghanistan, Iranian nuclear issue, Arab-Israeli conflict	Meeting with South American UNASUR leaders.
7th BRICS summit 8–9 July 2015 Ufa (BRICS, 2015)	NDB – CRA The Strategy for BRICS Economic Partnership (comprehensive framework for cooperation in trade and economic affairs). Documents: trade facilitation and cooperation in agriculture, communications, energy, security, tourism, and science and tech	Syria, ISIS, Ukraine, Yemen, and Afghanistan	Meeting with the Heads-of-State and Heads-of-Government of the Economic Eurasian Union (EEU) and with leaders of Shanghai Cooperation Organization (SCO)
8th BRICS summit 15–16 October 2016 Goa (BRICS, 2016)	1. Multipolar international order based on the central role of the United Nations, and on respect for international law 2. The operationalization of NDB-CRA (first year) 3. 2030 Agenda for Sustainable Development 4. Importance of public and private investments in infrastructure, including connectivity 5. Roadmap for Trade, Economic and Investment Cooperation until 2020 6. Possibility of setting up an independent BRICS Rating Agency 7. Cooperation through commercial and investment linkages and through financing infrastructure (Multilateral Development Banks) BRICS welcome the inclusion of the RMB into the Special Drawing Rights (SDR) currency basket in October 2016	Syria First meeting of counter-terrorism group Reform of UN including Security Council	Guest Invitees: BIMSTEC (Bay of Bengal Initiative for Multi-Sectoral Technical and Economic Cooperation) Bangladesh, Bhutan, Myanmar, Nepal, Sri Lanka, Thailand (and India) BRICS-BIMSTEC summit

(Continued)

Table 5.1 (Continued)

	IPE/development	*Security (main topics)*	*Outreach*
9th BRICS summit 3–5 September 2017 Xiamen (BRICS, 2017)	1. Reform of IMF's 15th General Review of Quotas and World Bank Group Shareholding 2. BRICS CRA 3. NDB Africa Regional Center 4. Open globalization/interconnectivity 5. Outcomes of G20 summits	Implementation of International Standards on Combating Money Laundering and the Financing of Terrorism and Proliferation in FATF Recognition of the presence of Pakistan-based terrorist groups 7th Meeting of the BRICS High Representatives for Security Issues Syria Reform of UN Security Council BRICS Intelligence Forum Israeli-Palestinian conflict Iranian nuclear issue Iraq/Mosul – Yemen	Guest invitees: Egypt, Guinea, Mexico, Thailand, and Tajikistan Dialogue of Emerging Market and Developing Countries on implementation of the 2030 Agenda for Sustainable Development and the building of broad partnerships BRICS Plus cooperation

Source: data from BRICS, 2011, 2012a, 2013, 2014, 2015, 2016, and 2017

context of the G7/8 – had an impact on BRICS. In the first place, since 2014 it can be noticed an intense engagement of Russia with the BRICS, that has influenced significantly the group agenda thereafter (Fortescue, 2014). In addition, there is a strong convergence of interests between India, Russia, and China in the fight against terrorism (Neelakantan, 2016).

In terms of the relative engagement of each of the BRICS countries, Brazil and South Africa seem to be trailing behind, despite their more proactive roles at certain moments in the history of the forum. Both countries behave as *norm-takers* rather than *norm-makers*.

Here, two noteworthy points deserve attention. First, there has been a noteworthy evolution in the prominence of international security issues. Throughout the history of BRICS, institutional consolidation has largely occurred in dealing with issues associated with international political economy, and in particular with the question of international development – a "path of least resistance" (Abdenur and Folly, 2015: 106). Nevertheless, the progress made in recent summits on international security issues should not be overlooked. The second noteworthy feature is the direct influence of host countries on the outreach process; host countries have often invited regional allies to BRICS meetings, thus strengthening the institutional densification of BRICS.

While these are important trends, the economic focus remains central for BRICS: "The BRICS have chosen to rely mainly on economic and financial capabilities in their collective financial statecraft, rather than on military power" (Roberts et al., 2018: 24). Economics is a strong centripetal force binding the BRICS countries together in terms of their goals. As Roberts et al. emphasize: "BRICS countries have cooperated to promote reforms of the Bretton Woods institutions, encourage internationalization of China's currency, the yuan or RMB, and build parallel international financial institutions" (Roberts et al., 2018: 4).

Such engagements represent a conservative behavior in relation to the Western liberal order, or to world capitalist order. In other words, BRICS can be seen as a typical *conservative globalizer* arrangement (Garcia and Bond, 2015; Kahler, 2013; Kahler, 2016). Thus, it is interesting to note that from Ekaterinburg to Xiamen, institutional progress has occurred in continuous dialogue with (and not against) existing international institutions. This trend is evident in a variety of issue areas: the constant demand for the reform of international financial institutions, especially the IMF; the emphasis on innovation for medium and long-term growth and sustainable development, reaffirming the G20 agenda expressed at the 2016 summit and the importance of the G20 as a forum for macro-economic cooperation; and the discussions on renewable energy, energy security, and climate change associated with the Paris Agreements on Climate Change (BRICS, 2016: §54, §70, and §92) – in addition to the statements made to the FATF and to the WTO. In political terms, the BRICS agenda is not confrontational; it is an attempt to claim "a place at the table" with the Western powers (G7), a stronger voice, and greater participation in existing institutions (Garcia and Bond, 2015).

It makes more and more sense to understand BRICS not as a collective challenge to global capitalism but as a group of emerging countries trying to modify the current balance of forces within the western liberal order: the Bretton Woods Institutions and the UN system (Security Council). This reformist character of BRICS expresses itself in the other two points: the gradual construction of parallel international institutions and encouragement of the internationalization of the RMB.

As Katada et al. (2017: 4) have pointed out, it might be that "the most striking feature of BRICS collaboration has been their ability to hang together in exercising 'financial statecraft'", which is defined as "the use of financial and monetary policies by sovereign governments for the purpose of achieving larger foreign policy goals" (Katada et al., 2017: 4). Thus financial statecraft is at the core of the institutional densification of BRICS, and the annual meetings have involved an institutional evolution and a gradual but consistent outreach process (Ramos et al., 2018). These two characteristics of the configuration of BRICS as an emerging bloc are the main features revealed by our analysis. A careful examination of the annual declarations reveals four main repeated demands made by BRICS members: a) a reform of IMF quotas and votes; b) a UNSC reform; c) a strong BRICS Bank – The New Development Bank (NDB-CRA); d) a strengthening of BRICS common political position in the G20 summit, including common political positions on security issues.

Brazil, China, and the BRICS' future

Some criticism of Western economic dominance was expressed publicly when BRICS countries complained that austerity in the West was holding back world growth. Furthermore, they complained that the unconventional monetary policy of central banks was encouraging speculation worldwide rather than domestic growth.

Nevertheless, the critical position of BRICS regarding global neoliberalism contrasts with the political path adopted by Brazil since the coup in August 2016 (the so-called "impeachment"). Since then, Brazil has been applying severe austerity policies based on a neoliberal script, thus showing the intrinsic contradiction at the heart of the evolving institutional consolidation of BRICS. Regarding the foreign policy of Brazil as an emerging middle and regional country (Huelsz, 2009; Lima and Hirst, 2006), BRICS has given visibility to the nation, has contributed to the decentralization of world order, and has exerted extra pressure behind demands for reforms of the IFIs and the UN Security Council.

Since 2013, however, the Brazilian domestic economic and political situation has faced serious difficulties. The parliamentary coup installed a low-legitimacy right-wing government supported by congressmen, corporate media, and the business class. This situation might also be perceived as a political and economic crisis. Economically, the rise of the right wing has led to the implementation of neoliberal adjustment policies designed to cope with the crisis and to attract financial transnational capital. Such measures are establishing a new relationship between society, state, and market, with uncertain political consequences. When it comes to Brazilian President Michel Temer foreign policy, there is an ambivalent relationship between *desire* and *reality*. That is, the Brazilian government *desires* investments from the United States and Western Europe, but it faces the *reality* of material forces: the capitalist system, the current role of China in this global scenario, and the short-term and medium-term problems faced by the Brazilian economy.

Such ambivalence has affected Brazil's position in BRICS. At the 8th BRICS summit, President Michel Temer was almost ignored by Putin (Netto, 2016), and the role played by the country in the summit was insignificant. At the 9th BRICS summit in Xiamen, Brazil proactively encouraged China to invest and to improve trade deals (Campos, 2017; BrazilGovNews, 2017). The attempts of the current Brazilian Government to strengthen Brazil's ties with BRICS, especially with

China, were evident at the last BRICS meeting. The bilateral meeting between Temer and Xi Jinping before the summit was crucial. It seems that Temer was selling the country to China, promoting privatizations, and attempting to sell devalued state-owned companies (Fontdeglòria, 2017). Both countries signed 14 agreements and various memoranda (Itamaraty, 2017) focusing on Chinese investments, and they ratified the Chinese banker role in Brazil. China received a new line of credit to *Banco do Brasil* of US$ 300 million, and approval was secured for another preparatory accord between BNDES[5] and the China Development Bank (CDB) to deepen strategic cooperation and to define the parameters for the establishment of a future US$ 3 billion credit line. It seems that the Brazilian crisis brought the two countries closer together. In August, approval was granted for a South African regional office of the New Development Bank, and the plan is to launch the next one in Brazil in 2018 (Nogueira Batista, 2017; Bo, 2018). As a result of such institutional expansion of the NDB, the New Development Bank President, Mr. K.V. Kamath, met Mr. Aloysio Nunes Ferreira, the Minister of Foreign Relations of Brazil on 21 May, 2018, and they agreed to open an NDB Americas Regional Office (ARO) (NDB, 2018).

The possibilities of the BRICS outreach process (Figure 5.1) reflect the current Brazilian foreign policy dilemma: in following a neoliberal ideology and promoting the weakening of Mercosur and Unasur, Brazil would be weakening its own leadership as a regional power. This is critical when it comes to its regional representativeness and the possibilities of future BRICS outreach as promoted by president Xi Jinping in the "BRICS Plus" project. As discussed earlier, the outreach process has been highly influenced by the interests of the host countries; however,

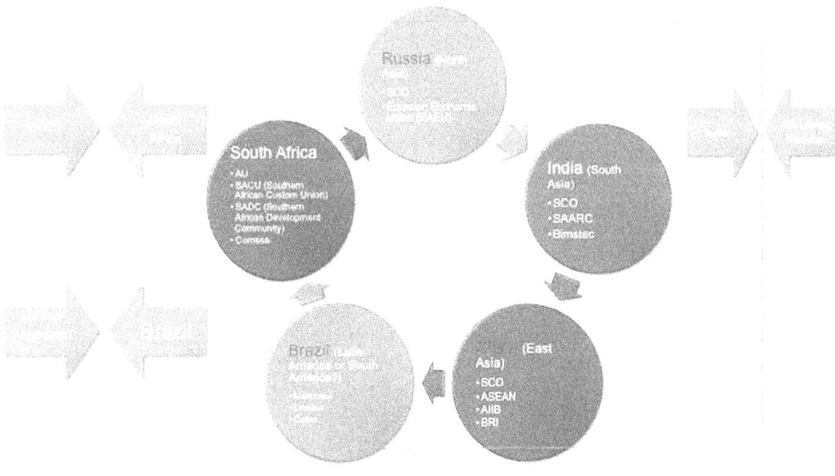

Figure 5.1 Dilemmas of "BRIC plus" and its regional implications

Source: authors' own elaboration

the current Chinese interest in outreach as expressed in the "BRICS Plus" project can introduce another political variable into the process. In this sense, for political and economic reasons, the "natural" candidates in Latin America would be Argentina[6] (MercoPress, 2014) and Mexico (Xinhua, 2017). If we add to this the reduction of Brazilian international prominence, it is possible to foresee problems affecting the role of Brazil in BRICS in a near future.

Conclusion

The economic agenda of BRICS is a clear priority for China, but as the security agenda is of growing importance with each summit, Russia plays an increasingly central role. Another interesting question for future research is whether the BRICS common agenda is wresting international economic governance away from neoliberalism and Western dominance. Despite a fragmentation of desires, disintegration seems unlikely. In this context, it is important to take into account the coexistence of two distinct logics: (i) the Chinese logic and economic leadership, which emphasizes the interregional dynamics evidenced by the outreach mechanism of BRICS-plus (BRICS, 2017); and (ii) the Russian logic, which advocates the return of geopolitics and the balance of power. This is the broader structural context of the Brazilian logic of survival in the short term. In the outreach process up to the Xiamen summit, there was no consensus on procedures or on how many and which members could be incorporated into the bloc, nor on how the outreach process might affect the trajectory of the bloc. Nevertheless, "BRICS Plus" is an important innovation that must be taken seriously.

In the quest for a place in the sun, stronger BRICS financial institutionalization and the possibilities of gradual outreach are the core points of consensus that will mark the future paths of the forum and its gradual mutation into an economic bloc in search of a more balanced correlation of forces in the current multilateral and multipolar world – with crucial consequences for Brazilian's place in the world order.

Notes

1 Its theme was "BRICS and Africa: Partnership for Development, Integration and Industrialisation".
2 NDB disbursed USD 1.5 billion for seven projects in 2016: BNDES ($300 million for renewable energy), Canara Bank of India ($250 million), a project of the Eskom energy company in Africa ($180 million), a solar energy project in China ($81 million) and the construction of a highway in Russia. For more information, see www.ndb.int/newsroom/medias/.
3 The AIIB was created in the same year as the NDB. It is made up of 57 founding members (some of them historical US allies such as England, Germany, and France) and is clearly dominated by China, which has a veto right, the presidency of the bank, and the location of its seat in Beijing (www.aiib.org/en/news-events/news/2016/20160625_003.html).
4 This is explicitly stated in the following: "We are committed to further strengthen and support South-South cooperation, while emphasizing that South-South cooperation is not a substitute but rather a complement to North-South cooperation, which continues to be the main channel for international development cooperation" (BRICS, 2015: §66).

5 Brazilian Bank of Development.
6 It is important to notice that in 2014, there were the first signs that Argentina might possibly become part of the BRICS, with the support of India, Brazil, and South Africa – although the true extent of real support from Brazil on that occasion is not entirely clear (MercoPress, 2014).

References

Abdenur, Adriana Erthal, and Maiara Folly (2015) "O Novo Banco de Desenvolvimento e a Institucionalização do Brics." In Renato Baumann, Flávio Damico, Adriana Erthal Abdenur, Maiara Folly, Carlos Márcio Cozendey, and Renato G Flôres Jr. (eds.) *Brics: Estudos e Documentos*. Brasilia: FUNAG.

Alexandroff, Alan S., and Andrew Fenton Cooper (2010) *Rising States, Rising Institutions: Challenges for Global Governance*. Waterloo and Washington, DC: Brookings Institution Press.

Ambrosio, Thomas (2017) "The Architecture of Alignment: The Russia-China Relationship and International Agreements." *Europe-Asia Studies*, 69(1): 110–156.

Bo, Xiang (2018) "Brics New Development Bank Plans to Launch Americas Regional Office in Brazil." *XinhuaNet*, May 22. Available at www.xinhuanet.com/english/2018-05/22/c_137197986.htm.

BrazilGovNews (2017) "Brazil and China Sign 14 Cooperation Acts." Available at www.brazilgovnews.gov.br/news/2017/09/brazil-and-china-sign-14-cooperation-acts.

BRICS (2009) "First Summit: Joint Statement of the Bric Countries Leaders." Available at http://brics.itamaraty.gov.br/pt_br/categoria-portugues/20-documentos/73-primeiro-declaracao.

BRICS (2010) "Second Summit: Joint Statement." Available at http://brics.itamaraty.gov.br/category-english/21-documents/66-second-summit.

BRICS (2011) "Third Summit: Sanya Declaration and Action Plan." Available at http://brics.itamaraty.gov.br/category-english/21-documents/67-third-summit.

BRICS (2012a) "Fourth Summit: Delhi Declaration and Action Plan." Available at http://brics.itamaraty.gov.br/category-english/21-documents/68-fourth-summit.

BRICS (2012b) "Agreements between Brics Develoment Banks, Nova Delhi." Available at www.brics.utoronto.ca/docs/120329-devbank-agreement.pdf.

BRICS (2013) "Fifth Summit: Ethekwini Declaration and Action Plan." Available at http://brics.itamaraty.gov.br/category-english/21-documents/69-fifth-summit.

BRICS (2014) "Sixth Summit: Fortaleza Declaration and Action Plan." Available at http://brics.itamaraty.gov.br/category-english/21-documents/223-sixth-summit-declaration-and-action-plan.

BRICS (2015) "VII Brics Summit: Ufa Declaration." Available at http://brics.itamaraty.gov.br/category-english/21-documents/253-vii-brics-summit-ufa-declaration.

BRICS (2016) "8th Brics Summit Goa Declaration." Available at http://brics.itamaraty.gov.br/images/pdf/GoaDeclarationandActionPlan.pdf.

BRICS (2017) "Brics Leaders Xiamen Declaration." Available at www.brics.utoronto.ca/docs/170904-xiamen.pdf.

Campos, Ana Cristina (2017) "Temer: Chinese Entrepreneurs Seeking to Expand Investments in Brazil." *Agência Brasil*, August 31. Available at http://agenciabrasil.ebc.com.br/en/internacional/noticia/2017-08/temer-chinese-entrepreneurs-seeking-expand-investments-brazil

Cooper, Andrew F. (1997) *Niche Diplomacy: Middle Powers after the Cold War*. Studies in Diplomacy. Basingstoke: Macmillan.

Cooper, Andrew F. (2013) "Squeezed or Revitalised? Middle Powers, the G20 and the Evolution of Global Governance." *Third World Quarterly*, 34(6): 963–984.

Cooper, Julian M. (2006) "Russia as a Bric: Only a Dream?" *European Research Working Paper Series No 13*, July. Available at www.download.bham.ac.uk/govsoc/eri/working-papers/wp13-cooper.pdf.

Cox, Robert W. (1989) "Middlepowermanship, Japan, and Future World Order." *International Journal*, 44(4): 823–862.

Desai, Radhika (2013) "The Brics Are Building a Challenge to Western Economic Supremacy." *The Guardian*, April 2. Available at www.theguardian.com/commentisfree/2013/apr/02/brics-challenge-western-supremacy.

Desai, Radhika (2015) "Geopolitical Economy: The Discipline of Multipolarity." *Valdai Discussion Club*, 24. Available at http://valdaiclub.com/files/10943/.

Fontdeglòria, Xavier (2017) "China Promete a Temer Participar do Programa de Privatizações Brasileiro." *El País*, Set 1. Available at https://brasil.elpais.com/brasil/2017/09/01/internacional/1504279321_972453.html.

Fortescue, Stephen (2014) "The Brics and Russia." In Vai Io Lo and Mary Hiscock (eds.) *The Rise of the BRICS in the Global Political Economy: Changing Paradigms?* Cheltenham: Edward Elgar.

Garcia, Ana, and Patrick Bond (2015) "Introduction." In Ana Garcia and Patrick Bond (eds.) *Brics: An Anti-Capitalist Critique*. Sunnyside: Jacana.

Giaccaglia, Clarisa (2013) "Estrategias de 'Quodlíbet' en el Escenario Internacional Contemporáneo: Las Acciones ye India, Brasil y Sudáfrica (IBSA) en los Ámbitos Multilaterales." *Revista Brasileira de Política Internacional*, 55(2): 90–108.

Gilley, Bruce, and Andrew O'Neil (2014) *Middle Powers and the Rise of China*. Washington, DC: Georgetown University Press.

Huelsz, Cornelia (2009) "Middle Power Theories and Emerging Powers in International Political Economy: A Case Study of Brazil." PhD Thesis, University of Manchester, Faculty of Humanities. Available at http://hummedia.manchester.ac.uk/institutes/gdi/research/research-programmes/BeyondtheBICsdocs/Cornelia%20Huelsz%20Thesis.pdf

Hurrell, Andrew (2000) "Paths to Power: Foreign Policy Strategies of Intermediate States." In Andrew Hurrell, Andrew F. Cooper, Guadalupe González González, Ricardo Ubiraci Sennes, and Srini Sitaraman (eds.) *Some Reflections on the Role of Intermediate Powers in International Institutions*. Washington, DC: Latin American Program, Woodrow Wilson International Centre.

Itamaraty (2017) "Atos Assinados por Ocasião da Visita do Presidente Michel Temer à China-Pequim, 31 de Agosto a 3 de Setembro de 2017." Brasília. Available at www.itamaraty.gov.br/pt-BR/notas-a-imprensa/17378-atos-assinados-por-ocasiao-da-visita-do-presidente-michel-temer-a-china-pequim-31-de-agosto-a-3-de-setembro-de-2017.

Jordaan, Eduard (2017) "The Emerging Middle Power Concept: Time to Say Goodbye?". *South African Journal of International Affairs*, 24(3): 1–18.

Kahler, Miles (2013) "Rising Powers and Global Governance: Negotiating Change in a Resilient Status Quo." *International Affairs*, 89(3): 711–729.

Kahler, Miler (2016) "The Global Economic Multilaterals: Will Eighty Years Be Enough?". *Global Governance*, 22(1): 1–9.

Katada, Saori N., Cynthia Roberts, and Leslie Elliott Armijo (2017) "The Varieties of Collective Financial Statecraft: The Brics and China." *Internations Studies Association*. Baltimore.

Khalid, Ahmed (2014) "The Power of the Brics in World Trade and Growth, Analysing the Macroeconomic Impacts within and across the Bloc." In Vai Io Lo and Mary Hiscock (eds.) *The Rise of the BRICS in the Global Political Economy: Changing Paradigms?* Cheltenham: Edward Elgar.

Kiely, Ray (2016) *The Rise and Fall of Emerging Powers*. London: Palgrave Macmillan.

Lima, Maria Regina Soares de, and Monica Hirst (2006) "Brazil as an Intermediate State and Regional Power: Action, Choice and Responsabilities." *International Affairs*, 82(1): 21–40.

Li, Xing (2017) "The Rise of Emerging Powers & China and the Enlargement of 'Room for Maneuver' and 'Upward Mobility'". *Rising Powers in Global Governance*. Available athttp://risingpowersproject.com/the-rise-of-emerging-powers-china-and-the-enlargement-of-room-for-maneuver-and-upward-mobility/.

MacFarlane, Neil S. (2006) "The 'R' in Brics: Is Russia an Emerging Power?". *International Affairs*, 82(1): 41–57.

MercoPress (2014) "India, Brazil and South Africa Want Argentina to Join the Brics Club." *MercoPress*, May 6. Available at http://en.mercopress.com/2014/05/06/india-brazil-and-south-africa-want-argentina-to-join-the-brics-club.

Naidoo, Sharda (2012) "South Africa's Presence 'Drags Down Brics.'" *Mail & Guardian*, March 23. Available at https://mg.co.za/article/2012-03-23-sa-presence-drags-down-brics.

NDB (2018) "Ndb President Meets Brazil's Minister of Foreign Relations in Shanghai." *New Development Bank*. Available at www.ndb.int/press_release/ndb-president-meets-brazils-minister-foreign-relations-shanghai/.

Neelakantan, Shailaja (2016) "India Used Brics-Bimstec Summit to Outmanoeuvre Pakistan, Chinese Media Says." *The Times of India*. Available at http://timesofindia.indiatimes.com/india/India-used-Goa-Brics-meet-to-outmanoeuvre-Pakistan-Chinese-media-says/articleshow/54933030.cms.

Netto, Andrei (2016) "Temer foi o único dos representantes dos Brics a não ser recebido por Putin em Goa, Na Índia." *Estadão*, Outubro 18. Available at https://politica.estadao.com.br/noticias/geral,temer-foi-o-unico-dos-representantes-dos-brics-a-nao-ser-recebido-por-putin-em-goa-na-india,10000082946.

Nogueira Batista, Paulo (2017) "Brasil pode abrir representação do Novo Banco De Desenvolvimento já em 2018." *Sputnik*, September 9. Available at https://br.sputniknews.com/mundo/201709059282153-desenvolvimento-financiamento-infraestrutura-energia-comercio-exterior-geopolitica/.

Pandey, Pragya (2017) "2017 Brics Summit: Post-Doklam, India, China Meet in Xiamen." *The Diplomat*. Available at https://thediplomat.com/2017/09/2017-brics-summit-post-doklam-india-china-meet-in-xiamen/.

Pautasso, Diego, Gabriel Adam Adam, and Bruno Rocha Lima (2015) "A Política Externa Da Rússia Diante Da Crise Na Síria." *Tensões Mundiais*, 11(21): 147–168.

Polgreen, Lydia (2013) "Group of Emerging Nations Plans to form Development Bank." *New York Times*, March 26. Available at www.nytimes.com/2013/03/27/world/africa/brics-to-form-development-bank.html.

Ramos, Leonardo, Ana Garcia, Diego Pautasso, and Fernanda Rodrigues (2018) "A Decade of Emergence: The Brics' Institutional Densification Process." *Journal of China and International Relations*, Special Issue: 1–15.

Ramos, Leonardo, Rodrigo Corrêa Teixeira, Marcia Paiva Fernandes, and Rafaela Carnevali (2012a) "Objetivos, Contradições e Atuação da África Do Sul no G20." *Meridiano 47*, 13(132): 46–52.

Ramos, Leonardo, Javier Vadell, Ana Saggioro, and Márcia Fernandes (2012b) "A Governança Econômica Global e os Desafios do G-20 Pós-Crise Financeira: Análise das

Posições de Estados Unidos, China, Alemanha e Brasil." *Revista Brasileira de Política Internacional*, 55(2): 10–27.
Roberts, Cynthia, Leslie Armijo, and Saori Katada (2018) *The Brics and Collective Financial Statecraft*. Oxford: Oxford University Press.
Toloraya, Georgy T. (2016) "Goa as Today's Geopolitical Fulcrum." *The Brics Post*, October 17. Available at http://thebricspost.com/goa-as-todays-geopolitical-fulcrum/#.W4B7us5KiUk.
Wallerstein, Immanuel (1974) "The Rise and Future Demise of the World-Capitalist System: Concepts for Comparative Analysis." *Comparative Studies in Society and History*, 16: 387–415.
Wallerstein, Immanuel (2004) *World-Systems Analysis: An Introduction*. Durham and London: Duke University Press.
Wu, DD (2017) "Russia-China Relations Reach a New High." *The Diplomat*. Available at https://thediplomat.com/2017/07/russia-china-relations-reach-a-new-high/.
Xinhua (2017) "Mexico Open to Cooperation with Brics: Trade Group." *Xinhuanet*. Available at www.xinhuanet.com/english/2017-08/30/c_136567833.htm.

6 China's dual position in the capitalist world order

A dual complexity of hegemony and counter-hegemony

Li Xing

Research propositions

In studying the historical evolution or transformation of the world order, researchers of international relations (IR) and international political economy (IPE) are often facing a number of ontological and epistemological questions: How do states and markets hang together and interact with each other? What kinds of general rules of game govern interstate and intermarket relations? What are the causal factors that cause power shift? In which ways will the rise of a new global power alter IR and IPE relations, not only functionally but also structurally? Are changes taking place in IR and IPE in a direction of purposeful forward or backward movement, or are they in a dialectic process of waxing and waning, declining, and rising? Are IR and IPE relations continuously evolving in a state of flux and reflux, rather than in a deterministic logical progression?

World order is bluntly defined by Strange as "a set of global arrangements", and these arrangements are "not divinely ordained, nor are they outcome of blind chance"; rather, they are *imposed* as "the result of human decisions taken in the context of man-made institutions and sets of self-set rules and customs" (Strange, 1988: 18). Against the backdrop of China's global rise, it is less important to know whether or not the 21st century will be the Chinese century (perhaps it is important to policymakers and national elites), in view of the current decline of the United States and its withdrawal from international leadership and obligation. It is also less significant to know whether the GDPs of India, Russia, or Brazil will surpass those of Japan, Germany, or France in the first half of the 21st century. What is important – and this is the chapter's central thesis – is to study the extent to which the rise of China is "affecting" and "disturbing" a number of existing "global relationships" and "global arrangements" shaped by the "structural power" of the existing world order.

China's global rise has created a phenomenon with dual complexities. On the one hand, China is actively applying a strategy of both reviving and leading "South-South"[1] political and economic cooperation as the country has grown in economic importance and in political influence; on the other hand, however, it is taking advantage of its increasingly leveraged position in the global economy to change or modify the conventional norms and practices of the existing liberal institutions of global governance. In the former relationship, China seemed to be in the position of a new hegemon, whereas in the latter, it is seen to be taking the role of a counter-hegemon. Thus, the author deems it to be heuristic and inspiring for academic researchers to study the relationships between emerging powers and existing hegemons as a highly complex phenomenon. The chapter's research question and its main analytical framework propose an analysis of the present-day dual complexity brought about by the rise of China in a number of relationships. This dual complexity indicates two contrasting phenomena that reflect the theme of the chapter indicated by the title.

The discussions engaged in in this chapter are based on the conceptualization of China's rise as having different implications and impacts on different parts of the world. On the one hand, it may be argued that China is becoming a leading counter-hegemonic socio-political and socio-economic force to the "center" of the existing world order, while at the same time, it can be seen as a new emerging hegemon to the semi-peripheral and peripheral parts of the world order. This situation prompts the author to examine the dynamic and dialectic nexus between the following two open-ended research propositions:

Proposition A: "China's emergence as a counter-hegemonic power"

In line with the understanding of Realism, China's economic rise is premised on expanding and intensifying integration within the international system, China's rise presages an inevitable conflict within the current international system and a challenge to the US hegemony (Mearsheimer, 2006, 2014). Seen from the perspective of Liberalism, the liberal world order is an open, rule-and institution-based system founded on norms of non-discrimination and market openness, and the reason why emerging powers such as China are currently the winners in the era of globalization is precisely that their economic growth and wealth accumulation have been generated from within the order, not from without (Ikenberry, 2008, 2011). Thus, it is in the interest of both China and the core powers of the system to have China well integrated in the system, abiding by its norms and rules.

But ironically, China's current integration in the world economy, together with the strong role of the state, is strengthening China's comparative advantage and increasing its share of world wealth and resources. China's moving up in the global supply chain together with its increasing share in the possession of global resources has largely reduced the profit margin and resource access which used to be monopolized by the traditional core states. Beijing's struggle for a re-division of the already divided world is a menace. The Chinese state-led development model is ideologically unacceptable to the defined norms and values of the liberal order. Even today, China is not recognized as a "market economy" by the existing core powers of the liberal world, the US and EU.

China's double-track strategy of joining and modifying the existing international institutions and setting up the country's own global financial institutions is causing China's economic rise to be changing Beijing's position from a passive rule-follower to a proactive rule-maker, leading to an emerging world order "with Chinese characteristics". In other words, China has two options today: First, it can choose "to operate from within existing institutions to enhance its position through seeking the redistribution of decision-making authority, or by using its influence to obstruct and contain the progressive evolution of the liberal rules, practices, and norms of an institution in ways that threaten China's interests" (Ikenberry and Lim, 2017: 2). Second, if the first option does not give Beijing the expected result, Beijing can create its own international institution. Both options are affecting in different degrees the *patterns of global relationships* that generate gross inequalities in the world order and the tremendous privilege and power this global disparity of wealth and power has brought about for the core countries, especially the US. Currently China is implementing both options at the same time.

China's global economic rise and its increasing institutional roles are facilitating processes in which normative matrices and decisions in countries involved in economic relations with China are influenced by the thinking and practice of Chinese policymakers and intellectuals. As a result, the ideational components of Chinese policies, norms, values, and institutions will be diffused and intertwined in the emerging world order.

Proposition B: "China's emergence as a new hegemon"

According to other analysts, China's competition is seen to lead to peripherization of existing semi-periphery countries within the current world system, because "China's competition will completely undermine the relative monopoly of the existing semi-peripheral states in certain commodity chains. The value added will be squeezed, forcing the traditional semi-peripheral states to accept lower wage rates close to the Chinese rates" (Li, 2005: 436, 2008). China's competition breaks down the relative monopoly of the existing semi-peripheral states in certain global commodity chains, and causes a certain degree of deindustrialization or peripheralization of many existing semi-peripheral countries due to the change of their position from being an exporter of manufacturing goods to being a commodity supplier. This line of thinking and argument is also shared by many scholars in Latin America (Bernal-Meza, 2012; Dussel Peters, 2016; Guelar, 2013; Sevares, 2015)

Although this is contrary to China's long-standing self-identity as a leader of developing countries, paradoxically, China's new status as a world economic and political power is turning itself into a new world *hegemon* that is facing counter-hegemonic forces and constellations. China's capital expansion and production outsourcing to the world periphery, such as to Africa and other regions in the Global South, are seen to be bringing about a new circle of "unequal exchange" reflected in the conventional North-South dependent relationships. Economic relations between China and the Global South are increasingly portrayed by various media as "neo-colonialism" (*The Economist*, March 13, 2008; Sharife, 2009). Today, the debate as to whether China is a neo-colonialist predator or a development partner is still ongoing, especially in West-dominated mainstream media.

Conceptual and theoretical lenses

The economic rise of China is an integral part of the historical process of the global expansion of capitalism, and the rise and fall of world hegemons must be understood within the capitalist world system rather than outside of this. The premise of IPE is that all states and markets are connected in a globally defined capitalist system of production, exchange, and distribution, and IPE investigates the ways in which states and markets of the world are connected to one another and the "social, political, and economic arrangements" that have evolved to connect them. (Strange, 1988). The IPE approach provides the framework for understanding the global "structural power" that preserves those arrangements.

The analytical strength of IPE is that it provides the framework for understanding the global shift of "structural power". Structural power refers to "the power to decide how things shall be done, the power to shape frameworks within which states relate to each other, relate to people, or relate to corporate enterprises" (Strange, 1988: 25). Structural power is one of the key components of the concept of hegemony. It is on the basis of this broad IPE approach that this chapter studies how the rise of China has indeed "disturbed" the established global arrangements that are shaped by the conventional distribution of power and by the ways in which states and markets are structurally interrelated. The hegemony of the existing powers is fundamentally based on the possession of the structural power, while the rise of China is seen as challenging the status quo of such structural power.

The conceptual and analytical tools applied in this chapter constitute the instrumental lens of "hegemony", a concept that is often applied to describe different *enduring aspects* of an order in the capitalist world system. Realism perceives hegemony as the dominance by one leading state in interstate relations, whereas Liberalism identifies hegemony as being embedded in the interactions of each individual at the bottom, and in the norms and values of international institutions as rule-setters at the top. Constructivism sees hegemony as being rooted in the social foundation of international societies in which agent and structure, identity, and interest are transformable in various forms of norm-diffusion and norm-setting.

The critical school of the IR/IPE theories see hegemony both as a prevailing *order* among states and as a dominant *mode of production* that binds states together:

> hegemony at the international level is thus not merely an order amongst states. It's an order within a world economy with a dominant mode of production which penetrates into all countries and links into other subordinate modes of production. It is also a complex of international social relationships which connect the social classes of the different countries. World hegemony is describable as a social structure, and economic structure and a political structure; and it cannot be simply one of those things but must be all three.
>
> (Cox, 1983: 171–172)

Hegemony is always in a dynamic state, it symbolizes an evolving condition of the international system itself. It is a useful notion in conceptualizing and understanding the dynamic and dialectic interplays in the world order and the international relations/systems. It involves different interconnected components – ideas, material capacities, institutions, social forces, forms of state, world orders, and their interactions between national and international actors and institutions. However, "hegemony" is often perceived by mainstream IR theories as *status-quo realities*, and this perception is premised on the "existing arrangements" made by the US-led and West-dominated world order. The rise of China not only challenges the status-quo realities, it also necessitates a change of "perception" and ontological premise.

The chapter's conceptual IPE lens of "hegemony" is applied in combination with the theoretical tenet of the critical school of IR theory and the world system theory. There is an organic connection between the IPE conceptualization of the world order as "social, political, and economic arrangements" and the world system theory's identification of the world system as "global stratification". Both theories are aiming to explain social economic and political connections that tie the world's countries together and the endless movements taking place within the system in the position changes of countries in terms of "upward and downward mobility" and "room for maneuver". Along this line of thinking, the chapter intends to examine the change of position of China in the world system and the impact of this on global stratification.

Interdependent hegemony

As a contribution, the author places the concept of "hegemony" in the current context of globalization and transformation in the liberal world order, and introduces an alternative concept that can embrace the new situation, a concept coined by the author himself: "interdependent hegemony". What the world order is witnessing today is not the repeat of history manifested by the world wars (apart from some signs of great power rivalry) between the rising and the existing powers; nor is it the harmonious integration and accommodation of the late-comers into the established system. It is argued that the world order is entering into an era of interdependent hegemony, implying that the sources to feed and maintain the areas of structural power and monopoly are no longer dominated exclusively by the US/West, and that they are, to a large extent, dependent on the inputs from emerging powers.

Notwithstanding that the concept of "hegemony" is an important tool for understanding and analyzing politics and international relations, the chapter contends that "interdependent hegemony" is a better concept in describing, understanding, and analyzing the world order in transformation. The concept of "interdependent hegemony" implies a dialectic process of mutual challenge, mutual constraint, mutual need, and mutual accommodation. It symbolizes a dynamic situation in which the existing system's hegemons and the new emerging counter-hegemony powers are intertwined in a constant interactive process of shaping and reshaping the world order, whereby nation-states, global governance, transnational actors, civil societies, and interest groups are incorporated into the dominant project of global capitalism in various ways.

It is therefore necessary to adopt a dialectic approach to understanding the current world order, in which patterns of relationships among states are shaped by the historical evolution of the hegemonic structure, and within which emerging powers, such as China, are politically and economically integrated and embedded. The relationships between the counter-hegemonic challenges posed by emerging powers and the structural barriers of the existing order can be studied through the conceptual lens of "interdependent hegemony" in the current era of the capitalist world order. That is to say, interdependent hegemony brought about by the emerging power phenomenon is a dialectic dualism that demonstrates, on the one hand, the dynamic and inclusive nature of the capitalist liberal order, and, on the other hand, the contradictions and structural limits embedded in the existing order for accommodating and integrating emerging powers. As major power interests intertwine and the major emerging and existing powers rely heavily on one another, a virtuous cycle is becoming increasingly characteristic of the relations among countries.

China's rise: a dual role of hegemon and counter-hegemon

China's dual position as both hegemon and counter-hegemon proposed at the beginning of the chapter is conceptualized as dialectic, dynamic, and complex. One aspect of this inter-relationship is that it is an unintended consequence of *mutual generation*. The intensification of Proposition A, "China's emergence as a counter-hegemonic power", implies the increase of Proposition B, "China's emergence as a new hegemon", and vice versa (see Figure 6.1)

The background of Figure 6.1 is that the world capitalist system is embedded with fundamental features characterized by a series of cyclical rhythms, i.e.

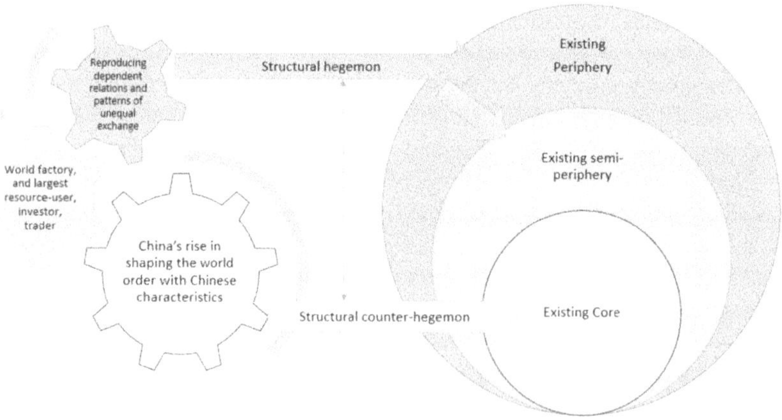

Figure 6.1 China's dual position in the capitalist world system

Source: author's own figure

prosperity or crisis, and upward or downward movement. This system expanded over a long historical spectrum and developed into a rigid division of labor that perpetuates a condition of economic core-semi-perphery-peripheral relations (Wallerstein, 1974, 1979, 1997, 2004). More importantly, this series of cyclical rhythms was followed by the decline of the existing hegemon(s) and the rise of new hegemon(s) (also called new "system guarantors" of the world system (Wallerstein, 1979).

Figure 6.1 explains that the emergence of China can be plausibly perceived as part of the system's rhythmic cycles in the upward mobility, and that China continues to follow the core features of the world capitalist system. It is believed that China is motivated or driven to act as a new political and economic system-guarantor, due to its economic integration and market dependence in the system's mode of production and capital accumulation (Ikenberry, 2008). This explains why the system's new hegemon will unavoidably have its own unique pattern of control; it will not be able to alter the fundamental features of the system's law of value (capital accumulation and profit-seeking) (Wallerstein, 1997). This is to posit that, in line with the Neo-Gramsican IR/IPE perspective and the world system theory's interpretation, even if the future world order were to be injected with Chinese characteristics, this would simply be a reflection of the expansive phenomena of China's internal economic, political, and cultural structures; the core architecture of the world capitalist order – *interstate relations shaped by a dominant mode of production* – would not be altered by this.

However, a common consensus today is that China is indeed challenging the hegemony of the power center of the world system. What has been underestimated is the impact of China's unique historical and cultural imprint on this common consensus. Gramscian analysis emphasizes the fact that hegemony is constantly competed over by contending social forces both within the country and without (Gramsci, 1971). Figure 6.1 can be interpreted to show that whereas in theoretical terms, China is a "status quo" power in line with the system's economic logic, in practical terms, it is increasingly perceived by the system's existing core powers as a rising "revisionist" hegemon, a counter-hegemonic econo-political force.

Figure 6.1 also indicates that China's emerging presence in the system's semi-periphery and periphery does not generate any fundamental "change" in the "hierarchy" of the capitalist world system. Rather, China's increasing role in the world system's semi-periphery and periphery further confirms the "cyclical rhythms" of the capitalist world system. The rise of a new hegemon successively incorporates new states into the system's division of labor, which repeats the "unequal exchange" mechanism originally conceptualized represented by "Latin American structuralism" of Prebisch and ECLA(C) as the source of the system's maintenance of its hierarchy, exploitation, and underdevelopment. Since both China and semi-periphery and periphery countries are conditioned on the dominant mode of production reflected by the exigencies of global commodity and capital markets, the argument is: *while China is successfully moving into the core, it still needs the semi-periphery and periphery*. Not only that; the point is that China will always need these two stratifications and perhaps even more so when China transforms itself into a highly developed capitalist country.

This is to say that the capitalist world order is not an accidental collection of unrelated individual states; rather, states are connected as a whole in a capitalist world order in which each actor is part and parcel of a historical process. Hence, a proper way to conceptualize hegemony is perhaps to perceive it as a dynamic and dialectic movement, and a highly multifaceted phenomenon. Competition for hegemony in a world order represents a dynamic process, or a constantly evolving condition of the international system itself, a condition involving shared or antagonistic visions, projects, strategies, and interest.

Surplus generated in the system is unevenly distributed among states, depending on their different *positions* in the world economy/market. Different positions denote the extent or degree to which each country can benefit from or suffer from the system's "room for maneuver" (increase or decrease) and "upward mobility" (upward or downward).

"Room for maneuver" refers to the external conditions for "upward mobility" in a world capitalist economy that is conducive to internal development. Seen from a long historical perspective, the global core-semi-periphery-periphery hierarchy defined by the world system theory has been a relatively stable structure over centuries. The system's rhythmic cycles and the rise or decline of hegemonic powers provide both upward and downward mobility. The rise of the US is the clear example of upward mobility, and so is China since the 1980s. A positive effect of upward mobility is reflected by the combination of external forces, e.g. "promotion by invitation", and internal forces, e.g. "seizing the chance". According to a World Bank report, China's capital expansion in Africa represents a new round of global capital mobility and production relocation (World Bank, 2015).

The fact that countries are in different hierarchical positions represented by the global core-semi-periphery-periphery structure is a potential source of conflict. As peripheral countries attempt to elevate their positions in the system by taking advantage of any possibility of "room for maneuver" and "upward mobility", semi-peripheral countries are struggling to move into the core without falling into the "downward mobility" trend, thus becoming peripherized. At the same time, the core countries are striving to maintain their dominant position in the system through trade relations and international institutions on the basis of the established rules of the game and their structural power.

The IPE structure of "global arrangement" has been sustained for decades by an institutional architecture consisting of major political and economic institutions such as the UN, the IMF, World Bank Group and GATT, which were created under the auspices of the Bretton Woods System led by the transatlantic alliance after World War II. It was the "US hegemony", i.e. its economic, political, and security-related leadership, and especially its global institutional "public goods", that shaped the postwar world order. This is also the Neo-Gramscian IR/IPE theoretical tenet in the conceptualization of the way in which the construction of hegemony driven by social forces occupying a leading position within a nation-state is then projected outwards on a world scale, leading to the shaping of the international order (Cox, 1981, 1983). Robert Cox (1983) uses precisely international institutions as empirical examples.

If the given sources of the existing hegemony are derived from the US-led world order, counter-hegemony is a dynamically inherent reflection or an extended consequence brought about by the ongoing global changes. China has been seen as a "revisionist power" because of the discrepancy between the increasingly multipolar world economy brought about by the rise of China in the recent decades and the mismatched representation of the organizations mandated with its governance, which causes much strain in global politics (Güven, 2017). The existing world order (politics, institutions, ideas, norms) should be understood as a product in a specific historical context, whereas new historical transformations (new contexts, such as globalization and the rise of new emerging powers) are generating new social and political forces that are shaping new politics, institutions, and ideas in a dialectic and dynamic nexus.

Obviously, the shift of the world economy from "unipolar" toward "multipolar" has not been translated into changes in hegemony (authority and influence) within multilateral organizations such as the World Bank and the International Monetary Fund (IMF). Consequently, policy coherence at the global level becomes problematic in this fragmented institutional milieu, while China is gradually gaining greater influence over the international decision-making process. Managing the rising influence of China and reforming multilateral institutions are becoming decisive and indispensable issues for the principal powers of the existing global governance system.

China as a counter-hegemon to the core of the world order

Historically, counter-hegemony forces or anti-systemic movements in world orders/disorders/ reorders have always resulted from the disturbing dynamics unleashed by recurrent crises of the order. Since the hegemony of an existing order is organically embedded with and constantly challenged by counter-hegemonic components, both hegemony and counter-hegemony are a constantly dual phenomenon. The relationships between the rise of China and the existing international institutions provide good opportunities for studying counter-hegemony aspects and interactions.

In his speech in 2015, Robert Zoellick, former US Deputy Secretary of State, anticipated China to become a "responsible stakeholder" in the existing liberal multilateral institution. Beijing's membership of the World Trade Organization (WTO), together with its constructive roles in a wide array of multilateral institutions, seemingly confirmed Zoellick's anticipation. For example, China has been a forerunner in accepting the existing neoliberal order and benefiting from that order, particularly in the area of free trade. This is contrary to the argument pursued by some classical critical theories such as Prebisch's "Theory of the Deterioration of the Terms of Trade" modeled in the core-periphery structure that peripheral countries do not benefit from free trade to the same extent as the core states, and that free trade prevents the development of the periphery. China has benefitted immensely from the open and competitive economic system, and it is believed that their continuous success is dependent on the functioning of the system. A good example is that China's economic success is seen as being premised on expanding and intensifying integration within the international system, and the internal and external factors of China's economic achievement are so intertwined and mutually dependent. Consequently, as a rising power, China's national interests and foreign policy behavior are increasingly reflecting and embracing the status quo. The reason why China is currently a winner in the era of globalization is precisely that its economic growth and wealth accumulation is generated from within, not from without, the capitalist world system (Ikenberry, 2008). As Ikenberry correctly explains,

> The struggle over international order today is not about fundamental principles. China and other emerging great powers do not want to contest the basic rules and principles of the liberal international order; they wish to gain more authority and leadership within it.
>
> (Ikenberry, 2011: 57)

However, critics see China's active participation in and engagement with the existing multilateral organizations has a hidden agenda. In other words, Beijing is seen to be using these pragmatic solutions as a strategy, employing its increasing leverage to extract concessions. And once the expected concessions are not received, China embarks on a search for an alternative counter-hegemony path to either undermine and bypass the existing system of multilateral institutions, or to establish China-led substitute institutions. The sources of China's alternative path are its "financial minilateralism", such as the Asian Infrastructure Investment Bank (AIIB), the New Development Bank (NDB, also called the BRICS Bank), and the Regional Comprehensive Economic Partnership trade agreement (RCEP) in the Pacific and East Asia (Ikenberry and Lim, 2017; Wang, 2014). These new institutions mark the borderline between China as a "revisionist power" and the existing US-led liberal world order.

These Beijing-led global financial institutions and regional development frameworks demonstrate "Beijing's challenge to the world of Bretton Woods" (*Financial Times*, 2014). China is increasingly deriving more hegemonic authority and legitimacy from setting up international financial institutions. Such a network of revisionist and "counter-hegemonic" institutions challenge or, to a large extent, oppose and undermine the US-led global and regional institutions. Even if Beijing claims that it does not have any counter-hegemonic purpose, it nevertheless has the counter-hegemonic economic structure. The latter will inevitably lead to the establishment of a counter-hegemonic super-structure in terms of norm diffusion and rule making.

However, China's state-led economic success with "Chinese characteristics" is seen a challenge to the ideational aspects of the existing system. As observed by Chris Patten, the last British Governor of Hong Kong, the rise of China is "a threat to democracy" and is "the first example of a country which has done astonishingly well in this international system, but challenges its basic foundations" (as quoted in *BBC News*, 2008, November 23). The Chinese economic success is not only leading the world into multipolarity, multilateralism, and diversity; it is also opening for alternative norms and values. The "Chinese model" is providing alternative factors and explanations regarding mechanisms that cause nations to grow, and regarding the set of mutually dependent relationships between property rights and economic growth, between the rule of law and a market economy, between a free currency flow and economic order, and, most importantly, between democracy and development. These "universal" norms and values are conventionally defined by the existing powers alone, and the rise of China is making them "non-universal" – open, less rigid, and non-universal.

The rise of China is generating a great deal of impact on the existing center of the world order due to its relationships with both the system's structure and agency. Neither Realism's "conflict and war" nor Liberalism's "cooperation and independence" is able to provide a correct analysis of China's impact. Beijing's counter-hegemonic constellations are seemingly perceived as a competitive rivalry to the existing structural arrangement, and especially to the agency that has created this structural arrangement. However, today's situation is neither the repeat of history manifested by world wars, apart from some signs of great power rivalry between China and the existing powers, nor is it the harmonious one-way integration and accommodation of the former into the established system.

For example, according to a study by Peng and Tok (2016), the China-led Asian Infrastructure Investment Bank (AIIB) can be identified as "China's normative power in international financial governance" from three angles:

> Based on the existing framework of normative power concept, the AIIB's role in China's normative power is examined from three angles: normative principles, norm diffusion, and external perception. As a Chinese initiative, the AIIB's policy framework has inherited Chinese norms of unconditionality and infrastructure construction. The management structure of this new bank also manifests China's preference of a lean internal arrangement. Moreover, Asian developing countries hold the majority of voting power of the AIIB. This distribution of votes also falls in line with China's appeal of a fair governance structure in international financial institutions.
>
> (Peng and Tok, 2016: 736)

This study shows that the conventional norms underlining these three angles have always been defined by the existing core powers, and they are the normative pillars of the World Bank and the IMF. However, they are now being rewritten and redefined by China as a set of new normative guidelines for the AIIB.

What can be regarded as "norm diffusion" from the Chinese success is the role of the socio-cultural and political "embeddedness" in a *governed market* reflected by a unique embedded integration of state-market-society relations (Li, 2016b). The Chinese relevance in this context has perhaps less to do with the attraction of the Chinese political system and cultural values and more to do with China as a metaphor for "doing it your own way", or China is seen as an example of what can be done (Breslin, 2010). Beijing's unique authoritarian *deliberative* mode of governance assisted by a "deliberative mechanism" and "authoritarian resilience" is one of the strongest enduring features of the Chinese political culture, which is characterized by dynamic adaptive skills and greater institutional capacity for political survival (Nathan, 2003; Li, 2017). Labeling China as a new "imperial power", the US Secretary of State Rex Tillerson recently warned Latin America against the new normal derived from the Chinese economic success, saying that "China's state-led model of development is reminiscent of the past. It doesn't have to be this hemisphere's future" (*Reuters*, February 1, 2018). Washington is really worried about the norm diffusion of the Chinese model.

While the existing core powers believe that China will be moulded and shaped to adapt to the neoliberal order, what they might forget is that this "adaptation" cannot be a one-way accommodation; rather, a two-way mutual adaptation must take place. The existing liberal order does not give a clear clue as to how the existing order can accommodate necessary changes or modifications brought about by the rise of China for the sake of its own survival. China is not just simply "joining the club of other leading powers"; instead, it is seeing itself as playing the new role of functioning as a representative of the developing world, with a grand objective of changing the existing order substantially in a direction that is more equally balanced and represented. The current crisis of liberal hegemony is a consequence of the deep and complex crisis of the neoliberal development model in which no new hegemonic project has imposed itself (Ougaard, 2013: 12). Thus, it is important to understand that whether the "late-comers" will accept or resist the established order or create a new world order also depends on the roles emerging powers, especially China, decide to play (Schweller and Pu, 2011; Li, 2016a).

China as a new hegemon to the semi-periphery and periphery of the world order

In the view of the world system theory, capital is always mobile in relocating the declining sectors to semi-periphery or periphery countries according to their labor conditions and technological level. Some of these countries will benefit from global capital mobility and production outsourcing. Historically, it was in such pivotal moments that opportunities for upward mobility within the system were generated and regenerated (Wallerstein, 1979). China's high economic growth in the past decades is a good story reflecting the positive spill-over effect of taking advantage of the system's upward mobility.

China and the semi-periphery

Following China's own capital and production outward expansion, the global rise of China seemingly represents another rhythmic cycle of the rise of a new hegemon. Such a rise is an opportunity for some countries in terms of enlarging their room for maneuver and increasing their upward mobility, while for other countries, it is a challenge and even has a downward impact. China's competition is seen to lead to the deindustrialization of existing semi-periphery countries within the current world system, because

> China's competition will completely undermine the relative monopoly of the existing semi-peripheral states in certain commodity chains. The value added will be squeezed, forcing the traditional semi-peripheral states to accept lower wage rates close to the Chinese rates [which they cannot do]
>
> (Li, 2005, p. 436)

The minimization of the semi-periphery space within the existing world capitalism system caused by the rise of China will eventually lead to the demise of the entire system.

For example, the economic relationship with China has been a source of substantial controversy in Brazil (Barbosa and Mendes, 2006; Maciel and Nedal, 2011; Jenkins, 2015). The Brazil-China trade relations represent two sides of the same coin – the coexistence of opportunities and constraints. On the one hand, China-Brazil trade relations are becoming increasingly important to Brazil because they are bringing many benefits to the country, particularly in the areas of commodities such as iron ore and soybeans. This situation is similar to that in many other developing countries that have benefited from China's rapid growth of demand for primary products and from rising world prices. On the other hand, the "unequal exchange of trade" between the two countries, with China exporting manufactured products and Brazil exporting commodities and raw material, is causing the "primarization" of Brazilian exports and the "deindustrialization" of its economy, thus generating negative impacts on Brazil's long-term economic development.

Both Figures 6.2a and 6.2b show that Brazil has experienced relative deindustrialization in terms of a falling share of the manufacturing sector in GDP. This situation is seen as being caused by the direct and indirect impacts of China-Brazilian trade relations, which generate the "primarization" and "deindustrialization" of Brazilian exports to and imports from China. The data in these Figures are claimed to add further evidence to the debate regarding whether the rise of China causes the peripheralization of existing semi-periphery countries.

China and the periphery

Much of the literature today which is critical of China's relations with less developed countries (the periphery), especially its increasing presence in Africa, applies largely the same theoretical and ideological discourses – *neo-imperialism* and *neo-colonialism* – on the historical economic relationship between the core Western countries and Africa. Reincarnation of the "dependency theory" is also claimed; according to this, Africa was seen as a victim of the unequal economic relationships imposed by external mercantilist forces. Accordingly, the Chinese

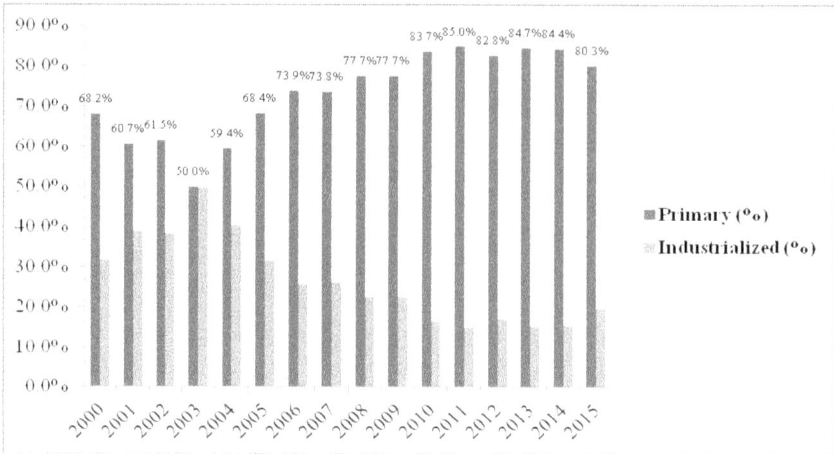

Figure 6.2a Brazilian exports to China 2000–2015

(Dantas and Jabbour, 2016: 319, fig. 8)

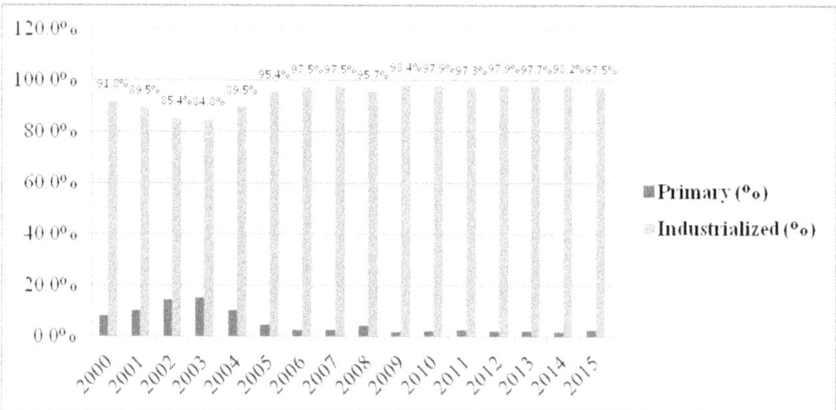

Figure 6.2b Brazilian imports from China 2000–2015

(Dantas and Jabbour, 2016: 320, fig. 9)

government is today perceived to be one actor amongst others, all of whom are engaged in a strategic pursuit of resources and in attempts to ensure raw material supplies. Figure 6.3a and 6.3b can be identified by the critics as evidence that China appears to be repeating the logic of the dependency theory's "unequal exchange" (manufacturing vis-à-vis raw material).

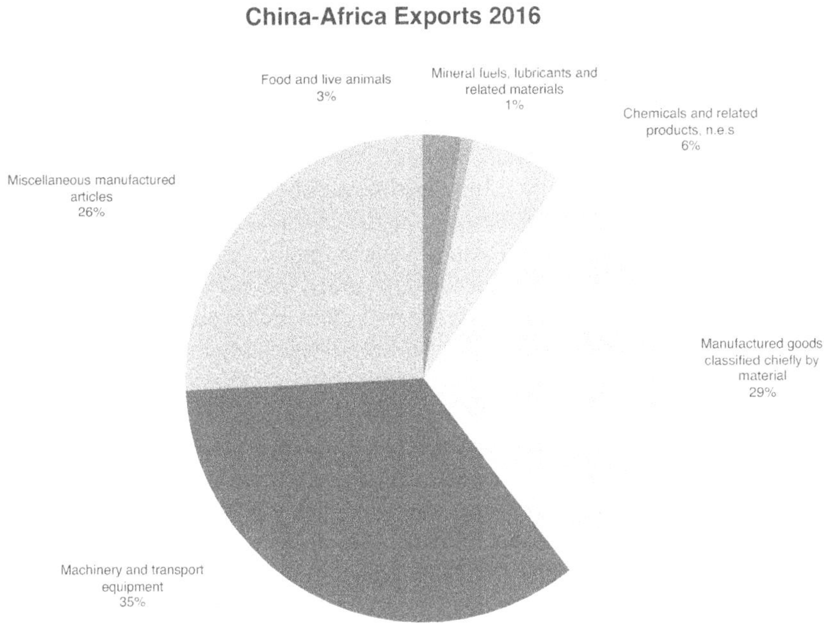

Figure 6.3a Recent data on China-Africa trade in 2016: exports

Source: World Bank (2018). World Integrated Trade Solutions. Retrieved from wits.worldbank.org

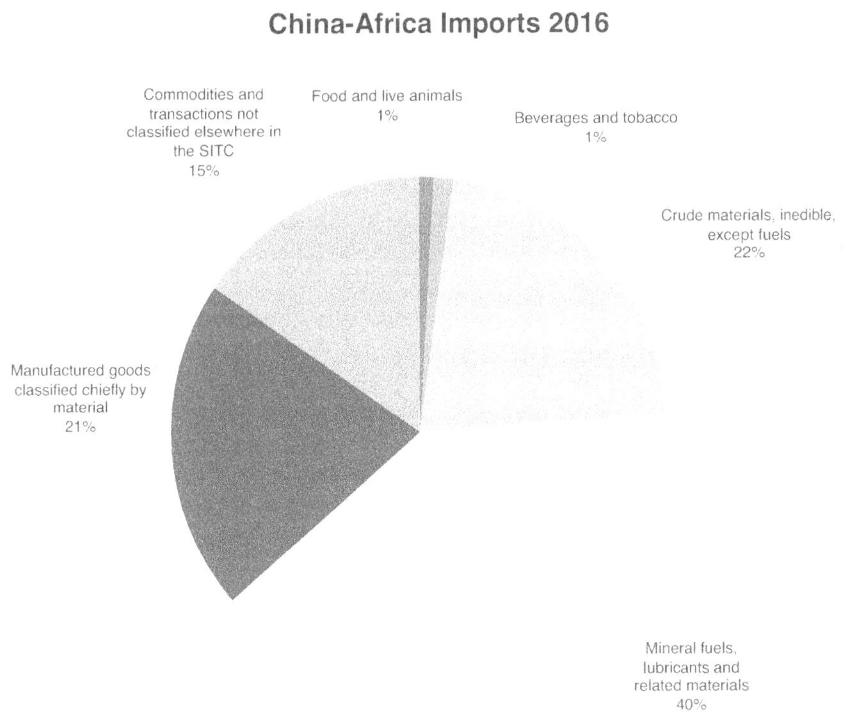

Figure 6.3b Recent data on China-Africa trade in 2016: imports

Source: World Bank (2018). World Integrated Trade Solutions. Retrieved from wits.worldbank.org

The centrality of the current debates and controversies lies in to the way in which China's merging relations with periphery countries are interpreted and analyzed in a balanced manner. One group of scholars represented by Ian Taylor (2016a, 2016b, 2016c) argue that China's economic relationships with the developing world can be conceptualized through the neo-Gramscian concept of "passive revolution". Seen from this perspective, the rise of China in the global order does not change the capitalist order, a similar view to that of the world system theory. In line with Taylor's argument, in a capitalist order, the interests of the emergent dominant forces within China rest on the terms that are favored by transnational elites and transnational capital. This is neoliberal hegemony that rests with transnational capitalism across the world. What the world is experiencing is a process of the adaptation and cooptation of China and its political and economic elites by traditional powers and leading transnational economic classes. The neo-liberal order's cooptation of China, together with China's outward financial and production-related expansion, neatly revitalized Kautsky-Lenin's debate on capitalism and imperialism. While from Kautsky's "ultra-imperialism" (1914) perspective, Chinese capital is forming a "cartel" with the capital of the core countries in order to jointly exploit the rest of the world, Lenin's "imperial capitalism" (1917) sees China as becoming a new imperial force which is expanding its exploitative sphere, leading to the acceleration of inter-core rivalry and imperialist conflicts.

In connection with the debates and controversies, some scholars, such as Ian Taylor (2016a, 2016b, 2016c), ask the question: "Does China's interests in cooperation with Africa provide the region with better development opportunities than those offered by traditional Northern partners?" They are doubtful as to whether the rise of BRICS and China's rising presence in Africa have provided the region with new and qualitatively different and better opportunities for a positive insertion in the global economy. Relations between BRICS/China and African countries are not substantially different from African relations with traditional Northern partners, and African countries are continuing to develop increasingly deep patterns of dependency with their external partners, as discussed. China's relations with Africa are seen to be as exploitative as the relations between the advanced industrial Western countries and Africa.

However, this type of view entirely contradicts China's self-perception of its role and impact in Africa:

> China, through its investment, financial and trade relations with Africa, has also provided African countries with more leverage in negotiating better investment, financial and trade deals with Western companies. Thanks to Sino-Africa relations, Western companies and governments face intensified competition. This provides African countries with more room for maneuver in their relations with the West. They now have a solid alternative to accepting the dictates of the international financial institutions. China is Africa's ally in promoting a global system in which Africa's interests are no longer taken for granted.
>
> Chinese companies are making goods available to Africans at prices that are relatively cheap compared with national and Western companies.

While national and Western companies make goods available mainly to the middle and upper classes, Chinese companies make them available to the working class and the poor. Is it true that this is against a further development of the textile industry of African countries? What is immoral about poor Africans improving their material conditions by buying relatively cheaper goods?

(*China Daily*, 2012)

China: a rising power with multifaceted positions

Despite a global consensus on China's emergence as a new hegemon, it is very important to conceptualize the nature of this type of hegemon. It is partly true that China's rise has been intensifying the minimization of the semi-periphery space within the existing world capitalism system, a situation that was predicted to lead to the collapse of the capitalist world system (Li, 2008). It is also partly true that China's own massive occupation of the semi-peripheral space (20% of the world population) has altered the world system theory's conventional stratification of the world economy, which was based on a three-layered structure with a small core, a comparatively larger semi-periphery, and the vast majority in the periphery (Grell-Brisk, 2017). China is making the semi-peripery stratus much bigger than ever!

In line with this understanding, China's gradual move to the core as a new hegemon should not be compared with the conventional "core" defined by the world system theory's three-layered structure. China should be seen as a different type of core – or a core with different characteristics. China's upward structural "positions" do not simply imply China's *hierarchical transition* to becoming a new member of the conventional core, but its occupation of the largest middle stratum of the world economy. The World-systems theory describes the middle stratum (semi-periphery) as a key structural element and a *stability pillar* in the world economy (Wallerstein, 1976).

Figure 6.4 indicates that due to the internal unequal development levels in China and by decomposing the Chinese hegemony, the Chinese economy is found to be simultaneously occupying important roles in all three stratifications of the capitalist world economy – core, semi-periphery, and periphery. China's multiple positions are enabling the country to compete with the conventional core countries in high-tech sectors and financial institutions, while still enjoying a comparative advantage in competing or cooperating with the conventional semi-periphery and periphery countries in manufacturing and commodity industries. In other words, China is exerting different impacts on countries located in the different stratifications. Thus, as a new hegemon, China is playing multiple roles, occupying multiple positions, and generating multiple impacts in the current world economy.

For example, China is simultaneously one of the largest and most important trading partners for all of the three stratifications – core, semi-periphery and periphery countries. As noted in an RT.com article: "As recently as 2006, America was the larger trading partner for 127 countries, versus just 70 for China. By 2011,

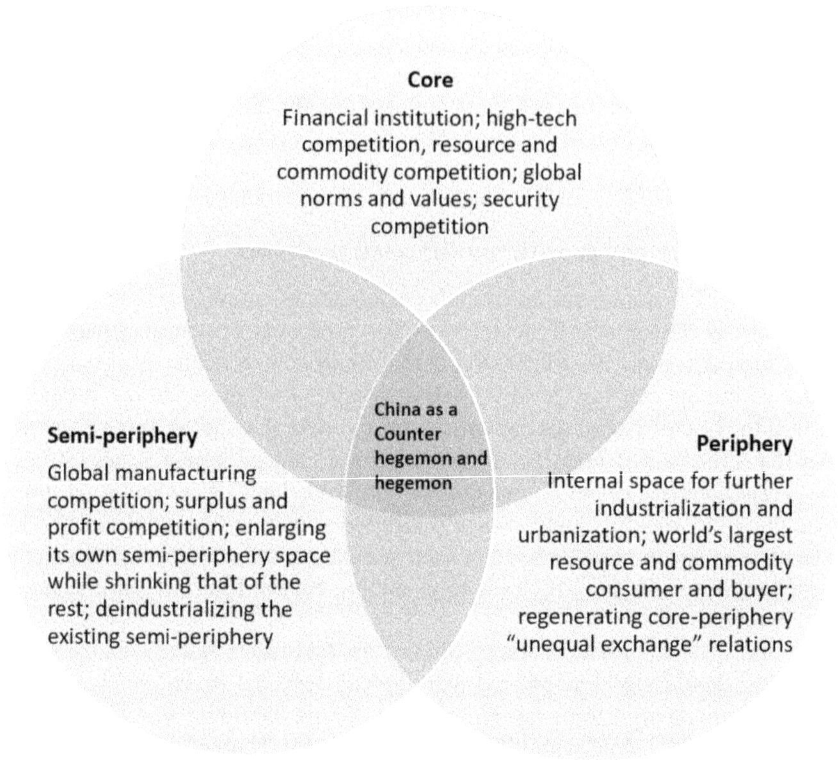

Figure 6.4 A holistic conceptualization of China as a hegemon with multifaceted positions

Source: author's own figure

the situation had changed drastically: 124 countries for China, 76 for the US" (quoted by *Forbes*, October 19, 2014). China is now virtually the No. 1 trading partner of most East and Southeast countries.

Conclusion

This chapter aims to provide a framework of understanding China's re-emergence in the nexus of the IPE and world system perspectives. The arguments for claiming China as a new hegemon are scrutinized from two perspectives that reflect dynamic and dialectic relationships. On the one hand, China's success is a strong indication of its movement toward a more positive structural position in the distribution of global wealth, while it also poses a challenge to many "enduring aspects" and "global arrangements" defined by the core powers of the existing world order. This positional improvement is enabling China to convert its economic wealth into political power and military capacity, to materialize its regional/global leadership formation, and to create an alternative and favorable normative world order. However, this development is unavoidably increasing the possibilities of conflicts with the existing core powers of the world system.

However, China's economic success is achieved by integration into the existing capitalist world order. The world system's law of value is still the *organic* foundation that shapes China's internal state-market mechanism as well as its external IPE relations. In other words, China is an emerging hegemon positioned *in* the conjuncture *of* a world order that is moving from hegemony to interdependent hegemony. Following its own positional upgrading in gaining more wealth and power in the world system, China's continuous rise will bring about the effect of enlarging the "room for maneuver" and increasing the "upward mobility" of semi-periphery and periphery countries. China as a "hegemon" must be understood not as a new member of the core, but as a nation whose power is characterized by global *relationship* and *relevance*. China is becoming an "indispensable country" to all countries of the different stratifications.

What is the economic relationship between China and the developing world? The situation is rather complicated and mixed. The consensus is that the rise of China's capital and trade expansion in developing countries of the Global South provides them with both opportunities and challenges. Economic relations between China and the developing world, albeit in a South-South context, do seem to reproduce some symptoms of North-South economic dependency under a core-periphery category. The conclusion reached by another study shows that the economic relationship between China and the Global South can be defined as a combination of increasing North-South trade and investment relations and growing South-South cooperation:

> The future scenario appears to be a consolidation of business partnerships between China and South America and between China and Africa. In fact, we observe the strengthening of North-South trade and investment network power overlapping with growing South-South Cooperation between the Asian Giant and the Global South. These developments are fostering more political and economic room of maneuver for developing countries. In the new century, Latin American and Africa, who went through hard economic crisis in the 1980s and 1990s, began to look for the Chinese trade, aid and investments opportunities. The failure of neoliberal policies after 2000s global financial crisis seems to have broken the possibility of univocal reforms and development policies for the less developed countries. It is in this context that the PRC emerges as a main factor for the economic recovery of most Latin America and African countries. China became the most important extra-regional actor for these states.
>
> (Vadell et al., 2014:102)

What the world is witnessing is an emerging world order of *interdependent hegemony* brought about by the rise of China (Li, 2014, 2016a). The concept of "interdependent hegemony" implies a dialectic process of mutual challenge, mutual constraint, mutual need, and mutual accommodation. Countries and country blocs (existing and emerging powers, existing and emerging international institutions) are intertwined in a constant process of shaping and reshaping the world order in the nexus of national interest, regional orientation, shared economic and political agendas, security alliances, and potential conflicts.

Note

1 The Chinese discourse on "South-South Cooperation" between China and the Global South is a controversy. There are two opposite opinions: In the first opinion, multi-levels and multi-platforms of economic cooperation between China, BRICS, and the Global South are seen (even by China itself) as a "resurgence of South–South cooperation", leading to the rise of the Global South (Gray and Gills, 2016). In the second opinion the above cooperation relationships are regarded as "North-South" competition. Some Latin American scholars even see China's trade relations with Latin America as an "unequal exchange", leading to deindustrialization of existing developing countries. The second view is substantially covered and discussed in the second part of this chapter.

References

Barbosa, Alexandre de Freitas, and Ricardo Camargo Mendes (2006) *Economic Relationships between Brazil and China: A Difficult Partnership*. São Paulo: Friedrich Ebert Stiftung.

Bernal-Meza, Raúl (2012) "*China-MERCOSUR and Chile Relations*." In Li Xing and Steen F. Christensen (eds.) *The Rise of China: The Impact on Semi-Periphery and Periphery Countries*. Aalborg: Aalborg University Press.

Breslin, Shaun (2010) "China Engages Asia: The Soft Notion of China's 'Soft Power'." *ETHOS*, 8: 5–11. Available at www2.warwick.ac.uk/fac/soc/pais/people/breslin/research/sbreslin-china_engages_asia-ethos_issue_8.pdf. (Accessed February 13, 2017).

China Daily (2012) "Africa Can Choose Its Own Friends." July 19. Available at http://europe.chinadaily.com.cn/opinion/2012-07/19/content_15598725.htm. (Accessed April 25, 2016).

Chris Patten (2008) "China is a Threat to Democracy." BBC News, November 23. Available at http://news.bbc.co.uk/2/hi/asia-pacific/7719420.stm.

Cox, Robert W. (1981) "Social Forces, States and World Orders: Beyond International Relations Theory." *Millennium: Journal of International Studies*, 10(2): 126–155.

Cox, Robert W. (1983) "Gramsci, Hegemony and International Relations: An Essay in Method." *Millennium: Journal of International Studies*, 12(2): 162–175.

Dantas, Alexis Toribio, and Elias Marco Khalil Jabbour (2016) "Brazil and China: An Assessment of Recent Trade Relations." *Economics of Agriculture*, 1/2016: 313–322.

Dussel Peters, Enrique (coord.) (2016) *La nueva relación comercial de América Latina y el Caribe con China. ¿Integración o desintegración regional?* México DF, Red Académica de América Latina y el Caribe sobre China, Universidad Nacional Autónoma de México, Unión de Universidades de América Latina y Caribe y Centro de Estudios China-México.

The Economist (2008) "China the New Colonialists." Available at www.economist.com/node/10853534.

Financial Times (2014) "Beijing's Challenge to the World of Bretton Woods." October 30. Available at www.ft.com/intl/cms/s/0/db2dcaf8-6042-11e4-88d1-00144feabdc0.html#axzz3lVvm7RvR.

Forbes (2014) "As the U.S. Sleeps, China Conquers Latin America." October 15. Available at www.forbes.com/sites/realspin/2014/10/15/as-the-u-s-sleeps-china-conquers-latin-america/.

Gramsci, Antonio (1971) *Selections from the Prison Notebooks*. Ed. Quintin Hoare and Geoffrey Nowell Smith. London: Lawrence & Wishart, New York: International Publisher.

Gray, Kevin, and Barry K. Gills (2016) "South-South Cooperation and the Rise of the Global South Journal." *Third World Quarterly*, 37(4): 557–574.

Grell-Brisk, Marilyn (2017) "China and Global Economic Stratification in an Interdependent World." *Palgrave Communications*, 3(17087): 1–12. doi: 10.1057/palcomms.2017.87.

Guelar, Diego (2013) *La invasión silenciosa. El desembarco chino en América del Sur*. Buenos Aires: Random House Mondadori S.A.; Ed. Debate.

Güven, Ali Burak (2017) "The World Bank and Emerging Powers: Beyond the Multipolarity-Multilateralism Conundrum." *New Political Economy*, 22(5): 496–520.

Ikenberry, John G. (2008) "The Rise of China and the Future of the West." *Foreign Affairs*, 87(1): 23–37.

Ikenberry, John G. (2011) "The Future of the Liberal World Order: Internationalism after America." *Foreign Affairs*, 90(3): 56–68.

Ikenberry, John G., and Darren J. Lim (2017) *China's Emerging Institutional Statecraft: The Asian Infrastructure Investment Bank and the Prospects for Counter-Hegemony*. Project on International Order and Strategy at BROOKINGS. Available at www.brookings.edu/wp-content/uploads/2017/04/chinas-emerging-institutional-statecraft.pdf.

Jenkins, Rhys (2015) "Is Chinese Competition Causing Deindustrialization in Brazil?" *Latin American Perspectives*, Issue 205, 42(6): 42–63.

Kautsky, Karl (1914) "Ultra-Imperialism." Available at www.marxists.org/archive/kautsky/1914/09/ultra-imp.htm. (Accessed April 25, 2016).

Lenin, Vladimir (1948[1917]) *Imperialism: The Highest Stage of Capitalism*. London: Lawrence and Wishart.

Li, Minqi (2005) "The Rise of China and the Demise of the Capitalist World-Economy: Exploring Historical Possibilities in the 21st Century." *Science & Society*, 69(3): 420–448.

Li, Minqi (2008) *The Rise of China and the Demise of the Capitalist World Economy*. London: Pluto Press.

Li, Xing (2014) "The Nexus of 'Interdependent Hegemony' between the Existing and the Emerging World Orders." *Fudan Journal of the Humanities and Social Sciences*, 7(3): 343–362.

Li, Xing (2016a) "From 'Hegemony and World Order' to 'Interdependent Hegemony and World Reorder'." In Steen F. Christensen and Li Xing (eds.) *Emerging Powers, Emerging Markets, Emerging Societies: Global Responses*. London: Palgrave Macmillan.

Li, Xing (2016b) "Understanding China's Economic Success: 'Embeddedness' with Chinese Characteristics." *Asian Culture and History*, 8(2): 18–31.

Li, Xing (2017) "The Endgame or Resilience of the Chinese Communist Party's Rule in China: A Gramscian Approach." *Journal of Chinese Political Science*, 23(1): 83–104.

Maciel, Rodrigo, and Dani K. Nedal (2011) "China and Brazil: Two Trajectories of a 'Strategic Partnership'." In A. Hearn and J.L. León-Manriquez (eds.) *China Engages Latin America: Tracing the Trajectory*. Boulder: Lynne Rienner.
Mearsheimer, John (2006) "China's Unpeaceful Rise." *Current History*, 105(690): 160–162.
Mearsheimer, John (2014) "Can China Rise Peacefully?" *The National Interest*, October 25. Available at http://nationalinterest.org/commentary/can-china-rise-peacefully-10204.
Nathan, Andrew J. (2003) "Authoritarian resilience." Journal of Democracy, 14(1): 6–17.
Ougaard, Morten (2013) "Hegemonikrise og kampen om den næste økonomiske verdensorden." *Økonomi og Politik*, 86(3): 3–20.
Peng, Zhongzhou, and Sow Keat Tok (2016) "The AIIB and China's Normative Power in International Financial Governance Structure." *Chinese Political Science Review*, 1(4): 736–753.
Reuters (2018) "Latin America Should not Rely on China: U.S. Secretary of State Tillerson." Febrary 1. Available at https://www.reuters.com/article/us-usa-diplomacy-latam-china/latin-america-should-not-rely-on-china-u-s-secretary-of-state-tillerson-idUSKBN1FL6D5.
Schweller, Randall L., and Xiaoyu Pu (2011) "After Unipolarity: China's Visions of International Order in an Era of U.S. Decline." *International Security*, 36(1): 41–72.
Sevares, Julio (2015) *China. Un socio imperial para Argentina y América Latina*. Buenos Aires: Editorial Edhasa.
Sharife, Khadija (2009) "China's New Colonialism." *Foreign Policy*. Available at http://foreignpolicy.com/2009/09/25/chinas-new-colonialism/.
Strange, Susan (1987) "The Persistent Myth of Lost Hegemony." *International Organization*, 41(4): 551–574.
Strange, Susan (1988) *States and Markets*. 2nd ed. London: Continuum.
Taylor, Ian (2016a) "BRICS and Capitalist Hegemony: Passive Revolution in Theory and Practice." In Steen F. Christensen and Li Xing (eds.) *Emerging Powers, Emerging Markets, Emerging Societies: Global Responses*. London: Palgrave Macmillan.
Taylor, Ian (2016b) "BRICS in Africa and Underdevelopment: How Different?" In Steen F. Christensen and Li Xing (eds.) *Emerging Powers, Emerging Markets, Emerging Societies: Global Responses*. London: Palgrave Macmillan.
Taylor, Ian (2016c) "The BRICS in Africa: Agents of Development?" In Justin van der Merwe, Ian Taylor, and Alexandra Arkhangelskaya and (eds.) *Emerging Powers in Africa: A New Wave in the Relationship*? London: Palgrave Macmillan.
Vadell, Javier, Leonardo Ramos, and Pedro Neves (2014) "The International Implications of the Chinese Model of Development in the Global South: Asian Consensus as a Network Power." *Revista Brasileira de Política Internacional*, 57: 91–107.
Wallerstein, Immanuel (1974) "The Rise and Future Demise of the World-Capitalist System: Concepts for Comparative Analysis." *Comparative Studies in Society and History*, 16: 387–415.
Wallerstein, Immanuel (1976) "Semi-Peripheral Countries and the Contemporary World Crisis." *Theory and Society*, 3(4): 461–83.
Wallerstein, Immanuel (1979) *The Capitalist World-Economy*. New York: Cambridge University Press.
Wallerstein, Immanuel (1997) "The Rise of East Asia, or the World-System in the Twenty-First Century." Available at www.binghamton.edu/fbc/archive/iwrise.htm.

Wallerstein, Immanuel (2004) *World-Systems Analysis: An Introduction.* Durham: Duke University Press.

Wang, Hongying (2014) "From 'Taoguang Yanghui' to 'Yousuo Zuowei': China's Engagement in Financial Minilateralism." *CIGI Papers No. 52.* Available at www.cigionline.org/sites/default/files/cigi_paper_no52.pdf.

World Bank Report (2015) "FDI and Manufacturing in Africa: Chinese FDI in Africa and Manufacturing FDI in Ethiopia and Rwanda." Available at www.worldbank.org/content/dam/Worldbank/Event/Africa/Investing%20in%20Africa%20Forum/2015/investing-in-africa-forum-fdi-and-manufacturing-in-africa.pdf.

7 Brazil as an emerging power

The impact of international and internal deteriorational effect on the BRICS

Raúl Bernal-Meza

Introduction

One of the central features of BRICS is that, except for South Africa, its members symbolize VoC or "new varieties of capitalism" (Becker, 2013). In this group of emerging economies, Brazil represents the South American region, bringing together an important economic development with a vocation of regional leadership. Simultaneously, through joining BRICS, Brazil was projected from the region to the world as part of the emergent power of the Second World in the international political economy and in the new world order. Brazil – a non-nuclear regional power – used the *soft power* of its regional leadership as a means of balancing its power against Russia, China, and India, which in turn had difficulties to impose themselves as leaders in their own regions. However, these conditions, which characterized the presence of Brazil since the birth of BRICS, are no longer present: Brazil is now a weak segment and its position within BRICS is weakening it as an emerging power.

In 1993, China established a relationship with Brazil, which was bilaterally as strategic. Since 2004, both countries have established the Sino-Brazilian High Level Agreement and Cooperation Commission (COSBAN) as the highest instance of bilateral political dialogue.

Brazil is the only country in the region that shares with China the aspiration to reformulate the global order and that participates with it in global alliances, such as BRICS (Christensen and Bernal-Meza, 2014; Bernal-Meza and Bizzozero, 2014). However, the content of the strategic relationship[1] was evident in the growth of trade flows but was not projected in other issues that were also of interest to Brazil. The bilateral political agenda regarding the international system would focus on the BRICS agendas. China has kept Brazil as a partner in South-South cooperation. China did not associate Brazil with the group of countries that dealt with the agenda of the main problems of world politics. China also did not support the Brazilian demand to be incorporated as a permanent member of the Security Council (Bernal-Meza, 2012, 2015).

Lula was the first PT government in the history of Brazil. The ideas on foreign policy, as of 2003, had as a regional and international strategy aimed at reviewing international institutions created under US hegemony.

Through a proactive policy in multilateral forums, the Lula's government tried to present itself as representative of the countries of the South and especially of South America. With this purpose, Lula's government developed a network of international and regional coalitions and promoted new instruments of regional governance – the South American Community of Nations (CSN), Unasur, CELAC – (Bernal-Meza, 2015; Saraiva, 2017), which after its second government it bequeathed to da Silva's successor, Dilma Rousseff. This policy was identified with a regional leadership.[2]

However, during the last two years of Lula's second term, Brazil's international and domestic conditions changed in a negative direction. Brazil's international political economy deteriorated, due to its external and internal fragility.

Internationally, the intra-BRICS reproduction of a core-periphery relationship, the disappointment of not having reached a peer relationship with China, and the fact that Beijing did not associate it with its global policy, thus holding a North-South relationship between China and Brazil beyond Brazil's aspirations, led to inside conditions of weakness in BRICS, affecting its capacities as an emerging power and a leader of the Second World in the construction of the new world order.

The relationship developed within BRICS weakens this group for three reasons. First, because the economic and commercial ties between Brazil and China reproduce a core-periphery relationship in their interior. This relationship, which is a structural characteristic of the capitalist economy that divides the world between development and underdevelopment by reproducing within BRICS, maintains the status quo of the world political economy. BRICS had in its origin the objective of modifying that unequal relationship. For this it takes a position as the preponderant segment of the Second World; second, because the foreign policy of Rousseff's government has abandoned the will to tie its destiny to that of South America and has neglected its vocation of regional leadership, thus losing its interest in the very schemes of regionalism that Lula had promoted, particularly UNASUR (the former South American Community of Nations); third, because its internal political, economic, and social crises have caused its status as an emerging economic power to deteriorate and has weakened its natural position as a political and economic regional leader.

The transition of the international order and the new emerging powers

Since the end of the cold war, the world system has undergone drastic changes, both in politics and in the world economy. One of the most important changes was the transition from the North-South axis to the new East-South axis, which revealed the emergence of an extraordinarily dynamic region, in which China appeared as the emerging great world power. Jan Pieterse (2011) calls attention to an East-South turn in the global system caused by an increasing shift in economic power toward Asia and the Global South. According to Pieterse, the changes in the global economy can be understood through the new relations between the semi-periphery and the periphery and the East-South relations, such as those developed by China with Africa and Latin America.

Lula da Silva decided to follow a policy that counterbalanced the power of the Western powers, and Brazilian diplomacy gave preference to the adoption of multipolar and anti-hegemonic positions (Gratius and Saraiva, 2013; García, 2013; Saraiva, 2017).

While Brazil's approach to China and India had begun in the mid-1980s, and the choice of preferential partners under the name of "strategic alliances" (or "strategic partnerships") began to take shape toward the end of that decade, Lessa and Altemani de Oliveira (2013: 9) point out that this expression became an important idea in the foreign policies of many countries, including that of Brazil. Albuquerque (2013) argues that the term "strategic partnership" was applied to Brazil's bilateral relations with China during the government of Itamar Franco (1992–1995), but the relationship attained a special character under Lula's government because of the combination of extraordinary growth in trade and investment flows between the two countries caused by to the importance that Lula ascribed to South-South relations – because Brazil always considered its relations with China as South-South relations, that is, between developing countries.

The purpose of strategic alliances could be explained by the need faced by diplomacies to give priority to certain bilateral relations. When Lula arrived to the government one of his objectives was to return Brazilian foreign policy to a universalist vocation that had been abandoned. This universalist policy had an important development under both its governments. Within this policy, bilateral relations with certain countries were strengthened and some of them received the qualification of "strategic" due to their importance (Lessa and Altemani de Oliveira, 2013: 10–11). For Brazil, China would be the most important strategic alliance outside of South America. The establishment of strategic partnerships was associated with the construction of large international alliances; first IBAS, then BRIC, and finally the latter with the inclusion of South Africa: BRICS.

BRIC's formal dialogues began only in 2006, and the Heads of Government of the nations involved met for the first time in June 2009. They had no definite positive agenda, only a negative and critical agenda regarding the international financial system. The immediate result of this meeting was a paper in favor of a new reference currency. According to Pfeifer (2013), from this we can deduce an understanding of BRIC according to which opportunistic incentives induced Brazil, Russia, India, and China to a adopt a conjunctural alignment policy devoid of any tangible bases of support, without common concrete interests or shared values that were sufficiently strong, which resulted in a collection of ethereal characteristics and reduced its potential of permanence. Fiori (2009) pointed out that the establishment of a political group engaging in diplomatic-economic cooperation with more or less significant trade and financial flows between Brazil, Russia, China, India, and South Africa was a new fact that could become the material basis for some sectoral and localized alliances, either among all of these countries or between some of them. However, it would be very unlikely that this alone was sufficient to justify a long-term strategic alliance between these five large countries. Nonetheless, BRICS became the most powerful collective platform that was presented to Brazil in the near future, although the United States would remain its primary bilateral partner (Pfeifer, 2013).

The establishment of a strategic partnership with China and an alliance with it, first called BRIC and then BRICS, became the most important objective of the foreign policy of the governments of Lula da Silva. Brazil proposed going "from the region – first with Mercosur, then with Unasur – to the world" (Bernal-Meza and Bizzozero, 2014) to build a new international scenario in which the regional powers had more influence. This involved acting on multiple fronts (García, 2013). One of them was the construction of "alliances and strategic groupings" at the South American level (CSN-UNASUR, South American Defence Council), the Latin American level (CELAC) and the global level (IBAS, BRICS).

Within the overall strategy, BRICS was an important goal of the governments of the Workers' Party (PT). Lula and Dilma Rousseff reiterated that Brazil wanted to link its destiny with that of South America (García, 2013). Leading their country to the great world politics required the building of alliances which were part of the great global government policy, whose objectives were to have a permanent seat in the United Nations Security Council, and to participate actively in the new international management.

Why did Brazil go to BRICS? In his book *Quinhentos anos de periferia*,[3] Guimarães gave some reasons as to why countries like China and Brazil should share a differentiated place within the international system. Brazil represented the South American region of this group of new emerging economies, joining an extraordinary economic development (Brainard and Martinez-Diaz, 2009) with a vocation of regional leadership (Bernal-Meza and Bizzozero, 2014; Bernal-Meza, 2011; Cervo and Lessa, 2010; Bernal-Meza, 2010; Lima, 2008). Simultaneously, through its incorporation into the BRICS group, Brazil projected itself from the region to the world, as part of the emergent power of the *Second World* in the international political economy and the new world order (Li, 2014; Christensen and Bernal-Meza, 2014). In this design, the alliance with China was a priority, and Beijing was seen as the new and most important global partner.

What Li Xing points out in his chapter in this book – "China's Double Positions in the Capitalist World Order: A Dual Complexity of Hegemon and Counter-hegemon" – is fulfilled in the China-Brazil bilateral relationship and in the participation of both countries within BRICS. While BRICS has carried out functions of counter-hegemonic power by promoting the strengthening of multilateralism – which in itself tends to limit hegemonic power – and some global agendas, such as the search for a reform of the Bretton Woods order and the reinforcement of the regional and collective strategic security, from an economic point of view, the China-Brazil bilateral relationship corresponds to the characteristics of a *core-periphery* structure.

Brazil had a special participation in this counter-hegemon policy. It promoted a new map of institutions – through the creation of Unasur, the South

American Defense Council, and CELAC – but it did not confront the traditional American Interamericanism (OAS). This policy was promoted by the Lula governments. Dilma Rousseff maintained this policy in political discourse, but not in actions.

Speech and praxis did not coincide. Under Rousseff's second term, Brazil's proactive policy was diluted, causing the political role of Brazil to decrease. The country was losing prominence both in world politics and at a regional level, moving from a proactive to a reactive dynamic (Saraiva, 2017; Cervo and Lessa, 2014).

Brazil and the relationship with China: the intra-BRICS reproduction of a core-periphery relationship

The original idea of Russia, China, India, and Brazil was to create a group of coincidences and political agreements, as a counterpoint to major international players such as the United States and the European Union (Thorstensen and Oliveira, 2012), and with the inclusion of South Africa, BRICS emerged as a political-diplomatic mechanism constituted at a time of redesign of global governance, when the perception of a deficit of representativeness and therefore of the legitimacy of the structures created in postwar was becoming increasingly acute (Reis, 2013). Following the inclusion of South Africa, "the BRICS countries focused on building a common identity around the need to manage the international financial crisis and reform of international institutions with greater participation of developing countries" (Becard, 2017: 404). However, Brazilian frustrations toward China and later the internal questioning of BRICS in Itamaraty – the headquarters of the Brazilian Ministry of Foreign Relations – (Saraiva, 2017) highlighted the crisis in the Brazil-BRICS relationship.

The failure of the "strategic alliance" with China

China introduced a factor of profound imbalance in the region and in the role played by Brazil in South America (Dussel, 2016; Bernal-Meza, 2016, 2012, 2012a; Medeiros and Cintra, 2015) by becoming a key player in the inclusion of Latin America – and particularly of South America – in the international economy.

According to the economist Barros de Castro, Brazil's concern was that the Sino-Brazilian relations were acquiring a global dimension, which came to reflect on how Brazil could react to the challenges and opportunities arising from Chinese dynamism (Oliveira, 2013). The result was that the first manifestation of the failure of the strategic alliance with China was the structure of bilateral trade. As Becard points out (2017: 405), "After applying the concept of strategic association to the empirical analysis of China-Brazil relations, it can be concluded that both countries are interested, but are not fully capable of promoting horizontal long-term relationships". Oliveira (2013: 60) points out that "for some time, our exports of durable goods grew significantly, but at the beginning of the new century, it was the raw material exports that were now growing, while sales of manufactured godos dropped". Albuquerque (2013: 72) argues that the main corollary about the existence of an exceptional relationship – qualified or not as strategic – came to be the existence of a very relevant trade flow. There was bilateral trade, but no other components to be considered a strategic relationship. That is, trade, but not other aspects so important for Brazil in the context of the global dimension to which this country aspired. A strategic relationship meant having an interindustrial trade. But what was happening was a core-periphery trade and that did not represent the example of a strategic relationship.

Although China is already recognized as Brazil's most important trading partner since 2009, it does not mean that China is the most important investment or loan partner. In addition, foreign direct and indirect investment flows are still a function of China's trade needs and preferences. "The Brazilian search for innovation and promotion of science and technology in various areas has not yet been considered and included in China's priorities" (Becard, 2017: 405). The accelerated process of development of a *core-periphery* or *north-south* relationship in the bilateral trade between the two countries has been mentioned in several works by different authors such as Ellis (2009), Jenkins and Barbosa (2012), Sevares (2007, 2012), Bernal-Meza (2012, 2012a), Vadell (2013, 2016), Oviedo (2014), Barbosa et al. (2011, 2014), Vadell et al. (2014), Altemani de Oliveira (2016), Hiratuka and Fernando (2016), who have already analyzed and described in their studies the primary exporting character of Brazil in the structure of Chinese international trade. The perception of threat related to the classical themes of the Cold War and the post-Cold War (democracy, human rights) have already been replaced by concerns about the negative or positive effects of the strong Chinese economic and trade presence (Altemani de Oliveira, 2012), which Uehara (2013: 36), described in terms that foretold the disappointment regarding the bilateral relationship:

> Nevertheless, coincidently after 2004, the year in which President Lula's statement promised to recognize China as a market economy, the trend in the trade relations was reversed, resulting in bigger growth in imports from China to Brazil than in exports from Brazil to China. Another disadvantage to Brazil is that its imports tend to include products of higher added value, while most of its exports are still commodities. The increase in imports of Chinese goods has been viewed as a threat by some industrial sectors and, in recent years, the Brazilian government started to develop defensive trade policies.

For Brazil, as for the rest of Latin America (Dussel Peters, 2016; Vadell et al., 2016; Medeiros and Cintra, 2015), the commercial complement produced by the harmony of interests between China and the South American countries constitutes the central axis of the relationship between both partners. The Chinese demand for raw materials harmonizes with the regional supply. However, this harmony is asymmetrical (Oviedo, 2014: 144), because its matrix responds to the classic model diagnosed by Prebish and ECLAC in the late 1940s. Brazil developed a core-periphery economic-trade relationship with China because, although China has become Brazil's main trading partner, "there is still no open, balanced and diversified trade in goods and services with high added value" (Becard, 2017: 405).

This declared strategic alliance between Brazil and China should also be ratified at the international level; in international politics. Albuquerque (2013: 74) argues that this dimension of partnership implies a division of common tasks and objectives that go beyond trade flows. In my view, this is the second aspect of Brazil's failure in its relationship with China, the first being the North-South character of bilateral economic-trade relations.

It can be concluded that there is no strategic partnership between Brazil and China because in the international political dimension, this association has a residual function. As Albuquerque argues,

> as a result of the tactic that would have one believe that Brazil's pretensions are methodological and relate to representation and efficiency rather than power, Lula undertakes, in his speech, to deflate the political nature of the UNSC. To his own rhetorical question – "how do you explain that Brazil is not part of it?" – Lula has no answer, because it would imply a discussion of power relations in the world order and the impossibility of a political partnership between Brazil and China in the case of UN reform.
>
> (2013: 87–88)

This objective envisaged by the Ministry of Foreign Affairs, according the Brazil at the new government – that China and Brazil should form a "strategic alliance" – has failed (Saraiva, 2017). In the beginning, their relationship included strengths, but the number of disagreements grew (Salama, 2017).

Thus, for Brazil, as for other Latin American countries, China went from "opportunity to challenge" (Bernal-Meza, 2016). The process of primarization and re-primarization of Latin American exports was reproduced throughout the region, as pointed out by Jenkins and Barbosa (2012), Vadell (2016), Lessa and Altemani de Oliveira (2013), Sevares (2014, 2015), Vadell and Neves (2014), ECLAC (2015), Medeiros and Cintra (2015), Vadell et al. (2016). The general conclusion is that the evolution of trade relations between Latin America and China has led to a strengthening of primary exports. According to ECLAC (2015: 41–42), Latin American and Caribbean exports to China are much less sophisticated than exports to the world in general. In 2013, primary products accounted for 73% of exports to China, versus 41% of its shipments to the world in general. By contrast, low, medium, and high technology manufactures accounted for only 6% of exports to China, versus 42% of shipments to the world in general. The opposite applies to imports: While low, medium, and high technology manufactures accounted for 91% of regional imports from China in 2013, they accounted for only 69% of imports from the world in general. In other words, trade between Latin America and the Caribbean and China is clearly interindustrial: raw materials for manufactures.[4]

The internal questioning of BRICS

Brazil went to BRICS looking for a strategic alliance with China in the field of international politics and economy, but it did not succeed. The first failure was that China did not associate Brazil with the issues of the great world politics (security, global negotiations on the international order). The second failure for Brazil was not to get Chinese support to occupy a permanent place in the United Nations Security Council. But the third failure was in economic relations. Brazil sought to associate China in the development of new technologies and in the joint production of high-tech goods, capital goods and manufactured goods. He hoped that China would make large investments to promote national industrial development and make advanced technology transfers, associating Brazilian companies with large Chinese companies. However, it ended up developing a core-periphery relationship with China, in which economic ties were transformed into an export trade of primary products and commodities and the importation of industrial goods and capital. Chinese exports were aimed at strengthening the infrastructure of that core-periphery relationship.

The fact that Brazil did not reach the expected objectives, in its relationship with China, led Itamaraty[5] to start questioning BRICS (which, under the two governments of Lula da Silva and the first years of Dilma Rousseff's government, its diplomats had supported), as seen in the analyses, diagnostics, proposals and initiatives of its diplomats and in various publications: Pimentel (2013, 2013a), Baumann et al. (2015).[6]

China did not associate Brazil with its global policy, the clearest sign being its refusal to support Brazil's candidacy for a permanent seat in the UN Security Council. A recent document prepared by the General Secretariat of the Presidency and the Special Secretariat for Strategic Affairs of the Presidency of the Republic,[7] strongly questions the foreign policy of the governments led by the PT (Lula da Silva and Dilma Rousseff). BRICS, Lula's South-South cooperation strategy, which replaced the South-North relationship promoted by the two Cardoso governments. The insistence on getting a place in the Security Council without seeking or having the support of the main countries. The regional trade policy, that is, toward the world and the South American integration promoted by Brazil, are considered errors of the Brazilian diplomacy of the PT. In summary, regarding BRICS, it points to this forum as a group of doubtful future.

The abandonment of the regional vocation of leadership

Brazil promoted BRICS, planning to represent South America as its leader. However, there were two problems. First, Brasilia never struck an agreement regarding positions with South American countries (Bernal-Meza, 2015), nor with its Mercosur partners – or even with Argentina, its "strategic partner" – on the international agendas of BRICS. Moreover, Brasilia did not bring to this forum the opinion of the countries of the region. Second, China's relationship with South American countries prevented Brazil from achieving the goal of becoming an indispensable trade partner, because the South American export offer of raw materials (copper, soybean, iron, oil) always harmonized with the Chinese demand, but not with that of Brazil.

At the same time, changes in priorities and actions occurred as the government of Lula went to Dilma. As Saraiva points out,

> From very early on the differences began to be felt, expanding during the course of the mandate. Presidential diplomacy and the role of the presidency as an incentive and balancing element of different foreign policy visions that had taken place during Lula's administration were abandoned. The political will demonstrated by President Lula to articulate visions in favor of building a leadership in the region was lost.
>
> (2016: 300)

Even the goal of obtaining a permanent seat in the United Nations Security Council ceased to be a priority of Brazil's foreign policy.

The impact of China on Mercosur, the strategic objective of Brazil

Brazil, through its strategy toward South America – through its relationship with Argentina since 1985, the creation of Mercosur, after the creation of Unasur – became an indispensable actor for the region. During his first government, President Lula defined South America as the starting point for a new insertion of Brazil into the international system (Lima, 2008: 99). Cervo (2008: 203) states that during the Lula government, South America became Brazil's external priority. However, it was China that became an indispensable country: first for the world political economy (Li, 2010, 2012, 2012a) and then in trade relations and, for several Mercosur countries (Argentina, Venezuela, Uruguay), also in foreign investment and in loans (Vadell et al., 2016; Medeiros and Cintra, 2015). Thus, the countries that should be "Brazil's natural partners" ended up being China's natural partners.

The creation of Mercosur was a strategic objective for Brazil. It transformed it into the centerpiece of future South American integration. That integration would revolve around Brazil because it was the most industrialized economy. That position and Mercosur would be the pillars of Brazil's regional leadership in the international system (Bandeira, 1996; Bernal-Meza, 2000; Saraiva, 2013).

However, China's entry into the political economy of South America displaced Brazil from its preponderant position within the bloc and in the regional context. Hiratuka points out that

> China consolidated itself as the region's main trading partner as of 2009, but this situation is associated with a typically intersectoral flow with very low levels of participation of industrial products in exports, beyond a very high

> concentration in a few products. By contrast, imports are dominated by more technologically sophisticated products, and the degree of concentration is not as high. If China's demand for primary products strongly affected Mercosur exports, imports from China clearly displaced the trade of the partners in the region.
>
> (2016: 237–238)

The author of this article adds that "China contributed to the difficulties experienced by regional integration within Mercosur. The Chinese emergence explains the insufficient progress in the constitution of a normative and institutional community apparatus. Intra-block economic flows lost ground to focus on an increasingly multilateral dimension" (Hiratuka, 2016: 238). China's commercial presence largely replaced Brazil as one of the regional suppliers of manufactured and industrial goods. As Hiratuka states, "the emergence of China competes and has displaced manufactured products in the region at extremely high levels" (Hiratuka, 2016: 239).

As noted at the beginning of the chapter, Brazil was considered a successful example of a variety of capitalism (Becker, 2013). However, the economic crisis that began during the last two years of the second Lula government was projected to the government of Dilma Rousseff. During the last two years of his government the crisis deepened and political and institutional elements were added to the economic ones. This process deterred the image of Brazil as a new model of capitalism.

This is a situation significantly influenced by the fall in prices and the Chinese demand for commodities as well as by the deterioration of regional political leadership (Saraiva, 2013, 2017; Cervo and Lessa, 2014).

The deterioration of Brazil's leadership and image has occurred not only because of the progressive loss of your regional political activism and your role as a structuring actor of regional institutions – Unasur, for example, which suffered the suspension of Brazilian financial contributions – but because of the reluctance of the two most recent presidents – Rousseff and Temer – to take positions toward South America (Saraiva, 2017). Moreover, it was caused by the fact that the regional exportation of corruption, through the large companies that were backed by the state bank BNDES, also deteriorated the political and economic image of Brazilian entrepreneurs. The fact that some large Brazilian services and civil construction companies with activities in a significant number of countries in South America and the Caribbean have been compromised in serious corruption crimes has seriously weakened the image of Brazilian businessmen within the region, and this deterioration of the image has directly affected the government, because the investments for the development of these projects were financed by the BNDES bank, under the direct control of the government. In short, Brazil exported to the region policies of corruption that had already been implemented internally from the governmental efforts of Lula da Silva.

Miriam Saraiva (2017) points out that under Rousseff's rule, the external political behavior in foreign policy gradually lost its pro-activist nature and assumed a pragmatic character. President Dilma sought short-term benefits. It emptied the content of the political dimension of Brazilian behavior toward the region in relation to Brazil's actions in the past, as a driving force for regional institutions. In international terms she opted for spasmodic and discontinuous movements.

The lack of regional leadership was noticed from the beginning of Dilma's government. This situation favored the emergence of alternative models of integration and regionalism, such as the Pacific Alliance. Mexico, a member of this alliance, did not compete with Brazil in the South American political space for the simple reason that this objective was not on the agenda of Mexican foreign policy.

Under the governors of Lula, Brazil made strong decisions in defense of sovereignty, security and non-intervention, through the action of Unasur. However, in the face of the crisis in Venezuela, the current Temer government has maintained a low-profile position and other South American governments have adopted leadership positions in the face of the Venezuelan situation.

The neglect of regional leadership can be seen by comparing three of the biggest crisis situations that Latin America experienced in the last decade: the crisis in Honduras, the issue of US military bases in Colombian territory and the crisis in Venezuela. While in the first two (both in 2009), Brazil took very strong positions in defence of sovereignty, security and democracy, through unilateral and via Unasur, when facing the Venezuelan crisis decisions, the Temer government has maintained a low-profile position.

The external impact of the internal crisis

Saraiva (2017) states that "as is often the case in crisis situations, foreign policy has been in second place". The internal political crisis, whose most dramatic points were the dismissal of Dilma Rousseff and Michel Temer's assumption of the presidency – a president in office strongly questioned by accusations of corruption –, as well as the political weakness derived from the way he reached the presidency, immobilized Brazil internationally.

The large business groups, which received a lot of economic and diplomatic assistance from Lula's governments, were a positive factor for the projection of Brazil's leadership image. They developed large ventures, investments, and other activities throughout the region. But many of those actions were the result of corruption, in association with the governments of the countries that received those investments. In this way, businessmen were associated with the image of widespread corruption that was already dominating Brazil internally and contributed to the fall of the country's regional image.

President Temer attended the next BRICS summit, but his short-term goal was to get resources to overcome the crisis. On his journey, he made mistakes that weakened his own image and that of his country.[8] Subsequently, BRICS lost support within the new government.

Conclusions

For Brazil, the relationship with China and its participation in BRICS were strategic decisions made by the governments of Lula da Silva. Through these decisions, the country was trying to ascend to positions of greater influence and prestige in international politics, whose first instrument was the creation of a "strategic alliance" with Beijing. As Saraiva (2017) points out, between 2003 and 2010 President Lula's government structured its foreign policy with the aim of bringing Brazil to the position of a world power. To this end, a policy of international initiatives and activism was adopted through the construction of international coalitions aimed at the revision of institutions of the global order. Moreover, actions aimed at structuring regional governance in South America under Brazilian leadership were taken. These initiatives were based on a favorable coincidence of external factors, such as the relationship with China and the creation of BRICS, and internal factors, such as the emergence of Brazil as an economic power, as described by Brainard and Martinez-Diaz (2009).

However, China became a disruptive player in the relations between Brazil and South American countries, weakening its position as a major trading partner. The fact that the document prepared by the current Presidency of the Republic points out as serious errors all initiatives characterizing the foreign policy of the governments of the Workers' Party (PT), calls into question the continuity of a Brazilian effort to strengthen BRICS. Miriam Saraiva (2017) concludes that the changes that occurred in the external behavior of Brazil between 2016 and 2017, added to the criticisms made in the Presidency document on the foreign policy of the PT governments, ended with the belief that the interior of Itamaraty – the Ministry of Foreign Affairs – there have been common or shared positions and that there has been a permanent foreign policy in it. There has been no monolithic position and the idea of a foreign policy of "national interest" turned out to be false.

It is evident that the failure of the "strategic alliance" with China, the lack of participatory commitments of the great members of the BRICS (China and Russia) with the least strong (Brazil and South Africa) to conduct joint strategies aimed at world politics have contributed to the fact that in Brazil today there is a very pessimistic view of the future of BRICS.

Politically, the fact that China does not support the accession of Brazil and India to the United Nations Security Council as permanent members has not only caused Brazil's and China's international strategic alliance to fail; this also prevents BRICS from becoming a group actor of very influential power in the international system. This political decision made by China tends to firmly maintain the status quo of the current distribution structure of world power.

The deterioration of the Brazilian economy called into question the image of an economic model identified as a "variety of capitalism", which has affected the Brazilian model in its credibility as an alternative path to development that differ from the Anglo-Saxon, Rhenian, and Japanese models, as an example for other countries of the Third World. The classic models of developed capitalism are the Anglo-Saxon, the Rhenish, and the Japanese. What some authors argue, for example Becker (2013), is that there are other models that could serve or be successful examples of capitalism. These are alternative paths to the historical development of capitalism. Among those models, Brazil was considered.

However, the causes are not in the model itself, but in the weaknesses of a leadership that was not able to continue the path of Lula da Silva and that are directly related to the political crisis, corruption and Dilma's personalist way of governing: not listening to advice or suggestions, lacking insight into the role of Brazil in regional and global spheres, displacing the best brains that accompanied the golden years of Lula and favoring the promotion to the presidency of a ruler weakened by the very conditions in which access to the Presidency was given.

Brazil remains the great country of the region, although rather because of its recent past than because of its present. Now it will have to reinsert its regional leadership aspirations in an area where it now has a national competitor, such as Macri, the president of Argentina, and models of regionalism, such as the Pacific Alliance, that have deprived projects promoted by Brazil of visibility and dynamism. However, what is crystal clear to Brazil is that China is not its strategic partner anymore, neither bilaterally nor internationally. The consequences are that BRICS will not be more than it already is, at least from the Brazilian perspective.

Notes

1 The text addresses the vision of what Brazil understands as a strategic alliance. This has been followed by the interpretation given by various authors. cf. Lessa and Altemani de Oliveira (org.), (2013), and Albuquerque (2013).
2 Here we understand leadership as summarized by Saraiva (2017) as the ability of a country to influence others so that they adopt a certain behavior.
3 *Quinhentos anos de periferia*, Rio Grande do Sul: UFRGS/Contraponto, 1999.
4 It is not that Brazil is not important to China, but that the economic and financial relationship that China has developed with Brazil tends to turn Brazil into a primary economy whose exchange is increasingly interindustrial, for which Brazil deepens its status as a primary exporter. That coincidence has a vast reference literature that sustains this affirmation. This literature includes Brazilian researchers, as well as ECLAC reports cited in the text. In the same way, Chinese direct foreign investment is directed, essentially, toward the sectors of the economy whose objective is export to China.
5 Name by which the Ministry of Foreign Affairs of Brazil is known and named, in homage to the name of the residence of the Baron of Rio Branco, the creator of the great foreign policy of Brazil.
6 Although not all the authors of the book are diplomats, the work has been edited by the Fundação Alexandre de Gusmão, which belongs to the Ministério das Relações Exteriores do Brasil.
7 See Miriam Gomes Saraiva (2017), "Política externa brasileira 2016/2017 – Da reversão ao declínio." Anuario de Política Internacional y Política Exterior. Montevideo: Universidad de la República. www.google.cl/search?q=BrasilUmPasemBuscadeumaGrandeEs tratgia.pdf&rlz=1C1CHBD_esCL811CL811&oq=BrasilUmPasemBuscadeumaGrandeE stratgia.pdf&aqs=chrome.69i57j69i60l3.3132j0j8&sourceid=chrome&ie=UTF-8.
8 Miriam Gomes Saraiva (2017) points out in that trip some incomprehensible errors for such a professional diplomacy as Brazilian.

References

Albuquerque, José Augusto Ghuilón (2013) "Business with China: The Three Elements of Brazil's Strategic Partnership with China." In Leila da Costa Ferreira and José Augusto Guilhon Albuquerque (eds.) *China & Brazil: Challenges and Opportunities*. São Paulo: Annablume.

Altemani de Oliveira, Henrique (2012) *Brasil e China, Cooperação Sul-Sul e parceria estratégica*. Belo Horizonte: Fino Traço Editora.

Altemani de Oliveira, Henrique (2016) "Brasil-China: uma parcería oredatória ou cooperativa?" *Revista Tempo do Mundo*, (29): 143–160.

Bandeira, Luiz Alberto Moniz (1996) "Política y relaciones internacionales en el Mercosur." *Ciclos*, 11(2): 103–122.

Barbosa, Alexandre de Freitas, Maria Neves Biancalana, and Angela Cristina Tepasé (2011) "A ascensão chinesa e os impactos sobre a América Latina e a Äfrica: objetivos comuns, estratégias diferenciadas." In Congreso Luso Afro Brasileiro de Ciências Sociais (ed.) *11 Diversidades e (Des)igualdades*. Salvador: UFBA: 1–15.

Barbosa, Alexandre de Freitas, Angela Cristina Tepasé, and Maria Neves Biancalama (2014) "Las relaciones económicas entre Brasil y China a partir del desempeño de las empresas State Grid y Lenovo." In Enrique Dussel Peters (coord.) *La inversión extranjera directa de China en América Latina. 10 estudios de caso*. México, DF: Unión de Universidades de América Latina y el Caribe.

Baumann, Renato, Flávio Damico, Adriana Erthal Abdenur, Maiara Folly, Carlos Márcio Cozendey, and Renato Flores (2015) *BRICS. Estudos e Documentos*. Brasília: Fundação Alexandre de Gusmão.

Becard, Danielly Siva R. (2017) "China and Brazil: Model of South-South Relations?" In Eduardo Pastrana B. and Hubert Gehring (eds.) *The Projection of China in Latin America and the Caribbean*. Bogotá: Editorial Javeriana.

Becker, Uwe (ed.) (2013) *The BRICs and Emerging Economic in Comparative Perspective: Political Economy, Liberalization and International Change*. London: Routledge.

Bernal-Meza, Raúl (2000) *Sistema mundial y Mercosur*. Buenos Aires: Grupo Editor Latinoamericano and Universidad Nacional del Centro de la Prvincia de Buenos Aires.

Bernal-Meza, Raúl (2010) "International Thought in the Lula Era." *Revista Brasileira de Política Internacional Brasilia*, 53: 193–213.

Bernal-Meza, Raúl (2011) "El pensamiento internacionalista en la era Lula." *Estudios Internacionales*, (167): 143–172.

Bernal-Meza, Raúl (2012) "China y la configuración del nuevo orden internacional: las relaciones China-MERCOSUR y Chile." In Raúl Bernal-Meza and Silvia Quintanar (eds.) *Regionalismo y Orden Mundial: Suramérica, Europa, China*, Buenos Aires: Universidad Nacional del Centro de la Provincia de Buenos Aires y Nuevohacer.

Bernal-Meza, Raúl (2012a) "China-MERCOSUR and Chile Relations." In Li Xing and Steen F. Christensen (eds.) *The Rise of China: The Impact on Semi-Periphery and Periphery Countries*. Aalborg: Aalborg University Press.

Raúl Bernal-Meza (2015), "La inserción internacional de Brasil: el papel de Brics y de la región", *Universum*, 30(2): 17–35.

Bernal-Meza, Raúl (2016) "China y América Latina: de la oportunidad al desafío." *Tempo do Mundo*. Brasília: Ipea.

Bernal-Meza, Raúl, and Lincoln Bizzozero (eds.) (2014) *La política internacional de Brasil: de la región al mundo*. Montevideo: Universidad de la República y Ediciones Cruz del Sur.

Brainard, Lael, and Leonardo Martinez-Diaz (2009) *Brazil as an Economic Superpower? Understanding Brazil's Changing Role in the Global Economy*. Washington, DC: Brookings Institution Press.
Cervo, Amado Luiz (2008) *Inserção Internacional. Formação dos conceitos brasileiros*. São Paulo: Saraiva.
Cervo, Amado Luiz, and Antônio Carlos Lessa (eds.) (2010) *Emerging Brazil under Lula: An Assessment on International Relations (2003–2010)*. Brasilia: IBRI-RBPI.
Cervo, Amado Luiz, and Antônio Carlos Lessa (2014) "O declínio: inserção internacional do Brasil (2011–2014)." *Revista brasileira de política internacional*, 57(2): 133–151.
Christensen, Steen F., and Raúl Bernal-Meza (2014) "Theorizing the Rise of the Second World and the Changing International System." In Li Xing (ed.) *The BRICS and Beyond: The International Political Economy of the Emergence of a New World Order*. Surrey: Ashgate.
Dussel Peters, Enrique (coord.) (2016) *La Nueva Relación Comercial de América Latina y el Caribe con China. ¿Integración o desintegración regional?* México, DF: Unión de Universidades de América Latina y el Caribe.
ECLAC (2015) *América Latina y el Caribe y China. Hacia una nueva era de cooperación económica*. Santiago: Cepal, Naciones Unidas, LC/L.4010, mayo.
Ellis, R. Evan (2009) *China in Latin America: The Whats & Wherefores*. Boulder: Lynne Rienner Publishers.
Fiori, José Luis (2009) "O Brasil e seu 'entorno estratégico' na primeira década do século XXI." In Emir Sader (org.) *Lula e Dilma*, São Paulo: Boitembo Editorial and FLACSO Brasil.
García, Marco Aurelio (2013) "Dez anos de política externa." In Emir Sader (org.) *Lula e Dilma*. São Paulo: Boitembo Editorial and FLACSO Brasil.
Gratius, Susanne, and Saraiva Miriam Gomes (2013) "Continental Regionalism: Brazil's Prominent Role in the Americas." In M. Emerson and R. Flores (eds.) *Enhancing the Brazil-EU Strategic Partnership: From the Bilateral and Regional to the Global*. Bruselas: CEPS.
Hiratuka, Celio (2016) "Impactos de China sobre el proceso de integración regional de Mercosur." In Enrique Dussel Peters (coord.) *La Nueva Relación Comercial de América Latina y el Caribe con China. ¿Integración o desintegración regional?* México, DF: Unión de Universidades de América Latina y el Caribe.
Hiratuka, Celio, and Fernando Sarti (2016) "Relações económicas entre Brasil e China: análise dos fluxos de comercio e investimento direito estrangeiro." *Revista Tempo do Mundo*, 2(1): 83–98.
Jenkins, Rhys, and Alexandre de Freitas Barbosa (2012) "Fear for Manifacturing? China and the Future of Industry in Brazil and Latin America." In Julia Strauss and Ariel Armony (eds.) *From the Great Wall to the New World, China and Latin America in the 21st Century*. Cambridge: Cambridge University Press.
Lessa, Antônio Carlos, and Henrique Altemani de Oliveira (2013) "Introdução. Parcerias Estartégicas do Brasil: uma busca por conceitos." In Antônio Carlos Lessa and Henrique Altemani de Oliveira (org.) *Parcerias Estratégicas do Brasil: os significados e as experiências tradicionais*. Vol. 1. Belo Horizonte: Fino Traço Editora.
Lima, María Regina Soares de (2008) "Liderazgo regional en América del Sur: ¿tiene Brasil un papel a jugar?" In Ricardo Lagos (comp.) *América Latina: ¿Integración o Fragmentación?* Buenos Aires: EDHASA.
Li, Xing (ed.) (2010) *The Rise of China and the Capitalist World Order*. Farnham: Ashgate.

Li, Xing (2012) "Introduction: The Unanticipated Fall and Rise of China and the Capitalist World System." In Li Xing and Steen F. Christensen (eds.) *The Rise of China: The Impact on Semi-Periphery and Periphery Countries*. Aalborg: Aalborg University Press.

Li, Xing (2012a) "China y el orden mundial capitalista el nexo de la transformación interna de China y su impacto externo." In Raúl Bernal-Meza and Silvia Quintanar (eds.) *Regionalismo y Orden Mundial: Suramérica, Europa, China*. Buenos Aires: Nuevohacer and Universidad Nacional del Centro de la Provincia de Buenos Aires.

Li, Xing (ed.) (2014) *The BRICS and Beyond: The International Political Economy of the Emergence of a New World Order*. Surrey: Ashgate.

Medeiros, Carlos A. de, and Maria R. Cintra (2015) "Impacto da asensão chinesa sobre os países latinoamericanos." *Revista de Economía Política*, 35(1): 28–42.

Oliveira, Amauri Porto de (2013) "Reinventar o Brasil para o pós China." In Leila da Costa Ferreira and José Augusto Guilhon Albuquerque (orgs.) *China & Brasil. Desafios e oportunidades*. São Paulo: Annablume.

Oviedo, Eduardo Daniel (2014) "Principales variables para el estudio de las relaciones entre Brasil y China." In Raúl Bernal-Meza and Lincoln Bizzozero (eds.) *La política internacional de Brasil: de la región al mundo*. Montevideo: Ediciones Cruz del Sur and Universidad de la República.

Pfeifer, Alberto (2013) "O Brasil, os BRICS e a agenda internacional." In José Vicente de Sá Pimentel (org.) *O Brasil, os BRICS e a agenda internacional*. Brasília: Fundação Alexandre de Gusmão.

Pieterse, Jan Nederveen (2011) "Global Rebalancing: Crisis and the East-South Turn." *Development and Change*, 42(1): 22–48.

Pimentel, José Vicente de Sá (org.) (2013) *O Brasil, os BRICS e a agenda internacional*. Brasília: Fundação Alexandre de Gusmão.

Pimentel, José Vicente de Sá (org.) (2013a) *Debatendo o BRICS*. Brasília: Fundação Alexandre de Gusmão.

Reis, Maria Fontenele (2013) "BRICS: surgimiento e evolução." In José Vicente de Sá Pimentel (org.) *O Brasil, os BRICS e a agenda internacional*, Brasília: Fundação Alexandre de Gusmão.

Salama, Pierre (2017) "Brasil y China: caminos de fortaleza y desconcierttos." *Problemas del Desarrollo*, México, DF, 188(98): 9–28.

Saraiva, Miriam Gomes (2013) "Continuidade e mudança na política externa brasileira. As especificidades do comportamento externo brasileiro de 2003 a 2010." *Relações Internacionais*, (37): 63–78.

Saraiva, Miriam Gomes (2017) "Política externa brasileira 2016/2017 – Da reversão ao declinio." *Anuario de Política Internacional y Política Exterior*. Montevideo: Universidad de la República.

Saraiva, Miriam Gomes (2016) "Estancamento e crise da liderança do Brasil no entorno regional." Anuario de Integración Coordinadora Regional de Investigaciones Económicas y Sociales (CRIES). Buenos Aires, Edición especial.

Sevares, Julio (2007) "¿Cooperación Sur-Sur o dependencia a la vieja usanza? América Latina en el comercio internacional." *Nueva Sociedad*, (207): 11–22.

Sevares, Julio (2012) "El ascenso de China y las oportunidades y desafíos para América Latina." In Raúl Bernal-Meza and Silvia Quintanar (eds.) *Regionalismo y Orden Mundial: Suramérica, Europa, China*. Buenos Aires: Nuevohacer and Universidad Nacional del Centro de la Provincia de Buenos Aires.

Sevares, Julio (2014) "Inversiones chinas en América Latina: una relación económica emergente." *Realidad Económica*, (284): 54–80.

Sevares, Julio (2015) *China. Un socio imperial para Argentina y América Latina*. Buenos Aires: Editorial Edhasa.
Thorstensen, Vera, and Oliveira Iván T. Machado de (2012) "Introdução." In Vera Thorstensen and Iván T. Machado Oliveira. *Os BRICS na OMC*. Brasília: IPEA.
Uehara, Alexandre Ratsuo Uehara (2013) "Política externa da China es al relações com o Brasil." In Leila da Costa Ferreira and José Augusto Ghuilonn Albuquerque (orgs.) *China & Brasil. Desafios e oportunidades*. São Paulo: Annablume.
Vadell, Javier A. (2013) "El norte del sur: las implicaciones geopolíticas del 'consenso del Pacífico' en América del Sur y el dilema brasileño." *Latin American Policy*, (4–1): 36–56.
Vadell, Javier A. (2016) "The North of the South: The Geopolitical Implications of Pacific Consensus in South America and the Brazilian Dilemma." *Latin American Policy*, (4): 36–56.
Vadell, Javier, Roberto Araújo, and Gustavo de Cerqueira César (2016) "China y la nueva ofensiva financiera en América Latina: los acuerdos con Argentina." In Gladys Lechini and Clarisa Giaccaglia (eds.) *Poderes Emergentes y Cooperación Sur-Sur*. Rosario: Universidad Nacional de Rosario.
Vadell, Javier, Leonardo Ramos, and Pedro Neves (2014) "The International Implications of the Chinese Model of Development in the Global South: Asian Consensus as a Network Power." *Revista Brasileira de Política Internacional*, (57): 91–107.

8 Brazil in the BRICS after ten years

Past, present, and near future perspectives

Danielly Silva Ramos Becard, Ana Flávia Barros-Platiau, and Antônio Carlos Lessa

Introduction

When Brazil received the formal invitation to join BRICS in 2008, the general perception in the country was that this coalition, in parallel with Mercosur and UNASUL, would be useful in forming part of the diplomatic effort to have more voice in the international scenario (Domingos, 2014; Amorim, 2016). In fact, becoming the regional leader was the main advantage for Brazil in order to "embrace the world", as phrased by former President Luiz Inácio Lula da Silva (2003–2011). With the country's robust economic growth, Brazil's ambition was to become a global player (Fonseca Jr, 2011). Ten years later, what were the main changes in the Brazilian diplomaticy toward BRICS? What main drivers may be useful analytical tools to understand BRICS' near future from a Brazilian perspective? Is it possible to outline clear macro trends?

Throughout this chapter, we have applied an eclectic theoretical contribution from the field of Foreign Policy,[1] which indicates that international relations are the product of a competitive environment in which dynamic interactions between governments, political and economic interest groups, decision makers and social and political-economic structures take place (Alden and Aran, 2012: 46–61). However, we emphasize two of these factors, i.e. the "presidential diplomacy" and the ministerial level; the first factor is essentially political and the second is more technical. We have combined two research agendas to answer the questions posed: Alfred Hirschman's (1970) approach on "voice, loyalty and exit" and Jochen Prantl and Evelyn Goh's "strategic diplomacy" concept (2016).

As Alfred Hirschman (1970) puts it, we contend that there is a link between political and economic factors that causes members of an organization to react whenever they consider this to be necessary; i.e. when the organization no longer yields the expected benefits. This could be by acting through formal or informal pathways for support or confrontation (voice) or by leaving the organization (exit). However, exit depends on two main factors: loyalty to the group and the external context. If commitment and voice are active, a member may consider all the other possible options before the exit option. If the external context is worse or more uncertain, exit is not a good option. Although Mercosur was losing efficiency as an instrument of foreign and economic policies and could be understood as a declining organization,[2] exit was never a significant option on the Brazilian diplomatic agenda. In this respect, Mercosur and BRICS coexist as complementary initiatives.[3]

In ten years, Brazil has evolved from a regional leader and an emergent country seeking international recognition to a declining lonely nation searching for giant investors. In this sense, the recent past scenario, i.e. the scenario seen under former Presidents Lula da Silva (2003–2011) and Dilma Rousseff (2011–2016), is very different from that presently seen under President Michel Temer (2016–2018). Therefore, future perspectives are even more uncertain. From a strategic diplomacy approach (Prantl and Goh, 2016), the end points (main goals) and the entry points (agendas from which to start acting) seem to have changed significantly since 2007.

To give a clearer picture of Brazilian foreign policy, Table 8.1 shows three different periods in which Brazilian presidential visions toward BRICS have been fundamental.

According to Table 8.1, BRICS was a highly politicized and typical issue of "presidential diplomacy" during some moments of these phases.[4] From 2003 to 2010, and especially from 2007 to 2010, President Lula and Foreign minister Celso

Table 8.1 Brazilian perceptions, expectations, and reactions toward BRICS from 2007 to 2018

	2007–2010	*2010–2016*	*2016–2018*
Perceptions	BRICS as a grouping for diplomatic talks with no initial consensus. Competition with Mercosur and IBSA in strategic foreign policy options.	BRICS as a much less important diplomatic initiative under Dilma's rule. Likewise, IBSA was not a priority. Mercosur and regional organizations were also considered less relevant to Brasilia.	Chinese leadership; BRICS as an economic and financial option with the New Development Bank and the Belt and Road Initiative.
Expectations	Search for spaces, voice, and reform of agendas in institutions and regimes at the global level.	Few expectations. The same for IBSA.	Bringing more investments to Brazil and intra-BRICS market deals, notably with China and India.
Reactions	Strong support and direct presidential involvement.	Poor presidential involvement, but incipient technical cooperation and support for the NDB.	Better presidential involvement and growing technical cooperation. Stronger support for the NDB and creation of a regional branch in São Paulo in 2018.

Amorim strongly supported Brazilian participation in BRICS. In contrast, from 2010 to 2016, President Dilma Rousseff gave little importance to BRICS at the level of presidential diplomacy, but some ministers were active in promoting agendas related to UN reforms, G20 and financing. In 2016–2018, both trends continued, but for different reasons. President Michel Temer was not always directly involved in the BRICS agendas, but a growing number of ministers were. As a result, an ever-increasing bottom-up process took place in Brazil until 2018 with ministries being involved in agendas related to trade and health (notably pharmaceuticals and tuberculosis). Moreover, in 2019 Brazil will host the BRICS presidency.

BRICS in the recent past (2003 to 2010)

In 2003, Brazil was rising as a world economy and a regional power, whereas multilateralism was in crisis (Lazarou, 2017), mainly because of the Iraq invasion, UN inefficiency, and the slow motion of the WTO. From a regional perspective, Mercosur was failing (Dabène, 2011; Saraiva, 2016) to promote the changes planned by Brazil, and Venezuela soon became a challenge to the vision of stability that Brazil was seeking to encourage in the South American region. Besides, the UN system needed deep reforms to enable the western liberal order to respond to global challenges such as crises related to economic downturns, migration, and climate change. According to the former Brazilian Minister of Foreign Affairs Celso Amorim (2016), it was a time of "multipolarity with no multilateralism", i.e. rising powers were eager to strengthen their voice (Narlikar, 2013). At the same time, Brazil was seeking to promote the view that multilateral institutions were suffering from a legitimacy gap since the established traditional powers no longer represented the global distribution of power. In this sense, Brazil's primary goal was to receive more recognition from international institutions, and Brazil was demanding reforms as a condition for reinforcing multilateralism under the UN auspices.

In this context, we can explain Brazilian diplomatic strategy of using the model proposed by Amorim (2014) of "autonomous and active diplomacy". This implied non-automatic alignment with traditional western powers related to the security agenda that bypassed the UN[5] and the search for new partners and markets in the so-called Global South (Saraiva, 2007). The primary goal of the diplomatic strategy was to pave the way toward a much more prominent role in the global agendas. The entry points, i.e. the first strategic moves, were to act in the agendas in which Brazil already possessed some legitimacy, such as within social development, health, and diplomatic/peaceful settling of disputes. This is why Brazil invested so much energy in the MINUSTAH mission in Haiti, the principle of Responsibility while Protecting (RwP), the 2012 Sustainable Development Summit, and the UN system reform in general, and the G4 related to the UN Security Council reform[6] in particular. Under Dilma Rousseff, the Brazilian government invested its time and energy in the election of Ambassador Roberto Azevêdo as Director General of the WTO in 2013.

Brazil was the only emerging power (Lima, 2008) that had no declared enemies and no regional disputes and could act as a bridge between the North and South (Burges, 2009). Seen as a peaceful regional leader, Brazil promoted nuclear disarmament[7] and diplomatic settling of disputes. President Lula could participate in the Davos World Economic Forum and the Porto Alegre Social Forum and be equally welcomed in both. Still, the country was seeking international recognition (Amorim, 2016; Ricupero, 2016).

Unsurprisingly, the proposal to create BRIC (without South Africa) was directly linked to this context and the creation of BASIC[8] (Hallding et al., 2011), UNASUR, and IBSA (Kurtz-Phelan, 2013), since their members were all countries demanding reforms in order to ensure that the liberal order would correspond better to the power diffusion of the new Millennium (Hagopian, 2015). More specifically, the BRIC members first considered this an excellent initiative to promote the reforms of the Bretton Woods institutions. Nevertheless, the members were so asymmetrical in many aspects that BRIC looked rather like an informal meeting of four heads of states aiming at coordinating their diplomatic positions. It is possible to say that BRIC developed from scratch since its members had no common formal diplomatic agenda and no big plans for the future; they were more like a coalition of like-minded emerging countries focused on a particular issue related to the IMF reform. Russia took the initiative to invite Brazil and India (Lavrov, 2012), but their geopolitical aims were, and still are, entirely different from those of the other nations, due to their relation to the US hegemony. Nevertheless, an analysis of their voting patterns related to the new economic order shows that only Russia sometimes differed from the rest of the BRIC members (Ferdinand, 2014; Montenegro and Mesquita, 2017).

This means that Brazil never saw BRIC as an anti-Western, anti-USA or anti-UN coalition. Thus, no alignment was easy nor automatic in several agendas regarding security, democracy or human rights, for instance. Brasilia still believed the Mercosur could be revived and that IBSA made more sense than BRIC, even after South Africa joined the coalition (henceforth called BRICS). Therefore, the search for the amplification of Brazil's international voice was the main reason for Brazil to participate in BRICS, not loyalty. Brazil made an opportunistic choice to join BRICS since loyalty was considered more important in relation to other organizations such as the UN, Mercosur, and IBSA.

Brazilian tectonic shifts in 2010

In 2010, two significant changes occurred in Brazil which had a direct impact on BRICS, and which were therefore the tipping points to the diplomatic strategy in Itamaraty: Dilma Rousseff was elected President of Brazil, and the Brazilian economy began to show clear signs of decline. President Rousseff did not ensure clear continuity of the work done by Lula da Silva, and therefore BRICS' objectives seemed to change completely. First, she did not devote her time to foreign policy in general, and to BRICS or IBSA in particular.[9] Therefore, her election may be considered the end of "presidential diplomacy" (Cervo and Lessa, 2014; Milani et al., 2017). Second,

Rousseff appointed Antonio Patriota as Minister of Foreign Affairs, but he did not have the same *marge de manoeuvre* as Celso Amorim, which clearly indicated that diplomacy was not a priority for Rousseff's government. From 2010 onwards, the diplomatic goals (end points) changed, resulting in a more economically results-oriented agenda (Becard et al., 2015), notably after the nomination of Mauro Vieira as Minister of Foreign Affairs in 2015, which represented the main tipping point[10] in Brazilian foreign policy. Brazilian expectations related to BRICS were ambiguous in the sense that BRICS was no longer a diplomatic priority, but China was the first trade partner. Nevertheless, other ministries involved in trade, investments, research, and health issues continued to work with the BRICS members. From an analysis of all the declarations of the BRICS summits[11] it appears that this horizontal expansion toward a more development-oriented agenda is unequivocal.

At the same time, Brazil restarted its straight talks with the OECD,[12] following the signing of their cooperation agreement in November 2015.[13] Even though entry points have changed only slowly, Brazil's priority has quickly shifted to the economic agenda under Rousseff (Fonseca Jr, 2011; Faria, 2012; Schmitz and Rocha, 2017). Therefore, Itamaraty saw BRICS as less important, whereas the Ministry fostered the negotiations with Mercosur and the European Union. Apart from the G20, Brazil reduced significantly its efforts to cooperate in coalitions and groups from the South, leaving Asia and Africa at the bottom of their diplomatic agenda. Besides, it chose not to take clear positions on the UN concerning several conflicts related to Crimea, Syria, Ukraine, and sensitive issues such as North Korean nuclear tests and the South China Sea dispute. With their focus only on trade and economic success through bilateral relations in particular, the Brazilian strategic partners were a couple of European countries and the USA, which were considered traditional investors, and unavoidably China (Cervo and Lessa, 2014).

However, three other drivers created conditions that were more conducive to a stronger Brazilian interest in BRICS: 1) the creation of the New Development Bank (NDB) and the Contingent Reserve Agreement (CRA)[14]; 2), the impeachment of President Rousseff in 2016, and 3) the Chinese leadership under President Xi Jinping and his enthusiasm to reinforce BRICS (Wang, 2016) .

The 2014 agreement on the creation of the NDB and the CRA was undoubtedly the primary driver that led Brazil to reassess its priority given to BRICS. Brazil was looking forward to receiving financing from the NDB for much-needed infrastructure projects. Not only could these loans arrive sooner with BRICS, they also represented an alternative to the World Bank and other development banks.

The assessment that there is a demand for resources for infrastructure investment that exceeds the potential available in existing multilateral institutions, the consideration that most of the available resources are being channeled to projects in advanced countries, and the likelihood that a capital increase will not occur in major financial institutions in the short term led to the creation of the NBD. According to Baumann (2017), there is an excess demand of more than USD 1 trillion per year, just for investments in infrastructure projects in developing countries. Associated with the purpose of having more expeditious project processes and conditionalities that were considered more appropriate by lenders, this is to no small extent the motivation that led BRICS members such as Brazil to create the NDB.

The two other drivers that caused Brazil to approach BRICS were the impeachment of President Rousseff in 2016 and the present Chinese leadership; the latter was caused by the fact that China represents around 75% of the group's GDP. When President Temer replaced Dilma Rousseff, the Brazilian Secretary of Strategic Affairs (SAE) published the first report stating that the country needed a new strategy for its foreign policy (Kalout and Degaut, 2017). Although succinct and not in line with Itamaraty's view, the SAE report stated that the results obtained with BRICS were limited as regards diplomatic and economic gains. Roughly speaking, it concluded that Brasilia needed a clear strategy to achieve better results from BRICS, i.e. it had to frame more precisely what the national interests were, in the short and long terms. Stated bluntly, the end of President Dilma Rousseff's rule represented a fragile context for the other BRICS members because Brazil did not improve its loyalty to the group, causing its voice in the group to be reduced.

Present and future perspectives for Brazil in BRICS

Since 2017, President Michel Temer has showed more interest in BRICS than his predecessor. However, due to domestic political turmoil,[15] he has been unable to deal adequately with foreign policy issues (Oliveira and Pennaforte, 2018). Minister of Foreign Affairs Aloysio Nunes and representatives of Itamaraty and the presidential cabinet[16] participated in most of the BRICS meetings promoted by China in 2017, even when Brazilian interests did not directly relate to them.[17]

In addition, many subnational initiatives and several technical cooperation projects undertaken by member country ministries help explain why the future of BRICS may still be bright (Stuenkel, 2017). Agendas related to trade, health, poverty alleviation, climate and education are in line with the UN 2030 Agenda (Sustainable Development Goals) and afford the BRICS members new opportunities to increase their cooperation efforts.[18] Brazil's government in particular has identified new opportunities for collaboration within BRICS, following China's organization of almost a hundred meetings in 2017 with agendas ranging from trade defence to academic exchanges. As a result, other actors are improving their loyalty to BRICS. So far, the central ministries involved in BRICS are responsible for trade defence (the Ministry of Development, Industry and Foreign Trade – MDIC and the Administrative Council for Economic Defence – CADE), budget planning (the Ministry of Planning, Development and Management – MPDG), agribusiness (the Ministry of Agriculture, Livestock and Supply – MAPA), science and technology (the Ministry of Science, Technology, Innovation and Communication – MCTIC), and health (Ministry of Health – MS).

At the present time, Brazil is viewing BRICS as a tool for the search for a more inclusive and effective multipolar international order, including the considerable strengthening of multilateralism. From an economic point of view, the Brazilian government is trying to expand global connectivity through the increase of trade, investment and development opportunities (Oliveira, 2017), and this is primarily due to China's stronger presence in BRICS and to the Belt and Road Initiative.

Brazil has not treated the entry points that Russia proposed in 2015 in the same manner. The point on strategic economic partnership received much attention, whereas the other point on emerging threats (terrorism, drug trafficking, and cyber-security) did not. This confirms that unlike Russia, Brasília has been focusing more on economic negotiations than on geopolitical issues since the creation of the BRIC.

Likewise, as BRICS' president in 2016, India proposed to reinforce the regional security agenda and views, but this is not a priority entry point for Brazil. During the Xiamen preparatory summit meetings, the Brazilian minister affirmed that "political coordination is a sensitive area, which must follow the principles of pragmatism, gradualism and reciprocity in the pursuit of convergence". (Madeira, 2017) The two other initiatives in the Goa Summit were related to the promotion of the BRICS brand, the "people-to-people events" on the one hand and the creation of institutions such as the NDB research institute, a credit assessment agency, a sports council, a railway research center, and a customs cooperation committee on the other (Madeira, 2017).

Sunny days ahead?

The Brazilian priorities for the 2017 Xiamen BRICS Summit were to improve the market-oriented, NDB and CRA initiatives, which were characterized by pragmatism (Madeira, 2017). Meanwhile, the endpoint was to strengthen BRICS concerning global financial governance, sustainable development and energy security, since the NDB projects will primarily finance renewable energy alternatives.

Since Brazil is concentrating its priorities on economic and financial measures, Brazil's government welcomed intra-bloc facilitation and growth in trade and investment,[19] the e-ports network[20] proposed by China, the creation of the working group on e-commerce, as well as the expansion of the NDB membership (Madeira, 2017). Besides, the industry and agriculture sectors, to mention but two, could benefit greatly from intra-bloc investments. Finally, Brazil is hosting an NDB branch established in São Paulo in 2018, so the prospects are slightly favorable. For the Brazilian government and the private sector, the creation of an NDB regional office in São Paulo is important, not only because Brazil is the most distant country from the Bank's headquarters in Shanghai, but also because this stimulates the elaboration of projects which can be financed by the NDB in other regions (Moreira, 2017).

In fact, Brazil was late in receiving funding from the NDB. In almost three years since NDB's operations started, Brazil had four projects approved, totalling USD 621 million: USD 50 million for Pará (urban development); USD 51 million for Maranhão (logistics and highway); USD 300 million for BNDES (renewable energy); and USD 200 million for Petrobras (sustainable infrastructure project) (Moreira, 2018b).

On 2 March 2018, the NDB held its 13th Board of Directors (BoD) meeting in Shanghai. During the meeting, the BoD approved the Pará Sustainable

Municipalities Project and the Maranhão Road Corridor, a South-North Integration Project in Brazil with aggregate loans of USD 121 million, subject to the completion of domestic requirements in Brazil (NDB, 2018c).

On 18 April 2018, the National Bank for Economic and Social Development (BNDES) and the New Development Bank (NDB) made their first joint disbursement for a financing operation in Brazil. The release of USD 67.3 million was the largest ever made by the NDB. It is part of a USD 300 million contract signed between NDB and BNDES a year before to support NDB's investments in Brazil's wind, solar, hydroelectric power generation (small hydropower plants), and biomass (biogas and agricultural waste). The funds disbursed will go to six wind farms in the states of Piauí and Pernambuco. They are part of the Araripe 3 Wind Farm Complex of the Casa dos Ventos Group, comprising 14 parks in the municipalities of Simões, Currais Novos (PI) and Araripina (PE). In total, the complex will have an installed capacity of 358 megawatts generated by 156 power turbines. The expected impact of the project is the production of 600 MW of renewable energy and the elimination of 1,000,000 tons of CO_2 per year. In this context, the new partnership is seeking to foster alternative energies by supporting the diversification of the matrix and enhancing the security of the system in the future in order to ensure supply to all sectors of the Brazilian economy (Estadão Conteúdo, 2018; BNDES, 2018).

In May 2018, the NDB Board of Governors (composed of finance ministers and central bank presidents) approved a project with Petrobras of US $ 200 million (NDB, 2018b). This is the first NDB project that directly finances companies in Brazil without sovereign guarantee. The project with Petrobras is in line with NDB's priority to support sustainable infrastructure projects. It will result in the reduction of sulfuric oxide emissions and the implementation of infrastructure to separate rainwater and water rejects (Moreira, 2018b).

The credits granted to Brazil so far represent 12% of the NDB portfolio. China and India have received much more, as they are the fastest growing economies (see Figure 8.1).

The NDB's directors say the bank is working to bridge the funding gap for Brazil and South Africa and establish a balanced portfolio between the five partners. The NDB also announced on 10 January 2018 a commercial partnership with Santander Bank in Brazil to finance regional projects. This is the first agreement between a bank in Brazil and the NDB. The agreement includes the concession of credit lines for the infrastructure and sustainable development projects, for services such as the structuring of bond transmission, exchange, and secondary operations and transfer of values (Moreira, 2018a).

From a broader sustainable development perspective, Madeira (2017) stressed that the Technology Facilitation Mechanism (MFT) might contribute to the UN 2030 Agenda and to intra-BRICS cooperation. However, the coherence of the BRICS declarations with the UN development agendas is not very strong, but there is growing convergence between them. Other "softer" programmes aimed at deepening loyalty and strengthening the voices of various members within BRICS have been introduced in Xiamen, such as film and culture festivals and collaboration within sports and traditional medicine. Such programmes may soon give Brasilia

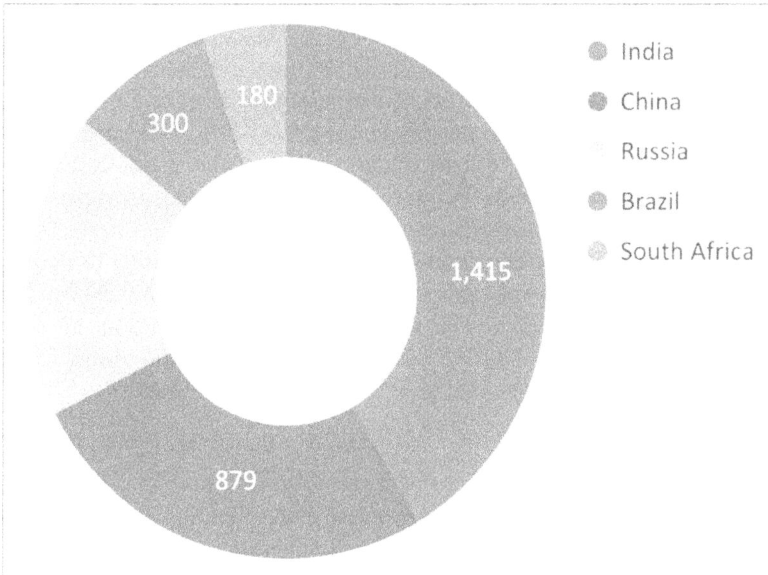

Figure 8.1 NDB's projects by country (USD million)

Source: NDB website (2018d), accessed on 1 June 2018

opportunities to set new entry points in their diplomatic strategy toward BRICS. In these efforts, Brasilia is not only struggling to build a shared vision with other members, but also to involve more private actors in the market and in society (Franco and Oliveira, 2017) in an effort to render BRICS' political and economic processes less top-down controlled than at present. Finally, this type of approach highlights the Brazilian effort to attempt to create a shift of focus in BRICS common agenda – causing this to become less focused on security issues and more focused on pragmatic issues, some of which may cause immediate economic repercussions.

According to the current Brazilian Foreign Minister Aloysio Nunes Ferreira, the global economy's center of gravity has shifted to Asia. For this reason, Brazilian foreign policy is seeking to strengthen the country's ties with the region. In meetings scheduled with politicians and business people from China, South Korea, Indonesia, Japan, Singapore, Thailand, and Vietnam, the Chancellor sought to attract more investment, expand trade and encourage partnerships that could contribute to better integration of Brazil in global value chains. In this respect, his trip to Asia in May 2018 was the expression of a foreign policy that contributes to the sustained expansion of the Brazilian economy, promotion of international trade and stimulation of the internationalization of Brazilian companies (Ferreira, 2018).

In this context, there are three macro trends for Brazil's future in BRICS. First, Brazil is becoming more involved in technical agendas within BRICS, whereas robust presidential diplomacy belongs to the past. One clear sign of this is that the political debate about the 2018 presidential elections did not mention BRICS or the international agenda as priorities. A second macro trend is the rise of China within BRICS, the country's accounting for more than 75% of the coalition's GDP and China's emergence as a bilateral trading partner, which could lead to serious disagreements.[21] In other words, Beijing is so powerful that Brasilia is increasingly worried about Brazil's dependence on Chinese trade and investments (Angelo, 2018; Arbache, 2012). A third trend is that Brazil is also more dependent on BRICS, and is looking forward to improving trade relations with India and Russia in the short term. In this vein, exit is not an option. At the same time, the country is losing its voice within BRICS and the NDB. So the question for the future is: will loyalty increase in this path of growing Brazilian dependency?

Conclusion

Brazil accepted to participate in BRIC because of the coalition's strong relation to the Brazilian strategy of "active and autonomous diplomacy" targeted at rendering Brazil a global player, which was coined by Minister Amorim during Lula da Silva's term, and continued with less impetus by the Rousseff and Temer governments. However, the disappointment with the UN reform in 2005 and the reforms of the Bretton Woods institutions later contributed to the Brazilian strategy of investing in the IBSA and Mercosur as well. After 2010, the Brazilian economic decline, together with the weaknesses of Mercosur and the collapse of IBSA, led to new diplomatic goals based on market-oriented results. Therefore, the perception of BRICS as a less interesting project caused Brazil to return to its traditional trade and investment partners. Focusing mainly on the country's economic recovery, Brazil also approached the main OECD members. Although mitigated results have been reached, it can be said that BRICS has acquired a growing priority in the Brazilian diplomatic agenda since its inception, notably because of trade and financing opportunities.

In 2017, the Xiamen summit consolidated more institutionalized collaboration between BRICS members concerning the creation of new agendas, working groups, and issue-area institutions. However, these horizontal and technical expansions are not yet the priority entry points for Brazil, probably because of the failures experienced by Mercosur. They rather reflect the political will of China and India.

Finally, if exit is not an option, and Brazil's influence within BRICS has decreased since 2010, what will be the future scenario? The latter seems to be linked to the direct involvement of the Brazilian private sector and related to technology and sustainable development in specific agendas such as those relating to infrastructure, energy, and health. However, the future scenario will depend on the ability of Brazilian ministries to build strong projects with other BRICS ministries and attract investments. In this respect, the strength of the Brazilian government to expedite approval and work closely with the NDB regional bank in São Paulo may result in an increase in investments, the facilitation of investment processes and better adaptation of NBD conditionality to the Brazilian profile. The Agenda 2030 could also be a useful path in this direction. Given the Brazilian presidential elections of 2018 and the substantial changes Brazil has experienced since the creation of BRICS, we will need more research to adjust the long-term scenarios.

Notes

1 The empirical work aimed to explore how structural, behavioral, and historical factors shaped the way in which Brazil responded to the political and economic presence of BRICS. We collected data mainly through official documents from Brazil's government and BRICS. We also conducted interviews with key Brazilian government officials from the Ministry of Foreign Affairs (Itamaraty); the Ministry of Industry, Development and Foreign Trade (MDIC); the Ministry of Science, Technology, Innovation and Culture (MCTIC); the Ministry of Health (MS); the Ministry of Agriculture (MAPA); and the Strategic Affairs Office (SAE), among others. We have mainly interviewed government agents who have participated directly in the BRICS negotiations over the past few years.

2 According to this reasoning, Gonçalves (2013) and Barbosa (2014) affirmed that the rhetoric of a positive framework of the current Mercosur was, in most cases, based on misinformation and distortions about what happened in practice. In their opinion, Mercosur totally ignored what happened in a world that has changed greatly from 1991 to the present, and this trade bloc had nothing to do with what was negotiated in connection with the 1991 Treaty of Asunción. The suspension of Paraguay and the admission of Venezuela in Mercosur in 2012, for example, are often cited as illegal decisions that have contributed to undermining Brazilian credibility and leadership.

3 According to the Itamaraty website, BRICS is not a group, bloc or alliance. It is an informal grouping, and it must remain so. Besides, rather than an acronym that identified emerging countries in the international economic order, Itamaraty saw BRICS as a promising new political-diplomatic entity, quite distinct from the original concept formulated for the financial market. See: MRE. Note on the BRICS (Informação sobre o BRICS) Available at http://brics.itamaraty.gov.br/pt-br/sobre-o-brics/informacao-sobre-o-brics.

4 See Preto, Alessandra Falcão (2006) "O conceito de diplomacia presidencial: o papel da Presidência da República na formulação de política externa". Master's dissertation. University of São Paulo, Brazil.

5 Notably the Iraqi invasion by the USA and allies. However, it also applies to the use of force in general, even before President Lula took office. Brazil followed the same pattern (or diplomatic principles) for other crises such as those in Libya, Iran, Ukraine, and Syria.

6 Brazil, Japan, Germany, and India.

7 With five other countries, Brazil strongly supported the UN Treaty on the total ban of nuclear weapons, and President Temer was the first to sign this in September 2017. See: de ORTE, Paola. Brazil signs Treaty on Prohibition of Nuclear Weapons. Agência Brasil. Available at http://agenciabrasil.ebc.com.br/en/internacional/noticia/2017-09/brazil-signs-treaty-prohibition-nuclear-weapons.

8 BASIC is the bloc of four countries – Brazil, South Africa, India, and China – formed in 2009 to discuss burden-sharing at the Copenhagen climate summit. See Hochstetler and Milkoreit (2015).

9 IBSA's last meeting was held in 2011, due to a large extent to President Rousseff's unwillingness to participate in the summit.

10 Tipping points are thresholds, trigger mechanisms or significant shifts that change the trajectory of a system or break the path dependence grip (Young, 2017: 5; Sheffer, 2009)

11 I Summit (June, 2009) – Yekaterinburg, Russia; II Summit (April, 2010) – Brasilia, Brazil; III Summit (March, 2011) – Sanya, China; IV Summit (March, 2012) – New Delhi, India; V Summit (March, 2013) – Durban, South Africa; VI Summit (July, 2014) – Fortaleza, Brazil; VII Summit (July, 2015) – Ufa, Russia; VIII Summit (October, 2016) – Goa, India; IX Summit (September, 2017) – Xiamen, China; X Summit (July, 2018) – Johannesburg, South Africa.

12 In fact, Brazil has been discussing with OECD staff since the 1990s, under President Fernando Henrique Cardoso. Subsequently, Presidents Lula and Rousseff left the issue aside.

13 See: OECD (2015) "Active with Brazil". Online brochure, p. 56. Available at www.oecd.org/brazil/.

14 The key documents of BRICS Bank (NDB) and the Contingent Reserve Agreement (CRA) are available on the NDB website (www.ndb.int/) and on the website of Brazil's Ministry of Foreign Affairs (See: Brazil. MRE. Tratado para o Estabelecimento do Arranjo Contingente de Reservas dos BRICS. Available at http://brics.itamaraty.gov.br/images/ACR%20portugues.pdf.

15 Since 2014, Brazil has been hit by a corruption scandal that began with a state-owned oil company, PETROBRAS, and since then, the country's political and business elites have been investigated and prosecuted as never seen before, as a result of Car Wash Operation (Operação Lava Jato). This scandal is one of the most prominent corruption cases in the world.

16 Mostly from the Strategic Affairs Office (SAE in the acronym in Portuguese) and the Institutional Security Cabinet (GSI in Portuguese), both from the Presidential Cabinet (Casa Civil).

17 Two examples in 2017 are the meeting on cybersecurity and the meeting related to the Sino-Indian border conflict. We consider The Belt and Road Initiative another case, but this is more relevant for Brazil than security issues.

18 The Xiamen BRICS Declaration confirmed this trend in 2017.

19 Chinese President Xi Jinping announced on 4 September 2017, at the opening session of the 9th BRICS Heads of State and Government Summit in the Chinese city of Xiamen, that China would launch an economic cooperation plan providing 500 million yuan (USD 78,937 thousand) to facilitate intra bloc trade and investment. The Chinese President indicated that of the USD 197 billion in foreign investment by the five members in 2016, only 5.7% were to go to BRIC countries. To strengthen BRICS Bank, Xi Jinping also announced that China would allocate an additional USD 4 million to BRICS to finance infrastructure and sustainable development projects in member countries, see: CAMPOS, Ana Cristina. Xi Jinping anuncia 500 milhões de iuanes para plano de cooperação intra-Brics. Agência Brasil. Available at http://brics.itamaraty.gov.br/images/ACR%20portugues.pdf.

20 E-port appears as a particular form of integrated electronic platform for processing and monitoring the cross-border movement of goods and transport vessels at the port level. This one-stop shop approach requires closer cooperation between all relevant authorities and government agencies in the area of port trade. One of the priority areas will be to develop a shared understanding of the e-port network model, to promote cooperation and a knowledge-sharing network on e-ports among BRICS members, and to explore the connectivity of the e-port network, information sharing and technology sharing. See BRICS official website www.brics2017.org/wdfj/201708/t20170831_1830.html.

21 Since 2009, China has been the first Brazilian trade partner surpassing the United States and Argentina, but it is only interested in commodities, mainly soybean and iron ore. China is also one of the most prominent investors in Brazil, notably in the infrastructure and energy sectors.

References

Alden, Chris, and Amnon Aran (2012) *Foreign Policy Analysis: New Approaches*. London: Routledge.

Amorim, Celso (2014) *Teerã, Ramalá e Doha. Memórias da Política Externa Ativa e Altiva*. Rio de Janeiro: Benvirá.

Amorim, Celso (2016) *A Grande Estratégia do Brasil*. Brasília: FUNAG.

Angelo, Mauricio (2018) "Com estratégias sofisticadas, Chineses aumentam seu domínio sobre o Brasil." *INESC*. Available at http://amazonia.inesc.org.br/materias/um-pais-sob-influencia-com-estrategias-mais-sofisticadas-chineses-aumentam-seu-dominio-sobre-o-brasil/.

Arbache, Jorge (2012) "The Siren's Song: A Study of the Economic Relationship between Brazil and China." Available at www.ssrn.com/abstract=2047126.

Barbosa, Rubens (2014) "Mercosul: retórica e realidade." *Política Externa*, 22(4):17–27.

Baumann, Renato (2017) "Os novos bancos de desenvolvimento: Independência conflitiva ou parcerias estratégicas?" *Revista de Economia Política*, 37(2) (147): 287–303.

Becard, Danielly Silva Ramos, Ana FláviaBarros-Platiau, and Carina Oliveira (2015) "O Brasil, a China e a VI Cúpula do BRICS." *Contexto Internacional*, 37(1): 81–112.

Brasil, BNDES (2018) "BNDES e New Development Bank, o 'Banco dos BRICS', realizam o 1° desembolso a operação no Brasil." *BNDES/Energia/Institucional*, April 18. Available at www.bndes.gov.br/wps/portal/site/home/imprensa/noticias/conteudo/bndes-e-new-development-bank-o-banco-dos-brics-realizam-o-1-desembolso-a-operacao-no-brasil.

Brasil, Presidente da República Federativa do Brasil (2017) "Discurso do Presidente da República, Michel Temer, durante reunião dos Chefes de Estado e de Governo do BRICS – Hamburgo-Alemanha." July 7. Available at www.itamaraty.gov.br/pt-BR/discursos-artigos-e-entrevistas-categoria/presidente-da-republica-federativa-do-brasil-discursos/16786-discurso-do-presidente-da-republica-michel-temer-durante-a-reuniao-dos-chefes-de-estado-e-de-governo-do-brics-hamburgo-alemanha-07-de-julho-de-2017.

Burges, Sean (2009) *Brazilian Foreign Policy after the Cold War*. Gainesville: University Press of Florida.

Cervo, Amado Luiz, and Antônio Carlos Lessa(2014) "O declínio: inserção internacional do Brasil (2011–2014)." *Revista Brasileira de Política Internacional[online]*, 57(2):133–151. Available at www.scielo.br/scielo.php?script=sci_arttext&pid=S0034-73292014000200133&lng=en&nrm=iso. ISSN 0034-7329. http://dx.doi.org/10.1590/0034-7329201400308. (Accessed June 1, 2018).

Dabène, Olivier (2011) "1991. Les 20 ans du MERCOSUR Au-delà du clivage droite/gauche, un bilan décevant." *Études du CERI*, (179–180): 48–52.

Domingos, Nicole (2014) "Le Brésil comme Partenaire Stratégique de l'UE – une préférence partagée pour le multilatéralisme?" PhD Thesis. Sciences Po de Paris. Supervisors: Zaki Laïdi and Ana Flávia Barros-Platiau.

Estadão Conteúdo (2018) "BNDES e 'Banco dos BRICS' fazem 1° desembolso no Brasil." *Época Negócios*, April 18. Available at https://epocanegocios.globo.com/Economia/noticia/2018/04/epoca-negocios-bndes-e-banco-dos-brics-fazem-1o-desembolso-no-brasil-para-parques-eolicos.html.

Faria, Carlos Aurélio (2012) "O Itamaraty e a Política Externa Brasileira: do insulamento à busca de coordenação dos Atores Governamentais e de Cooperação com outros Agentes Societários." *Contexto Internacional*, 34(1): 311–355.

Ferdinand, Peter (2014) "Rising Powers at the UN: An Analysis of the Voting Behaviour of BRICS in the General Assembly." *Third World Quarterly*, 35(3): 376–391.

Ferreira, Aloysio Nunes (2018) "O Brasil em Direção à Ásia." *O Globo*, May 7. Available at www.itamaraty.gov.br/pt-BR/discursos-artigos-e-entrevistas-categoria/ministro-das-relacoes-exteriores-artigos/18796-o-brasil-em-direcao-a-asia-o-globo-07-05-2018.

Fonseca, Gelson, Jr. (2011) "Notes on the Evolution of Brazilian Multilateral Diplomacy." *Global Governance*, 17(3): 375–397.

Franco, Camila, and Renan Oliveira (2017) "Inputs and Outputs of Innovation: Analysis of the BRICS Theme 6:Innovation Technology and Competitiveness." *Revista de Administração e Inovação*, São Paulo, USP, 14: 79–89.

Gonçalves, José Botafogo (2013) "Vamos renegociar o Mercosul?" *Política Externa*, 22(2): 49–57.

Hagopian, Joachim (2015) "Global Shift in the Balance of Power Is Moving from West to East." *Global Research*. Available at www.globalresearch.ca/global-shift-in-the-balance-of-power-is-moving-from-west-to-east/5437388. (Accessed June 1, 2018).

Hallding, Karl, MarieOlsson, AaronAtteridge, AnttoVihma, MarcusCarson, and Mikael Román (2011) "Together Alone: BASIC Countries and the Climate Change Conundrum." Nordic Council of Ministers, Copenhagen. TemaNord 2011. Available at www.sei-international.org/publications?pid=1963.

Hirschman, Alfred (1970) *Exit, Voice, and Loyalty: Responses to Decline in Firms, Organizations, and States*. Cambridge: Harvard University Press.

Hochstetler, Kathryn, and Manjana Milkoreit (2015) "Responsibilities in Transition: Emerging Powers in the Climate Change Negotiations." *Global Governance*, 21(2): 205–226.

Kalout, Hussein, and Marcos Degaut (2017) "Brasil, um país em busca de uma grande estratégia." Secretaria de Assuntos Estratégicos, *Relatório de Conjuntura*, 1.

Kurtz-Phelan, Daniel (2013) "What Is IBSA Anyway?" *Americas Quarterly*, Spring. Available at www.americasquarterly.org/content/what-ibsa-anyway.

Lavrov, Sergei (2012) "BRICS: ANew-Generation Forum with a Global Reach. BRICS and the New Delhi Summit, 2012." Available at www.brics.utoronto.ca/newsdesk/BRICS-2012.pdf.

Lazarou, Elena (2017) "The Future of Multilateralism: Crisis or Opportunity?" *European Parliamentary Research Service/Member Research Service*, May. Available at www.europarl.europa.eu/RegData/etudes/BRIE/2017/603922/EPRS_BRI(2017)603922_EN.pdf.

Lima, Maria Regina (2008) "Brazil Rising." *Internationale Politik*, 9(3): 62–67.

Madeira, Mariana (2017) "BRICS Cooperation: Assessment and Next Steps." Seminar FUNAG and Renmin University of China, Ministry of Foreign Affairs, August 1. 7 pages. Mimeo.

Milani, Carlos, LetíciaPinheiro, and Maria Regina Lima(2017) "Brazil's Foreign Policy and the 'Graduation Dilemma'." *International Affairs*, 93(3): 585–605.

Montenegro, Renan, and Rafael Mesquita (2017) "Leaders or Loners? How Do the BRICS Countries and Their Regions Vote in the UN General Assembly?" *Brazilian Political Science Review*. Available atwww.journals4free.com/link.jsp?l=8350455.

Moreira, Assis (2017) "Banco dos Brics deve ter escritório no Brasil em 2 anos." *Valor Econômico*, September 4. Available at www.valor.com.br/brasil/5106090/banco-dos-brics-deve-ter-escritorio-no-brasil-em-2-anos.

Moreira, Assis (2018a) "Crédito do Banco dos Brics ao Brasil deve alcançar US$ 1 bilhão." *Valor Econômico*, May 29.Available at www.valor.com.br/financas/5555851/credito-do-banco-dos-brics-ao-brasil-deve-alcancar-us-1-bilhao.

Moreira, Talita (2018b) "Santander Brasil anuncia parceria com NDB, o 'banco dos Brics'." *Valor Econômico*, January 10.Available at www.valor.com.br/financas/5252129/santander-brasil-anuncia-parceria-com-ndb-o-banco-dos-brics.

Narlikar, Amrita (ed.) (2013) "Negotiating the Rise of New Powers." *International Affairs*, Special Issue, 89(3): 561–577.

NDB (2018a) "NDB President Meets Brazil's Minister of Foreign Relations in Shanghai." *Press Releases*, May 22. Available at www.ndb.int/press_release/ndb-president-meets-brazils-minister-foreign-relations-shanghai/.

NDB (2018b) "NDB Board of Governors and Board of Directors Meetings Held in Shanghai, China." *Press Releases*, May 28. Available atwww.ndb.int/press_release/ndb-board-governors-board-directors-meetings-held-shanghai-china/.

NDB (2018c) "13th Meeting of NDB Board of Directors Held in Shanghai." *Press Releases*, March 5. Available at www.ndb.int/press_release/13th-meeting-ndb-board-directors-held-shanghai/.

NDB (2018d) "List of All Projects." Available at www.ndb.int/projects/list-of-all-projects/

Oliveira, Fabiana de, and Charles Pennaforte (2018) "Da crise de governabilidade à crise de legitimidade: os impactos da crise política sobre a política externa brasileira." *Revista de Estudios Brasilenos*, 5(9): 148–160.

Oliveira, Susan (2017) "Is the Death of the TPP Good News for Brazil? Mega-Regional Agreements and the Quest for Development 'Policy Space'." *Journal of World Trade*, 51(5): 1–24.

Prantl, Jochen, and Evelyn Goh (2016) "Strategic Diplomacy in Northeast Asia." *Global Asia*, 11(4): 137–139.

Ricupero, Rubens (2016) *A Diplomacia na Construção do Brasil: 1750–2016*. São Paulo: Versal Editores.

Saraiva, Miriam (2007) "As estratégias de cooperação Sul-Sul nos marcos da política externa brasileira de 1993 a 2007." *Revista Brasileira de Política Internacional*, 50(2): 42–59.

Saraiva, Miriam (2016) "Estancamento e crise da liderança do Brasil no entorno regional." *Anuario de Integración*, Edición Especial, 295–310. Available at www.cries.org/wp-content/uploads/2016/03/017-saraiva.pdf.

Schmitz, Guilherme, and Rafael Rocha (2017) *Brasil e o Sistema das Nações Unidas. Desafios e Oportunidades na Governança Global*. Brasília: IPEA.

Sheffer, Marten (2009) *Critical Transitions in Nature and Society*. Princeton: Princeton University Press.

Stuenkel, Oliver (2017) *BRICS e o futuro da ordem global*. Paz e Terra: Rio de Janeiro/São Paulo.

Wang, Yong (2016) "Offensive for Defensive: The Belt and Road Initiative and China's New Grand Strategy." *Pacific Review*, 29(3): 455–463.

Young, Oran (2017) *Governing Complex Systems: Social Capital for the Anthropocene*. Cambridge: MIT Press.

9 Russia and the BRICS

On the actual performance of a 21st century great power concert

Mette Skak

> *BRICS is an interstate association created on the initiative of Russia* (sozdannoe po initsiative Rossii) *consisting of the Federal Republic of Brazil, The Russian Federation, The Republic of India, The People's Republic of China and (from December 2010) The South African Republic.*
>
> (Dossier. Russian Ministry of Foreign Affairs, 2017)

Assessments of the economic and global political achievements of BRICS differ across time and space and among experts. On the one hand, Indian scholar Harsh V. Pant (2013) criticizes BRICS for their "lack of seriousness" on the issues of stabilizing Afghanistan and combating terrorism and hence considers BRICS a dysfunctional great power concert. On the other hand, Australian formerly Moscow-based diplomat turned academic Bobo Lo (2016) takes a pragmatic view of BRICS' performance and highlights China and Russia as the sole drivers behind the BRICS concert. China's geo-economic clout turns her into a driver behind BRICS cooperation whereas Russia is a driver mainly due to the Kremlin's geopolitical zeal in balancing against the United States seeking to turn this into a common BRICS cause (Skak, 2010: 114–160, 2013). Pant (2013) represents the normative institutionalist approach of the International Society school as he implicitly reasons on the basis of responsible *great power management* (Bull, 1977; Knudsen, 2014). Conversely, Lo (2016) represents fiscal structuralism and the dialectics between geopolitics and geo-economics (Luttwak, 1990; Buzan and Lawson, 2014; Wigell and Vihma, 2016). The point is to combine these two theoretical perspectives, when the empirical topic is Russia as is the case in the next section.

The immediate object of analysis is the BRICS policy of the Kremlin, which I shall portray in terms of Lo (2016), so to say, but also place in an overarching Pant (2013) framework that turns the Russian policy regarding the other four BRICS powers into a test of their capacity for great power management. I shall argue that the Russian geopolitical driver is a liability even from BRICS' own perspective on the world order due to the Kremlin's obsession with balancing, which borders on disruption, as exemplified by cyber attacks (Windrem, 2016). The problem is not one that diminishes over time, on the contrary. Indeed, Russia is replacing soft balancing (Pape, 2005) with proxy wars, hard balancing and revisionism (Mead, 2014). Moreover, China may begin to take its cue from Russia regarding the resort to offensive means and ends. In addition, the bilateral Russia-China relationship contains a power transition drama of its own (Shaku, 2017).

I shall take on the Russian claim of having masterminded the BRICS great power concert quoted at the outset by process tracing BRICS back to the "RIC" concept of the late Russian Foreign Minister Evgeny Primakov, which refers to the troika Russia-India-China. I continue by going into the 21st century Russian BRICS diplomacy, highlighting Russian President Putin's 2012 and 2013 agendas for Russia and for BRICS. In the process, I shall dwell on Russian proxy wars against the U.S. in Russia's post-Soviet neighborhood as well as on Russia's unilateral intervention into the Syrian civil war and the concomitant "silence of the BRICS", to quote Indian ex-Minister and pundit Jaswant Singh (2014). I trace an evolution from a bullish to a more bearish Russian approach to BRICS and continue by going into the broader world order context, highlighting the Russian grand strategy. This will lead me to the concluding section, in which I assess the actual performance of the BRICS great power concert. As already indicated, my yardstick for measuring the global performance of BRICS is their exercise of prudence operationalized as their capacity for long-term great power management vis-à-vis Russia. I therefore begin by presenting this reasoning within the International Society tradition, following which I turn to the neorealist logic of balancing and some insightful realist criticisms of the equally realist power transition theory.

Great powers as managers of peace and security vs. the logic of balancing and power transition

The concept International Society implies a more or less mature anarchy based on fundamental institutions: sovereignty, balance of power, war, etc. Hedley Bull's understanding of the very term *great power* presupposes this qualitative twist as opposed to the Hobbesian term *international system* (Bull, 1977: 202). According to Bull, great powers enjoy special rights and duties in that they "[determine] the issues that affect the peace and security of the international system" (loc. cit.). The practical expression of these extraordinary rights and duties is these great powers' permanent membership of the United Nations' Security Council, says Bull. This privilege was granted to Russia immediately after the dissolution of the Soviet Union on 25 December 1991, meaning that Russia was granted once and for all the power to veto decisions on world security affairs. Moreover, Bull expects great powers in this exclusive sense to be "*modifying* their policies in the light of the managerial responsibilities they bear" (ibid.; my italics). This managerial role based on constraint is what Bull understands by a superpower (ibid.: 203). In a similar vein, Adam Watson (1992: 14) proposes the concept *raison de système* defined as "the belief that it pays to make the system work" in contrast to the opportunistic, short-sighted *raison d'état*.

China and the other non-Russian BRICS powers do occasionally pursue the *raison de système* as they are export-oriented developing economies practising state capitalism and hence depending upon stability in the world economy (Skak ed., 2010; Armijo and Roberts, 2014). Russia, by contrast, may best be termed an alienated modern state, as held by the Finnish scholar Tomas Ries (Skak, 2013: 88f.). However, all BRICS nations resent the unfair distribution of power within the Bretton Woods institutions, etc. and thus also practice some balancing against the United States in the shape of soft balancing (Skak, 2011). This, then, is the topic toward which I shall now turn.

When analyzing Russia's abandonment of its former benign practices of balancing for the sake of hard balancing and revisionism, I rely on the reformulation of the neorealist argument about balancing offered by Robert Pape (2005). To him, U.S. unipolarity and the American high-tech revolution in military affairs signal the end of hard, i.e. military, balancing against the dominant great power. What remains is *soft balancing* as the only option of thwarting U.S. global agendas. Pape identifies four distinctive ways of balancing softly:

- territorial denial
- entangling diplomacy
- economic strengthening
- signals of resolve to balance

(Pape, 2005: 36f.)

The first bullet point refers to denying the U.S. access to bases, a policy pursued by Brazil during the U.S. drug war against Colombia. Entangling diplomacy is often what occurs inside the United Nations' Security Council, namely when Russia and China veto Western proposals. Economic strengthening is synonymous with geo-economics, a term for economic statecraft pioneered by Edward N. Luttwak (1990). However, the crux of the matter concerning Russia is the last category, i.e. signals of resolve to balance, because, according to Pape, soft balancing may ultimately turn hard. One obvious step up the escalation ladder are proxy wars and hybrid types of warfare emerging from a neorealist zero-sum strategic culture, i.e. the pursuit of hawkish *raison d'etat* at the expense of *raison de système*.

The reason why Pape's opening toward a return to hard balancing and overt great power rivalry is critical for understanding the Russian case relates to the context of power transition, or rather: a cogent criticism of the mainstream power transition theory. I have in mind Steve Chan (2008: 61–62), who argues against the widely held idea that China as a rising power would launch war against the declining power, in casu the U.S. Only the opposite scenario makes sense: That the declining power launches war based on a simple "better war now than later" calculation, as also maintained by Jack Levy (1987). Russia has an unreformed resource curse economy and a dwindling population and hence represents a case of decline, except in military terms (Sutela, 2014). Russia's slide into aggression may thus be interpreted as partly despair – exploiting the windows of opportunity for autonomous action before the onset of Chinese hegemony over Eurasia (Lukin, 2015).

The soft balancing origins of BRICS: Primakov's RIC concept

It is a well-known fact that Putin is an ex-KGB colonel; it is much less known that Primakov served as a KGB general before he became Head of Russian Foreign Espionage (SVR). Accordingly, Primakov personified a "Chekist" strategic culture of upholding regime security and balancing against the U.S. (Skak, 2016). As an enlightened Eurasianist, he coined the RIC concept of cooperation among the big three in this region, i.e. Russia, India, and China in the mid-1990s while serving as Minister of Foreign Affairs. RIC cooperation, however, was mainly a non-starter due to for instance Sino-Indian grievances stemming from the 1962 war. As Primakov never published his vision, little is known about this, except for the revival of Eurasian ideology at home in Russia, which set the scene for this Primakov venture into entangling diplomacy. Thus, when presenting his plan for the Kremlin elites in 1996, Primakov offered a three-way strategic pivot between Russia, India, and, China, which amounted to a doctrine of multipolarity (Simha, 2015).

According to one fan of Primakov, he argued that the RIC troika would allow "protection for free-minded nations not allied to the West" (ibid.). Hereby Primakov anticipated today's Russian distinction between "truly sovereign states", counting only the BRICS nations, and "subservient countries" such as Denmark and France (Vanin, 2014; cf. Herd, In press). Moreover, Primakov articulated the Russian grand strategy of territorial denial concerning NATO expansion (Skak, 1996: 140). He invested his own person in snubbing NATO and the U.S. during the Kosovo crisis by turning his aircraft around mid-air en route to Washington DC. But he never went into overt hard balancing, i.e. direct military confrontation with the U.S. Instead, he wanted internal balancing – building up Russian economic and military strength from within. In all of this, Primakov was a mentor for Putin and invented his slogans, such as "all-vector foreign policy" and "multipolarity". Putin's Russia pays respect to the legacy from Primakov by citing RIC cooperation along with BRICS, CIS, SCO, and G20 in its current National Security Strategy (2015, §88). Remarkably, the recent Russian foreign policy concept dwells only on RIC cooperation, not on BRICS, by stating: "Russia considers it necessary to continue the further development of the mechanism for efficient and mutually beneficial foreign policy and practical cooperation in the RIC format" (Kontseptsia vneshnei politiki . . ., 2016, §86).

This may reflect reality: RIC cooperation continues, but only in the shape of annual foreign minister meetings, meaning that the Ministry is entrusted with only minor business. Given the thorny issue of next-door Afghanistan, this ritualistic outcome certainly vindicates Pant (2013). Nowadays, Russia itself appears to be arming the Taliban (Rasmussen, 2017; Rowlatt, 2018).

The onset of Russian BRICS diplomacy

The coining of the BRICS acronym by the Goldman Sachs analyst Jim O'Neill back in 2001 as shorthand for the non-Western economic powerhouses was soon seized upon by Putin. According to the Russian Dossier (2017), Putin invited the first ministerial meeting among the BRICS nations in the wings of the United Nations General Assembly on 20 September 2006. Likewise, Simha (2015) depicts a RIC diplomacy on the sidelines of global summits that was later expanded to include Brazil. Jørgen Dige Pedersen (2018), a scholarly expert on India, stresses that India wanted Brazil on board, reflecting India's preference for the IBSA forum uniting the Global South democracies of India, Brazil, and South Africa. Simha (2015) argues that even without the O'Neill spin, the BRICS concert would have been born, hereby confirming Russia's role as the real driver behind the forum – a purely geopolitical driver at that as O'Neill saw Russia as no economic powerhouse. This was also the point in an analysis of the world manufacturing export performance of Brazil, Russia, India, China, Turkey, and the U.S. made by the eminent British economist Julian Cooper (2006).

As for Putin's own soft balancing against the U.S. and its European allies, compare the following statement from his famous speech at the Wehrkunde conference in Munich:

> The combined GDP measured in purchasing power parity of countries such as India and China is already greater than that of the United States. And a similar calculation with the GDP of the BRIC countries Brazil, Russia, India and China surpasses the cumulative GDP of the EU. According to experts, this gap will only increase in the future. There is no reason to doubt that the economic potential of the new centres of global economic growth will inevitably be converted into political influence and will strengthen multipolarity.
>
> (Putin, 2007)

Accordingly, it was no coincidence that Russia hosted the first official BRICS summit in 2009 in the Siberian city Yekaterinburg, celebrating "the post-American world". The world economic crisis did inspire some great power crisis management by BRICS, which marked the strenghtening of the financial muscles of the IMF decided at the London summit of the G20 in April 2009. Prior to this, however, cracks began to appear in the BRICS building, insofar as none of Russia's newfound great power allies extended diplomatic recognition to South Ossetia and Abkhazia, two Russia-sponsored breakaway republics created through the brief Georgian-Russian war of August 2008. Although the Georgian party was not without guilt, Russia's resort to arms shook security experts because of the context, i.e. the April 2008 meeting of NATO defense ministers that shelved NATO membership for Georgia and Ukraine (Atarodi, 2008). Insofar as only the U.S. was pushing for their entry into NATO, the Russian warfare qualified as a prime case of proxy warfare in continuation of "signals of resolve to balance". All the more interesting, then, that China openly defied Kremlin's lobbying on behalf of South Ossetia and Abkhazia in the Shanghai Cooperation Organization (de Coning et al. (eds.), 2014: 175). Putin appeared to conclude that Russian was bereft of soft power, a power repository often associated with Brazil.

In a speech whose title translates into "Russia and the changing world", Putin argued that the Arab Spring demonstrated the power of new communication and information technologies, turning these into instruments of domestic and international politics (Putin, 2012). He juxtaposed normal political life in BRICS with the instrumental use of soft power through the working of "pseudo-NGOs" or "influence agents of the great powers", as he termed them. For Putin, soft power is no bottom-up, spontaneous magic surrounding a given state akin to some humans' sex appeal, but a state tool. This is evident in his definition of the concept: "Soft power is the complex of instruments and methods for the achievement of foreign policy goals without using weapons" (ibid.). The dramatic climax in the speech was Putin's condemnation of the killing of Gaddafi in the context of NATO's armed intervention in Libya. In Putin's words, the execution represented a shocking, "pre-Medieval apotheosis" (Putin, 2012). The problem is Putin's neglect of local Arab agency and the fact that UN Secretary General Ban Ki Moon rejected that NATO had overstepped its Libya mandate (Charbonneau, 2011). Nevertheless, Putin's and the entire Russian elite's misperceptions of cause and effect in Libya came to be shared by diplomats representing the other BRICS nations (ibid.). Putin seems to have taken the murder of Gaddafi on 20th December 2011 so much to heart that it amounted to a near-death experience for himself (cf. Bryanski, 2011). The reason is that the Arab Spring happened to coincide with large protest demonstrations against Putin's hold on power back in Moscow and St. Petersburg during the winter of 2011–2012. On this occasion, Putin misperceived in a similar manner the moral backing of U.S. Secretary of State Hilary Clinton of the demonstrations as full-blown interference aimed at bringing about regime change, the absolute red line in Kremlin's thinking (Skak, 2016).

In any event, it is worth noticing the revisionist turn in Russian foreign and security policies as a reaction to this new wave of so-called color revolutions. Putin's operational agenda for Russia became a counter-offensive of non-military warfare against Western agendas – an aggressive use of cyber and internet media technologies. Hereby Putin (2012) anticipated the subsequent "Gerasimov doctrine" of hybrid war as well as the design of the intervention in Ukraine in 2014 and onwards (Windrem, 2016). In short, a radicalization of the Russian practice of balancing. Already in 2007, Russia was the likely principal behind the cyber attack hitting Estonia, and cyber attacks for the sake of forcing not just Georgia, but also Kyrgyzstan to territorial denial are on the list (ibid.).

Emboldened by the BRICS consensus on holding NATO responsible for whatever happened in Libya, Putin now began to push for turning BRICS into a geopolitical, security policy forum. Prior to the yearly BRICS summit in March 2013, Putin endorsed a formal *Concept on the Russian Federation's Participation in the BRICS Association Cooperation*, reflecting his unique ambition and enthusiasm about BRICS; this document seems to no longer be publicly available. During the BRICS summit held in the South African city of Durban, he announced a vision of turning the great power club into a full-blown concert capable of coordinating policy on the conflicts in Syria and Afghanistan, and Iran's nuclear program (*The Moscow Times*, 24 March 2013). In Putin's words, BRICS should become "a full-scale strategic cooperation mechanism" (ibid.; *ITAR-TASS*, 22 March 2013) – a vision for great power management on Russian terms, as it were. However, the other BRICS nations were lukewarm as their priority for BRICS cooperation remained geo-economics (Skak, 2010), and so the outcome of the Durban summit was the practical preparation of the New Development Bank, launched officially at the subsequent BRICS summit in Fortaleza, Brazil.

At this point, the reader may already have observed the curious nexus between Russian domestic and foreign policies as the backdrop for Russian BRICS diplomacy. This is also discernible in the 2013 BRICS policy doctrine. The Concept turned Russia's cooperation with BRICS into a strategic, long-term direction of Russian foreign policy which was instrumental in bolstering Russia's standing in world affairs. In line with Putin's top-down approach to soft power, the BRICS Concept cited the broadening of Russia's "Russian language-based linguistic, cultural and information presence" as its target (Utverzhdena kontseptsiya . . ., 2013). Thus, it is no coincidence that the chairman of the Russkiy Mir society, which advances the cause of the Russian language worldwide, is a Kremlin mouthpiece on BRICS affairs (Nikonov, 2013). Only as a secondary priority did the Concept highlight geo-economic concerns such as stimulation of Russian exports, investment cooperation, and the pursuance of common trade interests. Also in 2013, Russia issued a foreign policy doctrine that highlighted soft power – in practice meaning soft balancing – as a Russian concern along with a new geopolitical emphasis on BRICS cooperation.

It was replaced by an outright hawkish foreign policy concept in 2016 that reserved for Russia the right to reciprocate U.S. measures in an asymmetrical way (Kontseptsia . . ., 2016, §72). Comparing the BRICS discourse in the 2013 foreign policy concept to similar phrases in the 2016 document, Russian experts conclude that the Kremlin has downgraded BRICS cooperation (Khlopyanova, 2016). Indeed, the Russian National Security Strategy (2015) and the Economic Security Strategy (2017) contain only ritualistic mentioning of BRICS. What lay between the euphoria of 2013 and the cooling of it now was the Russian resort to arms in Ukraine and Syria as a climax in hard balancing, bringing back the Kremlin preoccupation with the U.S. (Herd, In press).

The evolution within Russian BRICS policy since 2013: from bullish to bearish

During the spring of 2014, the BRICS nations supported Russia in its conflict with Ukraine over the Kremlin's breach of international law and the Budapest Memorandum of 1994 when annexing Crimea (Yost, 2015). Thus, the aforementioned Nikonov headed the Russian delegation to the 6th BRICS academic forum in Rio de Janeiro, telling journalists that "no word" was uttered "to denounce Russia for including Crimea and the city of Sebastopol into the federation" (*Russia beyond* . . ., 2014). He declared the meeting's focus to be information security, following the Snowden revelations "that brought to light bugging of Brazilian President Dilma Rousseff's phones" (ibid.). BRICS did contemplate an alternative internet and an underwater cable from Vladivostok to Fortaleza slated for completion by mid-2015, but it was never completed and has since been quietly shelved (Lee, 2016). To the same extent as the Brazilians were indignated by the digital eavesdropping of the NSA, they may have had second thoughts about the Russian conduct in Ukraine. Well-informed Russian interlocutors later told me that the Russians were furious about their unceremonial reception by their Brazilian hosts at the official BRICS summit in Fortaleza in mid-July 2014. Coinciding with the summit, a Malaysian Airways passenger jet operating flight MH17 was shot down over separatist-held eastern Ukraine. The fatal missile was fired either by the Russian-sponsored separatists or from positions in Russia proper as recently revealed. The disaster killed some 300 civilians, but BRICS kept silent about the Kremlin's obvious complicity.

This awkward "silence of the BRICS" was lambasted in one op-ed written by the Indian former statesman-turned-pundit Jaswant Singh (2014). In his words, the MH17 disaster "echoed the 1914 assassination of Archduke Franz Ferdinand in its recklessness" (ibid.). While not being uncritical about the Western response, Singh stressed that "the reaction of the world's rising powers has been one of willful blindness". He concluded in terms of Bull's great power duty to manage world order:

> When the foundations of the global order are threatened great powers must not adopt a policy of inaction and silence. For their part, emerging powers like India, Brazil, South Africa and Turkey must [. . .] loudly and categorically defend the fundamental rules of the international system that has enabled them to grow and prosper.
>
> (Singh, 2014)

Notwithstanding this, BRICS reacted angrily to Australia's campaign for ostracizing Russia at the G20 summit later that year. Furthermore, the following year's BRICS summit hosted by Russia itself in Ufa was business as usual and announced The Strategy for the BRICS Economic Partnership. It moved forward on security issues including information and communication security, e.g. in the shape of the Soviet-invented GLONASS and the China-invented BeiDou alternatives to GPS. Russia pushed for the BRICS undersea cable, but Brazil opted out for fiscal reasons (Ozores, 2015). Then, on 30 September 2015, Russia began its armed intervention into the Syrian civil war in order to save the Assad regime hereby waging another proxy war against the United States (Stent, 2016). In 2014, in the context of the Russian intervention in Ukraine, U.S. President Barack Obama perhaps fatally called Russia a mere "regional power". Given that the Middle East used to be the turf of the superpower, Obama's term may unintentionally have pushed Putin into the out of area-military escalation. The Syrian case, in turn, represents no routine hardening of Russian balancing, but became notorious in terms of civilian casualties, as documented by Amnesty International.

The other BRICS nations continued to not publicly criticize their Russian partner and let Russia frame the Syria discourse – and by implication the fate of Syria – as concluded by Adriana Erthal Abdenur (2016). Meanwhile, the Goa summit in 2016 among the BRICS powers revealed serious BRICS fatigue in the host nation India.

Indian pundits continue to see BRICS as failing in terms of counter-terrorism, as during the summit, Russia and China refused to endorse India's anti-terrorist message, which was largely aimed at Pakistan (Saran, 2016; Stratfor, 2017). Similarly, Kremlin-critical Russian media portrayed the Goa summit as the most difficult in BRICS' history because of the Beijing-New Delhi tension (*Kommersant*, 14 October 2016). Furthermore, Russia itself is courting both Pakistan and the Taliban, as pointed out previously. Russian experts perceive Brazil and South Africa as preoccupied with domestic trouble, and Chinese sources condemn India's flirtation with the West. American expert on Russian BRICS policy Rachel S. Salzman (2017) puts her finger on stronger defense ties between India and the U.S. and also mentions the Indian anxiety over Sino-Russian intimacy. What is more, Andrey Kortunov, Director of the Russian International Affairs Council, dismisses the entire idea of a BRICS alternative to Western institutions as illusory (*Kommersant*, 14 October, 2016).

The broader strategic context of Russian BRICS policy

Kortunov's critical assessment is telling in several ways. It reveals that Russian scholarly experts realize the limits to BRICS cooperation, not least now that China's power and clashes of interest are becoming tangible even in faraway Brazil (Leite and Li, 2018). It further suggests certain ambiguities in the Russian grand strategy of balancing against the United States and the liberal West. As maintained by one cogent Estonian observer of Russian foreign and security policy, Russia is "part of the same connected ecosystem" consisting of Western democracies and does not want to abandon this for good, notwithstanding current confrontations and disruption (Liik, 2017: 12). Russia depends on the predictability that stems from a rule-based world order for the sake of having "laws that can be broken", as Kadri Liik writes, because the latter represents the Russian great power DNA (ibid.: 9; cf. Clunan, 2018). Like the other BRICS nations, Russia is a consumer of the current world order and hence does not believe in alternative world order projects. The Kremlin considers the Soviet alternative political system to have been doomed from the beginning. This is not to say that the clash between Russia and the liberal European Union and NATO is not serious – it certainly is, due to the Kremlin disrespect for the sovereignty of small states.

As for Russia's real grand strategy, Putin may have toyed with the idea of creating "Moscow's own solar system", as held by the Russian scholar Dmitri Trenin already in 2005 when, according to Putin (2017) himself, Russia launched its BRICS initiative – immediately following the original color revolution in Ukraine (cf. Salzman, 2015: 9). Salzman (ibid.) also has a point when positing BRICS as Russia's "battering ram against the West", but not when arguing that Russia has left the West for good. The onset of Western sanctions upon the annexation of Crimea certainly led Russian diplomats to cite BRICS as a geopolitical bulwark (Vanin, 2014; Lukyanov, 2015). Putin continues to attend BRICS summits and to enjoy their prestige. However, journalists and scholars alike often forget how deeply U.S.-centric Russian foreign and security policy really is – not least in times of hardened strategic rivalry with Washington D.C. According to Graeme Herd (In Press), Putin's operational code is structured around the U.S. as "Russia's strategic benchmark" for the country's entire great power identity. Tellingly, Nikolay Patrushev, another "Chekist" Kremlin decision-maker in charge of the Russian National Security Council, reacted to the election of Donald Trump as President of the United States by proposing direct links between his forum and its American counterpart (*Reuters*, 16 January 2017) – in effect proposing something akin to the Gavrilov channel between the Soviet KGB and the CIA. Later, in reaction to the Trump Administration's strengthening of its sanctions against Russia, its hawkish National Security Strategy of December 2017, and Putin's equally hawkish follow-up on 1 March 2018 (BBC, 2018), Patrushev called for an outright offensive Russian foreign policy (Patrushev, 2018).

Underneath this grand strategy of pursuing the case of Russian greatpowerhood, or rather parity with the United States, there is another more operational grand strategy of ensuring regime security reflecting the "Chekist" strategic cultural DNA. This is what has been indicated through my analysis concerning Putin's Gaddafi trauma and the Ukrainian color revolution context for Putin's BRICS initiative of 2005. Several Russian scholars offer the same interpretation of the operational Kremlin priorities (Schelin, 2016; Gel'man, 2016; cf. *Kontseptsia*, 2016, §26). The implication is that like BRICS, Russia is revisionist and post-Western for purely domestic, opportunistic and, indeed, defensive reasons, but is still dangerously revisionist and disruptive in its great power practices (Yost, 2015). In other words, BRICS cooperation is more of a sideshow, a derivative of the Kremlin instinct of balancing and not in itself a grand strategy for Russia. This reflects the fact that the Kremlin is a deeply geopolitical actor locked in on U.S.-, NATO- and EU-centric foreign and security policy agendas, which is not the case of Brazil, India, and South Africa, or even China, let alone the rest of the Global South.

This does not mean, however, that BRICS cooperation is without momentum nowadays, but it is becoming tricky to capture the Kremlin's true priorities. A case in point is the new emphasis on BRICS cooperation between national secret services, a field in which Patrushev and Putin are cooperating closely, for instance at the BRICS meeting in Moscow in May 2015 on the topic, as displayed on press photos (*Reuters*, 16 January 2017). The formerly quoted Russian Dossier (2017) considers such "meetings of representatives monitoring questions of national security" a regular BRICS activity, and exactly intelligence cooperation was on China's agenda for the 2017 Xiamen summit. The preceding so-called Fuzhou Initiative (2017) called for not just intelligence sharing, but capacity building and cyber-security cooperation. Given Russia's and China's own record of cyber attacks, this is hardly good news from a world order perspective (Domingo, 2016).

According to Russian independent media, Patrushev's forum is proceeding with the development of a separate internet for BRICS. Putin further ordered his government to draw up a specific proposal by August 2018 (*Meduza*, 28 November 2017). Yet, academic experts perceive a BRICS divide on internet governance consisting of the three democracies India, Brazil, and South Africa versus the authoritarian duo China and Russia (Hurel and Santoro, 2018). What is more, Russian experts on the "Chekists" are deeply skeptical about the Kremlin's willingness to abandon the U.S.-invented internet, which is well known after all. Kremlin pundits did once hail "international and political escalations and the bifurcation into a Western world of decline" as benefitting the BRICS' "comprehensive global project" along with the "Moscow-Beijing axis" (Lukyanov, 2015). However, as for the security, intelligence, and cyber-security cooperation between Russia and China observed by Stratfor (2017), other experts on Russian and Chinese intelligence are silent on such practices, as are Western intelligence insiders (Oleson, 2016), leaving one in doubt about their actual significance. In short, one must exercise "Quellenkritik" concerning Russia and BRICS and beware of possible token signals of resolve to balance and of tangible, mostly Russian, escalation into hard balancing. As I have argued throughout, one overarching problem here is the other BRICS nations' complicity in it all.

Concluding thoughts on Russia, BRICS, and the great power management of world order

Admittedly, my analysis is biased toward exposing the offensive dimension of the Russian BRICS policy. However, the bias is necessary for the sake of raising attention to the Russian slide away from Primakov's soft balancing into hard balancing and revisionism, which is threatening both the world order and the cohesion among BRICS nations. As suggested in my earlier remarks on power transition theory, Russia's military interventionism and non-military aggression may be intimately related to Russia's decline and geographic location next to a rising Asia and China. However, there is little comfort in this interpretation as the radical turn in Kremlin policy dismantled the other BRICS nations' instinct for great power management in the understanding of Hedley Bull (1977: 202f.). On this account, the verdicts of Pant (2013) and Singh (2014) quoted previously are not outdated. To take the Russian annexation of Crimea, this was and remains a flagrant violation of international law as Russia itself happened to guarantee the integrity of Ukraine's borders in the Budapest memorandum of 1994 (Yost, 2015) in continuation of the *Uti Possidetis Iuris* principle guiding processes of decolonization. Moreover, the subsequent Russian intervention in Syria turns the R2P principle of 2005 upside down.

The curious fact about Russia as a pioneer and geopolitical driver of BRICS cooperation is that as regards grand strategy, the Kremlin priorities are regime security and strategic parity with the U.S., along with a focus on Europe. In a contradictory manner, Russia is "deeply legalistic" (Liik, 2017). Furthermore, whatever priority is attached to BRICS cooperation, Russian doctrines and strategy papers reveal that Moscow is a multitasking, forum-shopping actor that ultimately attaches much greater priority to the United Nations Security Council than to BRICS (*Kontseptsia*, 2016, §24).

The acrimony surrounding the Goa summit in 2016 suggests some climaxing of BRICS cooperation amidst apparent internet, intelligence, and cyber cooperation. The latter trend reflects China's agenda marketed through her Fuzhou Initiative (2017).

Still, China is also displaying great power responsibility and world order management in the shape of her battle against climate change, advancing this issue as a common BRICS cause (Aneja, 2017; cf. the Fuzhou Initiative). If I were to update Lo (2016), I would say that whereas Russia has been using its closing power transition window of opportunity to pull BRICS cooperation in the archaic direction of geopolitics, China may guarantee a future correction of the course for the benefit of more holistic climate change geo-economics. Given the regime security impulses of these two authoritarian anchors behind the BRICS great power concert, their disruptive zero-sum thinking may be what remains, however.

References

Abdenur, Adriana Erthal (2016) "Rising Powers and International Security: The BRICS and the Syrian Conflict." *Rising Powers Quarterly*, 1(1): 109–133.

Aneja, Atul (2017) "BRICS Must Write the Rules of a New Wave of Globalisation: Fuzhou Initiative." *The Hindu*, June 16. Available at www.thehindu.com/news/international/brics-must-write-the-rules-of-a-new-wave-of-globalisation-fuzhou-initiative/article19086713.ece.

Armijo, Leslie E., and Cynthia Roberts (2014) "The Emerging Powers and Global Governance: Why the BRICS Matter." In Robert Looney (ed.) *Handbook of Emerging Economies*, New York: Routledge.

Atarodi, Alexander (2008) *Det kaukasiska lackmustestet: konsekvenser och lärdomar av det rysk-georgiska kriget i augusti 2008*. Försvarsanalys. Totalförsvarets forskningsinstitut. Book available as E-book (editor: Robert L. Larsson). Stockholm: FOI.

BBC (2018) "Russia's Putin Unveils 'Invincible' Nuclear Weapons." March 1. Available at www.bbc.com/news/world-europe-43239331.

Bryanski, Gleb (2011) "Putin: Libya Coalition Has No Right to Kill Gaddafi." *Reuters*, April 26. Available at www.reuters.com/article/us-russia-putin-libya/putin-libya-coalition-has-no-right-to-kill-gaddafi-idUSTRE73P4L920110426.

Bull, Hedley (1977) *The Anarchical Society: A Study of Order in World Politics*. London: Macmillan.

Buzan, Barry, and George Lawson (2014) "Capitalism and the Emergent World Order." *International Affairs*, 90(1): 71–91.

Chan, Steve (2008) *China, the U.S. and the Power Transition Theory: A Critique*. London: Routledge.

Charbonneau, Louis (2011) "U.N. Chief Defends NATO from Critics of Libya War." *Reuters*, December 14. Available at www.reuters.com/article/us-libya-nato-un-idUSTRE7BD20C20111214.

Clunan, Anne L. (2018) "Russia and the Liberal World Order." *Ethics and International Affairs*, 32(1): 45–59.

Cooper, Julian (2006) "Can Russia Compete in the Global Economy?" *Eurasian Geography and Economics*, 47(4): 407–425.

de Coning, Cedric, Thomas Mandrup, and Liselotte Odgaard (eds.) (2014) *The BRICS and Coexistence: An Alternative Vision of World Order*. Abingdon: Routledge.

Domingo, Francis C. (2016) "China's Engagement in Cyber Space." *Journal of Asian Security and International Affairs*, 3(2): 245–259.

Dossier (2017) "Uchastie Rossii v BRIKS. Dosye." Russian Ministry of Foreign Affairs. Available at https://brics.mid.ru/rossia-v-briks.

Economic Security Strategy (2017) *Ukaz Prezidenta Rossiiskoi Federatsii O Strategii ekonomicheskoi bezopasnosti Rossiiskoi Federatsii na period do 2030 goda*. Moskva, Kreml' 13 maya 2017 goda.

Fuzhou Initiative (2017) "15-Point Document." Available at http://ris.org.in/fidc/sites/default/files/Fushou_Initiative.pdf.

Gel'man, Vladimir (2016) "The Politics of Fear: How Russia's Rulers Counter Their Rivals." *Russian Politics*, 1(1): 27–45.

Herd, Graeme (In Press) "Characterizing President Putin's Operational Code." In Roger E. Kanet (ed.) *Routledge Handbook of Russian Security*. Abingdon: Routledge.

Hurel, Louise Marie, and Mauricio Santoro (2018) "Brazil, China and Internet Governance: Mapping Divergence and Convergence." *Journal of China and International Relations*, 6(1): 98–115.

ITAR-TASS (2013) "Interview to the ITAR-TASS news agency." March 22. Available at, http://en.kremlin.ru/events/president/news/17723.

Khlopyanova, Ol'ga (2016) "Sravnenie Kontseptsii vneshniei politiki Rossiiskoi Federatsii 2013 I 2016. Ekspertnye Otsenki." *Vneshpolitekspert*, December 22.

Knudsen, Tonny Brems (2014) "Danish Contributions in Syria and Mali: Active Internationalism in a Changing World Order." In Nanna Hvidt and Hans Mouritzen (eds.) *Danish Foreign Policy Yearbook 2014*. Copenhagen: Danish Institute for International Studies.

Kommersant (2016) "BRICS Becomes Excessively Multipolar, Losing Weight." October 14, reprinted by *Johnson's Russia List*.

Kontseptsia (2016) *Kontseptsia vneshnei politiki Rossiiskoi Federatsii* (utverzhdena Prezidentom Rossiiskoi Federatsii V.V. Putinim 30 noyabria 2016 g). Available at http://publication.pravo.gov.ru/document/view/0001201612010045?index=1&rangeSize=1.

Lee, Stacia (2016) "International Reactions to U.S. Cybersecurity Policy: The BRICS Undersea Cable." *The Henry M. Jackson School of International Studies*, January 8. Available at https://jsis.washington.edu/news/reactions-u-s-cybersecurity-policy-bric-undersea-cable/.

Leite, Alexandre Cesar Cunha, and Li Xing (2018) "Introduction: China and Brazil at BRICS: Same Bed, Different Dreams?" *Journal of China and International Relations*, 6(1): i–vii.

Levy, Jack S. (1987) "Declining Power and the Preventive Motivation for War." *World Politics*, 40(1): 82–107.

Liik, Kadri (2017) "What Does Russia Want? Commentary." *European Council on Foreign Relations*, May 26. Available at www.ecfr.eu/article/commentary_what_does_russia_want_7297.

Lo, Bobo (2016) "The Illusions of Convergence: Russia, China, and the BRICS." *Russia. Nei.Visions No. 92*, March, 27 pp., Russia/NIS Center at IFRI, Paris.

Lukin, Artyom (2015) "Mackinder Revisited: Will China Establish Eurasian Empire 3.0?" *The Diplomat*, February 7. Available at https://thediplomat.com/2015/02/mackinder-revisited-will-china-establish-eurasian-empire-3-0/.

Lukyanov, Fyodor (ed.) (2015) "War and Peace in the 21st Century: International Stability and Balance of a New Type." *Valdai Discussion Club Report*. Available at http://valdaiclub.com/files/9635/.

Luttwak, Edward N. (1990) "From Geopolitics to Geo-Economics." *The National Interest*, 20: 17–23.

Mead, Walter Russell (2014) "The Return of Geopolitics: The Revenge of the Revisionist Powers." *Foreign Affairs*, May–June: 69–79.

Meduza (2017) "Russia's Security Council Tells the Government to Develop a Separate Internet for the BRICS." November 28. Available at https://meduza.io, reprinted by *Jonhson's Russia List*.

The Moscow Times (2013) "Putin BRICS Preamble Speaks of Greater Geopolitical Role." March 24. Available at https://themoscowtimes.com/articles/putin-brics-preamble-speaks-of-greater-geopolitical-role-22613.

National Security Strategy (2015) *Russian National Security Strategy*, December 31: Full-Text Translation. Available at www.ieee.es/Galerias/fichero/OtrasPublicaciones/Internacional/2016/Russian-National-Security-Strategy-31Dec2015.pdf.

Nikonov, Vyacheslav (2013) "BRICS: Analyzing the Security Dilemma." *BRICS Information Centre, University of Toronto*. Available at http://brics.utoronto.ca/newsdesk/durban/nikonov.html.

Oleson, Peter C. (ed.) (2016) *AFIO's Guide to the Study of Intelligence*. Falls Church, VA: Association of Former Intelligence Officials.

Ozores, Pedro (2015) "Russia Pushes for BRICS Undersea Cable." *BNAmericas*, October 27. Available at http://www.bnamericas.com/en/news/privatization/russia-pushes-for-brics-underseas-cable.

Pant, Harsh V. (2013) "The BRICS Fallacy." *The Washington Quarterly*, 36(3): 91–105.

Pape, Robert A. (2005) "Soft Balancing against the United States." *International Security*, 30(1): 7–45.

Patrushev, Nikolay (2018) "Russia Needs More Offensive Foreign Policy to Counter US: Security Council Chief." April 28. Available at www.rt.com as reprinted by *Johnson's Russia List*.

Pedersen, Jørgen Dige (2018) *Personal Interview*. Unpublished internal document.

Putin, Vladimir Vladimirovich (2007) "Putin's Prepared Remarks at 43rd Munich Conference on Security Policy." *Washington Post*, February 12. Available at www.washingtonpost.com/wp-dyn/content/article/2007/02/12/AR2007021200555.html??noredirect=on.

Putin, Vladimir Vladimirovich (2012) "Rossia i menyaushchiysya mir." *Moskovskie Novosti*, 27 fevralya.

Putin, Vladimir Vladimirovich (2017) "Vladimir Putin's News Conference Following BRICS Summit." September 5. Available at http://en.kremlin.ru/events/president/news/55535.

Rasmussen, Sune Engel (2017) "Russia Accused of Supplying Taliban as Power Shifts Create Strange Bedfellows." *The Guardian*, October 22. Available at www.theguardian.com/world/2017/oct/22/russia-supplying-taliban-afghanistan.

Reuters (2017) "Russia Ready to Rebuild Security Ties with U.S. under Trump: Putin Ally." January 16. Available at www.reuters.com/article/us-usa-trump-russia-security-idUSKBN1501F3.

Rowlatt, Justin (2018) "Russia 'Arming the Taliban', Says US." *BBC News*. March 23. Available at www.bbc.com/news/world-asia-43500299.

Russia beyond the Headlines (2014) "BRICS Oppose Idea of Unipolar World: Russian MP." March 29. Available at www.rbth.com/world/2014/03/29/brics_oppose_idea_of_unipolar_world_russian_mp_34119.

Salzman, Rachel (2015) "From Bridge to Bulwark: The Evolution of BRICS in Russian Grand Strategy." *Comillas Journal of International Relations*, (3). Available at https://doaj.org/article/c2b4d0095a73434281bfe5043a283b56.

Salzman, Rachel (2017) "Russian and Indian Approaches to BRICS and Global Governance." Wilson Center, March 17. Available at www.kennan-russiafile.org/2017/03/17/russian-and-indian-approaches-to-brics-and-global-governance/.

Saran, Shyam (2016) "Summit over Substance." *The Hindu*, September 17. Available at www.thehindu.com/opinion/lead/Summit-over-substance/article14983858.ece#!.
Schelin, Pavel (2016) "Russian National Security Strategy: Regime Security and Elite's Struggle for 'Great Power' Status." *Slovo*, 28(2): 85–105.
Shaku, Kanat (2017) "China Rising: Beijing Stirs Up Russia's Backyard." *bne IntelliNews*, July 11. Available at www.intellinews.com/china-rising-beijing-stirs-up-russia-s-backyard-125123/.
Simha, Rakesh Krishnan (2015) "Primakov: The Man Who Created Multipolarity." *Russia beyond the Headlines/Rossiiskaya Gazeta*, June 25. Available at www.rbth.com/blogs/2015/06/27/primakov_the_man_who_created_multipolarity_43919.
Singh, Jaswant (2014) "Silence of the BRICS." August 29, Prothom Alo/ Project Syndicate reprinted by NKI BRIKS Rossia. Available at http://nkibrics.ru/posts/show/540089206272691799070000.
Skak, Mette (1996) *From Empire to Anarchy: Postcommunist Foreign Policy and International Relations*. London: Hurst & Co.
Skak, Mette (ed.) (2010) *Fremtidens stormagter. BRIK'erne i det globale spil. Brasilien, Rusland, Indien og Kina*. Aarhus: Aarhus Universitetsforlag.
Skak, Mette (2011) "The BRIC Powers as Soft Balancers: Brazil, Russia, India and China." Paper for the 11th annual Aleksanteri Conference "the Dragon and the Bear: Strategic Choices of Russia and China". Available at the homepage of *BRICS Information Centre, University of Toronto*.
Skak, Mette (2013) "The BRICS and Denmark: Economics and High Politics." In Nanna Hvidt and Hans Mouritzen (eds.) *Danish Foreign Policy Yearbook 2013*. Copenhagen: DIIS.
Skak, Mette (2016) "Russian Strategic Culture: The Role of Today's Chekisty." *Contemporary Politics*, 22(3): 324–341.
Stent, Angela (2016) "Putin's Power Play in Syria." *Foreign Affairs*, 95(1): 106–113.
Stratfor (2017) "For China, BRICS Is a Means to an End." *Reflections*. Available at https://worldview.stratfor.com/article/china-brics-means-end.
Sutela, Pekka (2014) "Russia Shouldn't Expect a Prosperous Future." *Russia in Global Affairs*, September 16. Available at http://eng.globalaffairs.ru/book/Russia-Shouldnt-Expect-a-Prosperous-Future-16970.
Utverzhdena kontseptsiya uchastiya Rossii v BRIKS (2013) *International Centre for Trade and Sustainable Development*, March 21. Available at www.ictsd.org/bridges-news/мосты/news/утверждена-концепция-участия-россии-в-брикс.
Vanin, Mikhail (2014) "Rusland er overhovedet ikke isoleret." *Berlingske Tidende*, interview with the Russian Ambassador to Denmark, November 18. Available at www.b.dk/nationalt/rusland-er-overhovedet-ikke-isoleret.
Watson, Adam (1992) *The Evolution of International Society: A Comparative Historical Analysis*. London and New York: Routledge.
Wigell, Mikael, and Antto Vihma (2016) "Geopolitics versus Geoeconomics: The Case of Russia's Geostrategy and Its Effects on the EU." *International Affairs*, 92(3): 605–627.
Windrem, Robert (2016) "Timeline: Ten Years Russian Cyber Attacks on Other Nations." *NBC News*, December 18. Available at www.nbcnews.com/storyline/hacking-in-america/timeline-ten-years-russian-cyber-attacks-other-nations-n697111.
Yost, David S. (2015) "The Budapest Memorandum and the Russia's Intervention in Ukraine." *International Affairs*, 91(3): 505–538.

10 India – Dreaming with BRICS?

Jørgen Dige Pedersen

The BRICS group has been declared dead and gone several times (Sharma, 2012: Pant, 2013), and the group was met with skepticism from the very beginning due to its heterogeneous character. This chapter will outline the motives and interests of India regarding its membership of BRICS and will thereby contribute to clarifying if and why BRICS may persist well into the future. It will answer questions such as: Why is India a member; what role has it played in the BRICS group; what has it achieved from its membership; will its interest in the group persist, etc.

Not surprisingly, India had a mixture of motives for joining the BRIC group: political and strategic motives, economic motives, ideological motives, all mixed together to form a relatively coherent strategy with clear continuities in relation to India's past policies in the postcolonial era. India is thus a good example of how economic, political, and other motives work together to form a foreign policy strategy.

The chapter is divided into five parts. After setting the scene, part one reviews some of the main recent interpretations of India's rise; part two provides the historical background in India's foreign policy; part three describes the decisive turn in the international environment affecting India's foreign policy: that of the end of the Cold War and the increasing economic globalization. Part four deals with the emergence of the BRICS concept and its transformation into a real-life phenomenon. Part five describes the political economy of India's BRICS relationship. Finally, part six concludes by summing up the argument.

In the beginning of the new century, India took part in the establishment of two sets of trilateral arrangements: one with China and Russia (RIC), another with South Africa and Brazil (IBSA). The key argument in this chapter is that to India, BRICS represents a merger of the two already existing and distinct visions of these trilateral arrangements: the RIC coalition agenda of promoting multipolarity in global security matters, and the IBSA agenda of South-South cooperation on development and economic problems. These two agendas were both formed by India's historical past, its global ambitions and politico-strategic location, and by India's status as a poor developing country in need friends and allies in its quest for economic progress and for a great power status. It is remarkable, however, that motives based upon purely economic interests have played only a minor role.

In theoretical terms, the two agendas of India together represent a combination of a Realist concept of balance of power between major states in the global system on the one hand, and, on the other hand, a concern with advancing the interests of poor countries, inspired by centre-periphery theories. Both theoretical traditions are necessary to understand India's membership of the BRICS coalition.

Recent interpretations of India's rise

Today many observers regard India as a rising power in world affairs, and irrespective of political color, its own political leadership has over time been keen to embrace this image. The rise of India has been ascribed to mainly two different events or trends. According to one interpretation, the rise of India is primarily determined by the decision to openly go nuclear, as demonstrated by the series of nuclear tests in May 1998. This marked both India's ambition to be internationally accepted as a major, nuclear-armed power and demonstrated, of course, that India did indeed possess a military capability enabling it to perform a new and more significant role in world politics. This was the perspective advanced early on by influential scholars of India's foreign policy (Cohen, 2002; Nayar and Paul, 2003; Raja Mohan, 2003). India had "crossed the Rubicon" (Raja Mohan, 2003) or had decisively advanced in its "search for Major-Power Status" (Nayar and Paul, 2003).

The other interpretation of, and key argument for, India being regarded as an emerging power, are found in its economic advancement, which became more evident into the 2000s, when the Indian economy suddenly – and contrary to the expectations of most economic commentators at the time – began to grow at a rate close to 9% per year, starting in 2003. This economic "dream run" (Nagaraj, 2013) lasted for five or six years until the global financial crisis struck the world. Even after the onset of the crisis that also in India initially reduced economic growth rates, the Indian economy continued to surge at rates similar to or even above the growth rates of other "emerging" powers like China and far above the growth displayed by the crisis-ridden Western world. Recent academic writings have tended to view India as an "emerging market" rather than as a strong nuclear military power. One work that otherwise focused mostly on traditional security policy issues even called India's economy "Its Global Calling Card" (Malone, 2011: 75).

I would argue that the sources of India's newfound position as an (emerging) great power are best understood as a combination of primarily its economic advancement and its growing military capabilities, which play a secondary but still important role; its advancements in nuclear and missile technology, in naval power, etc. are also important in this respect (Basrur, 2017: 21f). India's advancement is thus a truly combined political-economic phenomenon that should be understood in political economy terms.

India's traditional foreign policy

The original vision of India and its future held by its founding fathers was that of a free nation. To be free from colonial British rule was the overarching objective of the Indian National Congress. To be a free nation first, and then to be able to advance economically. It was only after that first goal had been achieved that the defining figure of India's foreign policy, its first Prime Minister Jawarharlal Nehru, began to contemplate seriously the future of his newly independent nation. Having worked laboriously on interpreting India's glorious past, Nehru had been thinking less about the role that the new India would and should play in the wider world following independence. However, in his many comparisons with the other great Asian civilization, China, we may see the seed of a firm view that India deserved to play a role similar to that of China (Nehru, 1982). Back in the 1920s, the political movement fighting for independence, the Indian National Congress, had started to formulate the rudiments of a foreign policy (ibid.: Ch. 9) mainly in line with what later became known as the policy of non-alignment as the best way to defend its national interests. (p. 420ff). At this stage, India wanted to become part of the world of Free states (p. 523), and it wanted to play "an important part in world affairs" (p. 535). Shortly before the formal Independence, Nehru had outlined in a radio broadcast the key elements of India's future foreign policy:

> We propose, as far as possible, to keep away from the power politics of groups, aligned against one another. . . . We believe that peace and freedom are indivisible and the denial of freedom anywhere must endanger freedom elsewhere and lead to conflict and war. We are particularly interested in the emancipation of colonial and dependent countries and peoples. . . . We seek no dominion over others and we claim no privileged position over other peoples.
>
> ("Future Taking Shape", Broadcast from New Delhi, 7 September 1946. Nehru, 1961: 2)

In his much-celebrated speech at the dawn of Independence in 1947, Nehru furthermore spoke of India's dreams for the future and of its finding its "rightful place in the world" (ibid.: 14). While this is not spelled out as an explicit strategic goal in the country's foreign policy, there is thus little doubt about India's long-term aspiration to become a great power (Nayar and Paul, 2003).

The global East-West division of the world immediately following India's independence did not make it easy for the new state to achieve its goals. In its foreign policy, India was trying to navigate by following an official policy of Non-Alignment along with many other newly independent developing nations. The goal of achieving economic development was pursued by a policy of self-reliance, which in practice meant trading with both sides of the Cold War divide, state planning and a consistent policy of supporting indigenous entrepreneurs as much as possible vis-à-vis foreign competitors. Non-alignment and the quest for economic self-reliance naturally did not please the US, as these approaches frequently conflicted with the interests of the US government and the interests of US companies. Consequently, the US often sided with India's regional rival, Pakistan, but over time, India and the US did, nevertheless, develop quite strong economic ties without India compromising too much on its goals of economic and political independence.

After all, the political economy strategy of modern mercantilism was hardly unfamiliar to the US, who had developed economically using a similar strategy (Chang, 2002).

India's foreign policy after the Cold War

Fast forward to the collapse of the Soviet Union and the end of the Cold War. With the monumental changes in the global order triggered by these events, India found itself in a difficult situation. Coinciding with an economic crisis, this was a time of fundamental rethinking of both the country's economic strategy and its foreign policy. India was trying to preserve as much as it could of the old order, while simultaneously navigating forward toward great power status in the new circumstances. This would be a trial and error process.

In the economic sphere, the intensification of economic globalization was one of the impulses that led the Indian government to change, from 1991 onwards, its economic strategy away from the earlier state-directed and protective strategy toward an open and more market-oriented strategy without sacrificing the goal of self-reliance and the promotion of Indian-owned and Indian-managed private companies. India also eventually had to accept the new international rules for global trade inscribed into the new World Trade Organization (Pedersen, 2008). This new more open policy toward the global economy provided new opportunities for Indian companies, which increasingly began to invest abroad while establishing partnerships with international companies in their operations within India, most importantly through various forms of technological collaboration. In terms of foreign policy orientation, India tested different options. While generally upholding the basic principles of strategic autonomy and a "friends with all, allied with none" policy, India did establish closer relations with the US, while trying in the Asian region to establish a closer relationship with Southeast Asia (ASEAN) through a new "Look East" policy.

In 1997, a broad segment of the Indian foreign policy community surveyed the options available to India's foreign policy in the new world order and in the coming century. What is remarkable, seen in retrospect, in their assessment of the challenges and opportunities for India's foreign policy under the new circumstances is that none of the participants in the discussion foresaw that India would use the option of openly declaring itself a nuclear-armed power (Mansingh et al., 1997).[1] Nevertheless, this was exactly what the newly elected BJP government did in May 1998, shortly after coming to power. The decision to "cross the Rubicon" (Mohan, 2003) must be interpreted as a forceful application by India to be recognized by the international community as a great power.

The nuclear tests immediately led to reactions from especially Western countries and from Japan, ranging from official condemnation to economic sanctions. Russia's reaction was different, however. When the Russian prime minister at the time, Yevgeny Primakov, visited India later the same year, instead of condemning India, he aired the idea of forming a "strategic triangle" between Russia, India, and China (the RIC group). While positive toward the idea of promoting multipolarity in international affairs, India was hesitant in its response (Pant, 2004, 2006). A few years later, in 2002, however, the RIC group started to hold regular meetings, typically at foreign minister level. This has now become a regular feature of the interaction between the three powers and has been generally interpreted as an attempt to counterbalance the dominance of the US in international affairs (ibid.).[2] Moreover, mainly in the strategic realm, India was for a long time seeking to become a member of the Shanghai Cooperation Organization (SCO) established in 1996/2001 as a kind of quasi-military alliance between Russia, China and the Central Asian republics. In 2015, India was accepted as a full member, together with Pakistan, after a ten-year period as an observer.

In its role as a prominent developing country, India has also been trying to broaden and strengthen its international relations. In 2003, India, together with Brazil and South Africa, created the so-called IBSA Dialogue Forum for closer coordination of the policies of developing counties within various international fora, in particular the WTO and the trade negotiations in this forum (Stephen, 2012). IBSA has since been a forum for regular meetings at the highest political level between the three countries, with the general aim of promoting closer South-South relations.

Thus, around the turn of the century, India was busy realigning its foreign policy in two directions simultaneously, in terms of strategic cooperation and promotion of multipolarity as well as in terms of economic cooperation and development with other large and important countries.

Enter BRICS

It was in this context of India searching for new alliances and friends that the idea of a BRIC grouping of countries emerged. This was first envisaged in a report from Goldman Sachs in 2001 (Goldman Sachs, 2001) and later reported in greater detail (Goldman Sachs, 2003). The basic idea was that four rising powers (Brazil, Russia, India, and China) together were on their way to becoming, in economic terms, as important as, or perhaps more important (or at least larger) than, the leading six Western economies. This notion was received with a great deal of interest in India. Initially, it was mostly in financial circles that the BRIC acronym became known, but policymakers and the broader public soon became aware of the new acronym and its implications for India. The transformation of BRIC from an investment concept within the financial world into a concrete group of countries with regular political meetings was introduced by Russia at foreign minister level in 2006 and from 2009 onwards at annual head of state meetings. For India, BRIC came to represent a convenient merger of its earlier multilateral attempts at joining the RIC and the IBSA countries, respectively. This was of course especially evident from 2011, when South Africa was invited to join the BRIC group, turning it into a BRICS group. The support for multipolarity, the organizing of developing countries and the struggle against Western dominance in international institutions (primarily the World Bank and the IMF) were all elements in India's traditional foreign policy, and they now found a new and clear expression in the creation of the BRICS group. A former foreign secretary bluntly stated in a recent book that "India's best interests are served by its assistance in shaping a multipolar order with the support of other major powers. It should not hesitate in promoting and participating in a countervailing coalition to constrain any aspiring hegemon even while it expands its own economic and military capabilities" (Saran, 2017: 275).

Thus, from an Indian perspective, the BRICS coalition should be seen primarily as a group designed to put pressure on the key Western countries who dominate the Bretton Woods institutions. The joint statement made by the BRIC heads of state at their very first meeting in Yekatarinburg, Russia, in 2009 focused primarily on the international economic situation (financial crisis) and the need of the international financial institutions for governance reforms (read: the Bretton Woods institutions). The institutions needed reform of their governance structure so that they would better reflect the changes in the world economy (read: the rise of the BRIC countries). The statement also supported the demands of developing counties and called for "a more democratic and multipolar world order".[3] The arguments were closely linked to the analysis presented by the Goldman Sachs' reports on these rising economic powers. The subsequent summit meetings, however, broadened the agenda considerably, and the inclusion of South Africa into the group demonstrated a break with the perception of the group as an alliance of rising economies only.[4] From an Indian perspective, the inclusion of an African country that was traditionally closely linked to India was most welcome. Since then, there have been several indications that the inclusion of South Africa in the BRICS group has rendered the IBSA Dialogue Forum almost superfluous. Thus, no summit meetings have been held in the IBSA group since 2011; India was expected to invite the member states to the next meeting and to host this, but has not done so; however, the activities of the group do continue, albeit at lower levels. (For examples, see MEA annual reports).

The key argument here is that the strategy of joining the other members of the BRICS group has thus been perfectly aligned with both India's traditional and emerging foreign policies. One important element in India's new foreign policy – its much closer relationship with the US – is of course not consistent with the BRICS strategy. Moreover, other BRICS members also have coinciding close relationships with the US. Nevertheless, to India it makes perfect sense at the same time to befriend and to oppose selectively the US in order to preserve as much of its own strategic autonomy as possible.

Since the formation of the BRICS group, India has invested increasingly more energy and effort in the activities of the group. The higher priority given by India to the BRICS collaboration is indicated by the frequency with which the acronym is used in the annual reports of India's Ministry of External Affairs, see Figure 10.1. Following an increase in frequency up until around 2012, when India hosted the annual BRICS Summit for the first time, the frequency leveled off for some time and then culminated in 2016–17. This was when India (in 2016) for the second time hosted the BRICS Summit, this time in Goa on the west coast of India. India has also worked to expand the scope of collaboration among the BRICS member

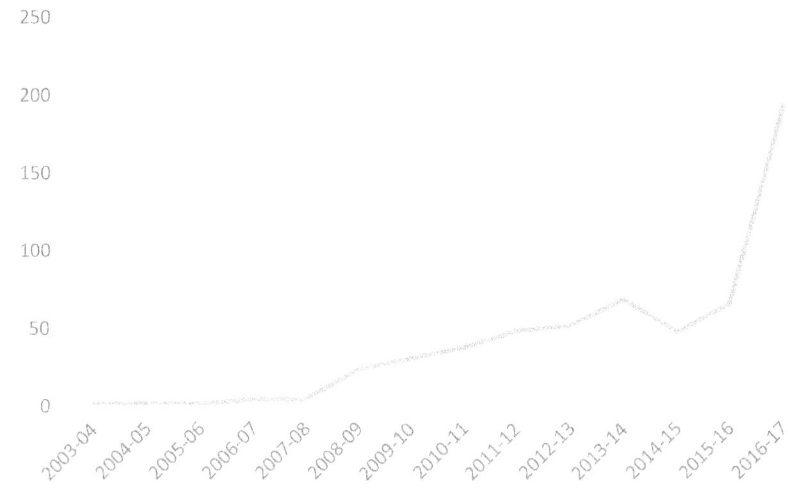

Figure 10.1 Frequency of the BRIC(S) term used in MEA Annual Reports

Source: Ministry of External Affairs, *Annual Report*, New Delhi: various years

countries in an attempt to harvest some of the potential benefits that the five countries might gain by collaborating across a wide range of social and economic activities. The issues and institutions mentioned as suitable for collaboration include national development banks, energy and agricultural issues, academic research, education, environmental issues, telecommunication, and a large number of other issues.[5]

India's interest in these forms of collaboration became evident at the fourth summit meeting, which took place in 2012 in New Delhi, hosted by the Indian government. As BRICS is organized without its own separate secretariat, it falls to the host government to initiate and coordinate the summit statement and the interest of the host country may well be reflected in the content and wording of the statements. For the first time in the BRICS summit history, the Delhi Declaration 2012 was accompanied by a separate Action Plan. Together, the two documents brought the collaboration between the five countries to a new and higher level of activity.

The early issues of international institutions, i.e. global finance and trade and development issues, were expanded to a summit agenda that included issues such as agriculture, education, security, statistics, and health. Now, summit declarations also routinely comment on a broad range of current issues in global politics. One need only mention issues like international piracy, tax evasion, drug control, terrorism, and even the use of outer space! In addition, more contentious issues relating to ongoing international conflicts in Africa and the Middle East, migration issues and, generally, all issues on the current international agenda are routinely mentioned. Even diplomatic phrases on the Ukraine crisis are included.

The foreign ministers of the group also meet regularly on the sidelines of UN meetings (General Assembly), World Bank /IMF meetings, G7/G20 meetings, and other international events. India has also been a very active driver behind the recent initiatives to establish new international institutions under the BRICS umbrella, such as a financial safety net, the Contingency Reserve Arrangement (CRA) to be used in times of crisis, and the New Development Bank (NDB). Both the CRA and the NDB operate in areas previously dominated by the Bretton Woods institutions, the IMF and the World Bank, respectively. At the suggestion of India, the BRICS countries are presently contemplating the creation of their own credit rating agency because of dissatisfaction (India's?) with the credit ratings, which BRICS members experience are biased against them by the dominant Western institutions (Fitch, Moody's, Standard & Poor's).

During the more than ten years that the BRICS group has been working, there have been many discussions, disputes, and clashes of interest, some of which have involved India. In particular, skeptics have always mentioned the troubled relationship between India and China, who have been traditional adversaries since the war in 1962, as a source of instability in the group. The size of China and especially the economic weight of China with a GDP larger than that of the rest of the group combined, has indeed been an issue with which the BRICS countries have had to struggle. The organization of the New Development Bank may serve as an illustration of this.

The idea of establishing a separate BRICS bank which provides loans for projects in emerging and developing countries was suggested by India during the 2012 Delhi summit hosted by them (Sinha, 2015: 167). The New Development Bank (NDB), as the bank was named, started operating in 2015 on the basis of an intricate agreement. The articles of agreement were finalized at the 2014 summit in Fortaleza, Brazil. China's much larger economic resources had meant that in the setup of the Contingent reserve arrangement (CRA), China would contribute more resources and consequently have a larger say in the running of the arrangement. In the case of the NDB, the situation was different, however. All the BRICS' member states would contribute an equal amount of financial resources – USD 50 billion of share capital – and they would consequently have equal representation and vote in the organization. Furthermore, although new members could be admitted later, the founding members would always possess at least 55% of total voting power. Rich countries could, as a maximum, obtain 20% of the voting powers. For the most likely clients of the Bank – and they would most likely include poorer members like India, Brazil, and South Africa – it was important to have a significant say in the running of the bank and to balance China's huge economic strength. There are indications that China had an interest in a much bigger investment bank than could be realized within the BRICS group. The subsequent setting up by China of the Asian Infrastructure Investment Bank (AIIB) could plausibly be seen as a consequence of the limited size of the NDB. However, India, who had been a driving force behind the NDB, did also contribute quite significantly to the AIIB, but for political reasons, India did not participate in another large Chinese infrastructure-related initiative – the Belt and Road Initiative. The traditional strategic rivalry between India and Pakistan (a China ally) was obviously a hindrance in this context as some of the projects were located in areas of Pakistan which were also claimed by India. The headquarters of the NDB became located in Shanghai, while the bank's first president is from India, which confirms India's strong interest in the running of the institution.

While the setting up of the Contingent Reserve Arrangement and the New Development Bank by the BRICS countries could be seen as an outcome of their lack of success in reforming the governance structure of the existing Bretton Woods institutions, their demands for changes in the institutions have not been completely ignored. China and India have both had their (small) voting shares increased in the IMF and in the World Bank. They were not successful, however, in changing the informal norms stating that the managing director of the IMF should be a European and the President of the World Bank should be an American citizen (see Güven, 2017). However, the World Bank has accommodated the two BRICS member countries in other ways. The bank's highly profiled chief economist had always been a Western economist, but recently this has changed in order to enable economists from the two BRICS members, China and India, to fill the position.

The first non-Western chief economist of the World Bank was the Chinese economist Justin Yifu Lin, who served in 2008–2012, and his successor was an Indian economist, Kaushik Basu, who served from 2012 to 2016. It may also be noted that the Director General of the World Trade Organization (WTO) since 2013 is a Brazilian, Roberto Azevêdo, which probably reflects the fact that the BRICS countries already have a significant say in the governance of this more democratic and comparatively recent institution. While none of these mentioned individuals are obliged to represent their countries of origin, they nevertheless signify small but symbolically important changes in key international institutions. Along with these changes in personnel, modest changes in the lending practices and other policies of the World Bank and the IMF may be detected, which accommodates some of the criticism voiced by BRICS members. In particular, lending policies have become more client-friendly and less standardized than previously (Güven, 2017).

In sum, India has had clear political and strategic interests in joining the BRICS coalition. India has gained from this and has been able to work to advance its own interests by shaping, to the extent possible, the international economic institutions, forming new alternative institutions and generally securing for itself a role in global consultations on a variety of international political and economic issues.

The political economy of India's BRICS membership

A separate but related motive for India has been the potential benefits for all the BRICS countries in promoting mutual economic and commercial relations, but also collaboration and mutual inspiration in a number of different social sectors.

The argument for this collaboration – as seen by India – was precisely to try to take advantage of the different levels of development and different experiences of the involved countries. Mutual collaboration formed a part of the summit declarations from the very beginning in 2009, and this took a more concrete form in the Delhi Action Plan issued in 2012.[6] While probably often ceremonial and symbolic in nature, this form of cooperation has nevertheless expanded tremendously. The declaration from the 2017 meeting in Xiamen lists 40 different elements of economic collaboration, 20 types of "people-to-people" exchanges and a host of new planned initiatives involving meetings of ministers, experts, and senior officials from the five countries.

In terms of actual commercial interaction in trade and investments, the BRICS group has been much less successful. Intra-BRICS trade has increased, and so has India's trade with the other BRICS countries, but India has also experienced a substantial and growing deficit in this trade, largely because of their trade deficit with China (EXIM Bank, 2016). Since 2011–12, India-BRICS trade has stagnated because of the economic slowdown in Brazil, Russia, and South Africa. While the economic structures of the five countries are largely complementary in nature, and their trade pattern is a reflection of this, the expected increase in mutual trade, which was also hoped for, has not yet materialized to any satisfactory degree (ibid.). China's strength as a trading nation is evident in the trade among BRICS nations, and for India this is also apparent, as clearly seen from the data in Figures 10.2 and 10.3. India has benefitted by increasing its trade with especially Brazil and South Africa, but the severe economic downturn in both countries after 2014 has reduced India's export significantly. Given the two countries' history of close commercial ties, it is remarkable that India's trade

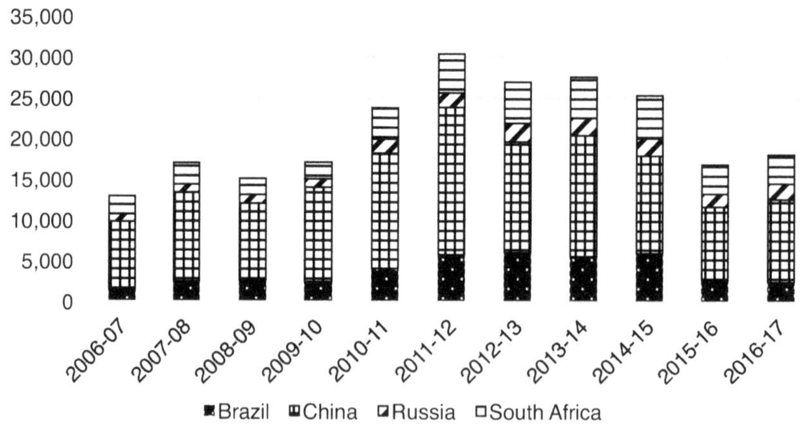

Figure 10.2 India's export to BRICS member countries, Mio. US$

Source: Ministry of Commerce, *Export-Import Data Bank* (http://commerce.nic.in/eidb/default.asp)

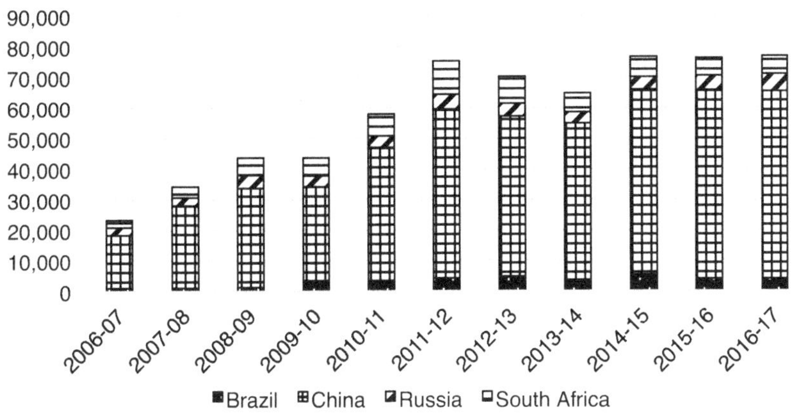

Figure 10.3 India's import from BRICS member countries, Mio. US$

Source: Ibid.

with Russia is and has remained quite small. India's large import of military equipment from Russia is not included in the data, however.

In relation to India's international trade, their trade with BRICS has struggled to keep pace. With the exception of imports from China, India's trade (both export and import) with Russia, Brazil, and South Africa has not increased in significance, compared to India's trade with the rest of the world. Their export to BRICS countries has actually declined from around 10% to less than 7% of India's total export. The share of total imports has risen from around 12% to almost 20%, but only because of a huge increase in imports from China. The share of total imports originating from the other BRICS countries has only increased from around 3% to slightly over 4%.[7]

Other economic ties than trade between the countries are of increasing importance. Foreign direct investments (FDI) from private and state-owned companies have increased in importance, but the size of the increase is difficult to assess. It is not possible to obtain solid data on FDI flows into India from other BRICS member countries, and it is equally difficult to acquire precise data on investments by Indian companies in other BRICS countries. According to official figures on investment flows, the BRICS countries do not play any significant role as neither suppliers of equity investment nor as hosts for Indian investments abroad.[8] The BRICS countries combined have supplied less than 1% of all foreign direct investments into India since 2000, and annual Indian investments into the four other BRICS member countries have rarely amounted to more than 2% of total outflows. Around half of all investments both in and out of India have been routed through international tax havens (Mauritius, Singapore, British Virgin Islands, etc.);

however, little is known about their origin or final destination. Scattered information obtained from the Indian embassies and the High Commissioner in South Africa shows that an increasing number of Indian companies are becoming active in these markets.

Many Indian companies in the IT sector, in pharmaceuticals and in the transport sector are known to be active in Brazil, China, and South Africa, whereas large state-owned companies in the oil and gas industries have dominated Indian investments into Russia. There is little doubt more Indian companies are active in Brazil, South Africa and Russia than vice versa, and there are probably also more Indian companies in China than there are Chinese companies in India. The Chinese companies operating in India are much larger, though.[9]

Generally speaking, the growth of the mutual investment links between India and the other BRICS countries have probably benefitted to some extent from the creation and development of the BRICS group. Realistically speaking, most trade and investment relations would probably have developed anyway because of the increasing globalization of India's economy and of Indian business activities. Nevertheless, the growing number of investment links naturally implies that India's purely economic self-interests in building and nurturing good relations with the other BRICS countries is slowly expanding. This has been a motivating factor behind India's attempt to broaden the scope of the collaboration efforts within BRICS, but these still tend to be largely potential economic interests rather than actual and direct material interests. Critics of the BRICS project have long been pointing toward the disparity of the economic structures and the level of development of the involved countries and have seen this as a factor which is detrimental to the collaboration in the group. It has also been pointed out that for all member countries, their relations with the US and with the rest of the Western world in economic terms are still much more important than their mutual connections (Pant, 2013).

Conclusion

India has always been a central member of the BRICS group of countries. The country forms a kind of bridge between the Eurasian continental powers of Russia and China on the one hand, and the traditional members of the coalition of developing countries, Brazil and South Africa, on the other. For India itself, the establishment and consolidation of the BRICS group and its many activities has been a natural continuation of long-term policies seeking to promote multipolarity and secure the best possible environment for its economic and political advancement in the world. The advent of the BRICS group has so far been a dream for India in two different ways. It has been a dream because it quite unexpectedly created better conditions for India to continue its already existing policies that had been traumatized by the fall of the Soviet Union and shaken by the advent of economic globalization. However, it has also been a dream of elevation to great power status – which for India remains an aspiration for the long-term future. BRICS has helped India become recognized as a potential great power in world politics and potentially an economically developed country, but India is still a long distance away from realizing these potentials, both politically and economically (Bardhan, 2010). This also means that India is far from achieving its "rightful place" in the world as envisaged by the country's founding fathers.

Whether the BRICS group will endure for a long time is of course uncertain, and many obstacles and events may still undermine the coherence of the group. For India, the group is still useful, and the country will undoubtedly try to preserve the unity and progress of BRICS, while at the same time remaining apprehensive of the rise and dominance of China.

In line with the Realist tradition of international relations, BRICS may be understood as a balance of power device against the dominance of the West and with an emphasis on multipolarity. This Realist perspective should be combined, however, with a theoretical perspective that focuses on centre-periphery relations with BRICS as an organization that represents the periphery and opposes the hegemony of the center. BRICS is an embodiment of this unique combination, and within BRICS, India is a perfect example of the very same combination. For this reason, India will remain as an indispensable core of the group.

Notes

1 Among the challenges discussed by the participants were the (perceived) shrinking room for foreign policy maneuvering, the rise of China, the dominance of the US, the increasing importance of economic issues in general, international terrorism, energy and environmental issues, etc.

2 Pant argues that the triangle is hardly likely to succeed as a true counterbalance to the US, given the importance of US relations for all three countries. Nevertheless, the RIC members have continued their regular meetings.

3 The different statements from the BRICS summit meetings have been collected by the BRICS Information Center at the University of Toronto (www.brics.utoronto.ca/docs/index.html).

4 The inventor of the acronym BRIC, the economist Jim O'Neill, protested strongly against the inclusion of a relatively small economy like South Africa into a group of countries with large and growing economies.

5 For an overview of the activities, see the action plans from the summit meetings (note 3). See also Stuenkel (2013).

6 A much smaller action plan was incorporated into the declaration from the summit in Sanya 2010.

7 Based on data from the Ministry of Commerce, *Export-Import Data Bank*. The period is from 2006–07 to 2016–17.

8 Data on foreign investments into India are available on the Department of Industrial Policy and Promotion (DIPP) website (http://dipp.nic.in/publications/fdi-statistics). Data on Indian investment abroad (approval data) are available from the Reserve Bank of India (www.rbi.org.in).

9 Based on information from websites of Indian diplomatic representations in the countries. According to the Consulate General of India in São Paulo, Brazil, there are around 55 Indian companies operating in Brazil and 12 Brazilian companies in India. See also EXIM Bank (2014) and Pradhan (2017). Large Chinese companies are especially prominent in construction and in electronics in India.

References

Bardhan, Pranab (2010) *Awakening Giants, Feet of Clay: Assessing the Economic Rise of China and India*. New Delhi: Oxford University Press.

Basrur, Rajesh (2017) "Modi's Foreign Policy Fundamentals: A Trajectory Unchanged." *International Affairs*, 93(1): 7–26.

Chang, Ha-Joon (2002) *Kicking Away the Ladder: Development Strategy in Historical Perspective*. London: Anthem Press.

Cohen, Stephen (2002) *India: Emerging Power*. New Delhi: Oxford University Press.

Export-Import Bank of India (EXIM Bank) (2014) "Outward Direct Investment from India: Trends, Objectives and Policy Perspectives." *Occasional Paper No. 165*, Mumbai.

Export-Import Bank of India (EXIM Bank) (2016) "Intra-BRICS Trade: An Indian Perspective." *Working Paper No. 56*, Mumbai.

Goldman Sachs (2001) "Building Better Global Economic BRICs," by Jim O'Neill. *Global Economics Paper No. 66*, London.

Goldman Sachs (2003) "Dreaming with BRICs: The Path to 2050," by Dominic Wilson and Roopa Purushothaman. *Global Economics Paper No. 99*, London.

Güven, Ali Burak (2017) "Defending Supremacy: How the IMF and the World Bank Navigate the Challenges of Rising Powers." *International Affairs*, 93(5): 1149–1166.

Malone, David M. (2011) *Does the Elephant Dance? Contemporary Indian Foreign Policy*. New Delhi: Oxford University Press.

Mansingh, Lalit et al. (eds.) (1997) *Indian Foreign Policy: Agenda for the 21st Century*. Vol. 1. New Delhi: Foreign Service Institute (in collaboration with Konark Publishers).

Ministry of External Affairs (MEA) (various years) *Annual Report*. New Delhi.

Mohan, C. Raja (2003) *Crossing the Rubicon: The Shaping of India's New Foreign Policy*. New Delhi: Penguin.

Nagaraj, Rayaprolu (2013) "India's Dream Run, 2003–08: Understanding the Boom and Its Aftermath." *Economic and Political Weekly*, 48(20): 39–51.

Nayar, Baldev Raj, and Thazha Varkey Paul (2003) *India in the World Order: Searching for Major-Power Status*. Cambridge: Cambridge University Press.

Nehru, Jawarharlal (1961) *India's Foreign Policy: Selected Speeches, September 1946–April 1961*. New Delhi: Government of India, The Publications Division.

Nehru, Jawaharlal (1982) *The Discovery of India*. New Delhi: Oxford University Press. (First edition 1946).

Pant, Harsh V. (2004) "The Moscow-Beijing-Delhi 'Strategic Triangle': An Idea Whose Time May Never Come." *Security Dialogue*, 35(3): 311–328.

Pant, Harsh V. (2006) "Feasibility of the Russia-China-India 'Strategic Triangle': Assessment of Theoretical and Empirical Issues." *International Studies*, 43(1): 51–72.

Pant, Harsh V. (2013) "The BRICS Fallacy." *The Washington Quarterly*, 36(3): 91–105.

Pedersen, Jørgen Dige (2008) *Globalization, Development and the State: The Performance of India and Brazil since 1990*. London: Palgrave.

Pradhan, Jaya Prakash (2017) "Indian Outward FDI: A Review of Recent Developments." *Transnational Corporations*, 24(2): 43–70.

Saran, Shyam (2017) *How India Sees the Wold: From Kautiliya to the 21st Century*. New Delhi: Juggernaut.

Sharma, Ruchir (2012) "Broken BRICs: Why the Rest Stopped Rising." *Foreign Affairs*, 91(2): 2–7.

Sinha, Dilip (2015) "India, BRICS and the World Economy." *Indian Foreign Affairs Journal*, 10(2): 160–173.

Stephen, Matthew D. (2012) "Rising Regional Powers and International Institutions: The Foreign Policy Orientations of India, Brazil and South Africa." *Global Society*, 26(3): 289–309.

Stuenkel, Oliver (2013) "The Financial Crisis, Contested Legitimacy, and the Genesis of Intra-BRICS Cooperation." *Global Governance*, 19(4): 611–630.

11 Geographies of hope and exploitation

South Africa, Africa rising, and the global turn to the BRICS

Justin van der Merwe

Introduction

It has been noted that the Africa rising phenomenon is an important and central manifestation of the broader rise of the Global South (Taylor, 2014; Van der Merwe et al., 2016). However, South Africa's place in this narrative is often overlooked or downplayed. This chapter will discuss the nuances and spatial-temporal assumptions of "Africa rising" as an important strand within the broader rising South narrative. The chapter will also demonstrate the subtle shifts and intersections between these manifestations, as the various capitalist blocs ebb and flow within the African space. What will be revealed are the subtle shifts which take place as these blocs of emerging capital generate interest in, and then look to concentrate their spatial fixes on, the continent.

The net result is that Africa loses yet again, largely because of illicit and licit capital outflow and accelerated forms of accumulation by dispossession (Bond, 2017). By now most commentators and analysts agree that the "Africa rising" narrative was misguided and built on the back of a commodity boom fuelled by rising demand in China, it will be argued that, despite its supposed usurping into the BRICS narrative through South Africa's involvement, Africa has certainly not benefitted from these growth cycles. The Africa rising narrative should also be viewed within the broader sweep of imperialism's gaze toward the South. The enabling role that imperialism played in spurring on sub-imperialisms and giving agency to its global Southern counterparts within the capitalist system will be focused upon. This is also consistent with the shifting gaze of global capital toward Southern sites more generally. It was the spatio-temporal impulses of capital itself that gave rise to the phenomena of Africa rising and BRICS, fabricated to extract maximum value out of these spaces.

How does one explain these growth cycles – the creation of entirely new geographies of growth and the blocs of capital that are melded into and animate these spatio-temporal phenomena?

The wandering "spatial fix" of global capital: the BRICS as a geopolitical "god trick"

At capitalism's core is a sense of trickery. To reveal these tricks, the government-business-media (GBM) complex brings to light the workings of the covert practices embedded in global capitalism. The key is human deception through geographies of hope and fear. For optimal exploitation of Africa, as one of capitalism's last frontiers, the Africa rising narrative and more broadly the rise of the "Global South" was peddled by the GBM complex. The overall geopolitical script constructed by mostly Western interests was one of "talking left" and "walking right" to shore up processes of accumulation and generate expanded rounds of accumulation during otherwise difficult times, and given the general remoteness of financial imperialism.

What follows in this chapter is, therefore, an exposition of the shift in the spatio-temporal fix of the GBM complex toward Africa and the South around the late nineties, as the last major round of expanded accumulation which was halted by the global recession, became fixated on the African space as a vehicle for exploitation and continued growth. The movement toward the South gained in importance during the global financial recession as the traditional poles experienced slower growth and tightening restrictions. Tragically, this cycle of accumulation was "sold" to Africa and the South as *their* chance to develop. In truth, this remained a way to sub-contract growth out to other poles while the West regained its footing. The hype preceded the reality, and the BRICS are now experiencing the fallout as a result of believing these tales.

Effectively, this chapter will describe the notion of BRICS as a geopolitical "god-trick" – a spatial trick, or more accurately, space-time trick, used by geopoliticians and finance capital which is at once magnanimous and imperialistic. Similar to the tropes of an American century, and then on a lesser scale, an African century, the time of the Global South had allegedly arrived. Although appearing magnanimous, these amorphous and aggrandizing spatial markers are typically employed as discursive devices used by progenitors of capital to further spatially expanded rounds of accumulation. Their purpose is to cloak imperial ambition.

These cycles will be elucidated through discussion of how the GBM complex as a system of accumulation has sought to speed up and facilitate increased accumulation across the globe, and how the mechanisms in the system work in synchronicity to create a self-perpetuating machine built around the accumulation of capital. This will be prefaced by a discussion of what can loosely be called "complex theory" as an approach to political economy, animated by various capitalist blocs, sectors, and actors, working through a matrix of power networks.

The government-business-media complex *writ large*: applying the concept to structural analysis

The GBM "complex" is effectively a network of elites based in the sectors of government, business, and media who support each other, collaborate and collude for purposes of capital accumulation within a fixed space (Van der Merwe, 2016a).

These patterns of accumulation perpetuate the interests of the dominant class, achieving this through "infrastructural" and "affective" labor. Infrastructural labor is used to fix extractive and transactional arrangements within a particular space, whereas affective labor is used to buttress accumulation practices within target spaces. Infrastructural labor rests on formalizing exchanges through contractual arrangements – largely through the building of physical infrastructure, financial arrangements, and trade agreements, not to mention the threat of litigation linked to intellectual property rights.

Affective labor is used to shore up consent for accumulation through processes of cultural imperialism or hegemonic practices. Generally the media component of the GBM refers not only to the conventional media (as collective noun for state-linked or commercially oriented print, broadcast and other digital media) but also to think tanks, commercial research, academia, government platforms such as summits, foreign affairs divisions, or even Corporate Social Responsibility (CSR) initiatives.

There are two heuristic applications of the GBM concept: in structural and descriptive analyses (although this paper focuses on the former). Structural analysis is more suited to the sectoral or systemic analysis of accumulation processes operating at the global and regional scales, while descriptive analysis is more focused on a bloc or the interaction between blocs (such as in the case of a particular country but not necessarily fixed to the borders of that country). Accordingly, one could say that countries have their own unique or dominant GBM complexes, such as in the case of South Africa (Van der Merwe, 2016b), India (Taylor et al., 2016), and Russia (Arkhangelskaya and Dodd, 2016). The idea of competing, yet interconnected systems of accumulation also echoes Wallerstein's (1979) world-systems theory. World-systems theory attempts to explain that nation-states have quite different positions within the global capitalist system, and more importantly, the system has been historically embedded with a series of cyclical rhythms, which is followed by the rise and decline of new global powers (new system guarantors) of world order, and each one has its own unique pattern of control and governance.

This chapter uses the GBM in structural analysis by focusing on systemic global capital accumulation or "big picture" involvement between government, business, and media actors and sectors, and how their involvement is representative or an embodiment of transnational bourgeoisie interests. This draws inspiration from the restoration of class power as captured in the turn to neoliberalism in the 1970s and strongly linked to the fortunes of Western economies. Capitalism's perpetual quest to acquire new territories and assets to exploit, is effectively what lies at the heart of these spatially expanded rounds accumulation as they spin out as an unstoppable centrifugal force over space and time (Harvey, 2007; see Taylor, 2017 for an exposition of the restoration of class power in the Global South).

(South) Africa rising? The rise of the Global South and its focus on Africa

After the fall of the Berlin wall and global dominance by neoliberalism, the GBM complex focused on market penetration and the general spread of Western-supported neoliberalism throughout the world. This proved particularly successful throughout the late twentieth and early twenty-first centuries, especially at the sub-imperial and inter-imperial levels as hitherto excluded geographies were openly integrated into the Western-led system of accumulation (see, for example, Bond 2014; Harvey, 2007; Van der Merwe, 2014a). Due to successive crises in the West, and especially the global financial crisis, these alternate centers of capital started to gain in importance as a means of maintaining growth during otherwise difficult times. Faced with the prospect of slower growth in the established poles and an all-out recession, new spaces for accumulation needed to be found, and the emerging markets and especially Africa, presented themselves as a "fixed space" to absorb this excess capital. Africa, in particular, presented the opportunity to provide cheap resources for their emerging market peers, giving rise to a phenomenon typically referred to as a "new scramble for Africa" (Carmody, 2011). This was further marked by a return to regional geopolitics where local regional powers were bestowed with the role of furthering the interests of a dominant system of accumulation within their respective regions (see South Africa in the discussion on Africa in this chapter). Through the (self-perpetuated and self-believed) rhetoric of Africa rising and the rise of the South, and with support from Western-backed banks and consultancies, the emerging markets and especially the BRICS were to concentrate and sharpen their focus within their respective "African spatial fixes" (see Harvey 2007, for definition of spatio-temporal fix).

Although by global standards, South Africa is a small player, its influence on the continent was significant in the early 90s and first decade of the twenty-first century. Between 1990 and 2000, South Africa was the largest investor in Africa, investing an average of US$ 1.14 billion of its annual foreign direct investment (FDI) in the continent (The South African Foundation, 2004). South Africa's role in the 1990s and 2000s of wedging open and leveraging the African continent for further penetration by global capital, should not be underestimated (Bond, 2004). South Africa achieved this through peddling its own geographies of hope, while seeking to further the interests of the GBM complex (for a descriptive analysis of the rise and fall of South Africa's post-apartheid GBM in the region see Van der Merwe, 2014b; and for an historical-geographical materialist perspective see Van der Merwe, 2016b). In a nutshell, the somewhat over-subscribed "South Africa in Africa literature" detailing South Africa's corporate and state expansion into Africa during the post-apartheid era (see, for example, Ahwireng-Obeng and McGowan, 1998a, 1998b; Daniel et al., 2003, 2007), is more elegantly captured through the GBM framework, where state, business, and media elements were engaged in focusing South Africa's African "spatial fix".

Although not the mandate of this chapter, a brief descriptive analysis of South Africa's GBM in the region illustrates the general logic of the complex over space and time. South Africa's dominance in the region also provided the base from which South Africa sought to project itself globally. The strong post-apartheid movement of South Africa's parastatals (such as Eskom and Transnet) into Africa, facilitated and aided the movement of its corporates into the region. South African mining houses, retailers, telecommunication companies, and food outlets soon became dominant in places like Zambia and Tanzania, even penetrating as far as north as Nigeria. These corporates were supported (at least tacitly) by government policy in the region, with the occasional disjuncture between state and capital discourses causing embarrassment for the South African government. South African banks (notably Stanbic) provided the financing to public-private partnerships and private ventures within these spaces. This was further supported by South Africa's policy-oriented think tanks and commercial research environment, with persuasive links to universities, institutes, and centers throughout the region. The multi-year "South Africa in Africa" project led by the Human Sciences Research Council (HSRC) and the corporate mapping project at Business Map, often inspired by the business press, drove interest and informed policy. With the strong focus on digital media and interconnectedness in the era of neoliberal globalization, the South African telecommunication giants (Naspers and MTN) further buttressed this northwards expansion. They provided the connectivity for capitalism but also fulfilled a consent-building role. MultiChoice, a subsidiary of Naspers, through their pay-television service, Digital Satellite Television (DSTV), carried the South African Broadcasting Corporation (SABC) into these territories. SABC had created a channel dedicated to the continent with the goal being to project a benign if not magnanimous image of the country (Van der Merwe, 2014b).

As a continental and regional power, there were three key initiatives driven by South Africa which were to facilitate capital accumulation on the continent: the African Renaissance, NEPAD, and its broader "multilateral imperialism". All of these channels provided South Africa with avenues whereby it could strongly champion the opening up of Africa within the global political economy. Mbeki himself was to play the leading role in these initiatives by formulating grand visions for Africa's development, taking it upon himself to detail and expound these plans in rousing speeches. He also acted as chairman of regional and international organizations. Mbeki was often termed a "foreign policy president" and was certainly the most prominent, if not important, African leader of the early twenty-first century.

The African Renaissance was launched in 1998. It was effectively a vision of African economic and social rejuvenation. The African Renaissance was to provide the motivation and ideational power behind its capital accumulation. The African Renaissance was the perfect "foil" for the GBM complex as it acted to allay fears concerning South Africa's hegemony, and by implication Western hegemony more broadly. The presidency hosted a conference on the African Renaissance, out of which a book was published. Mbeki opened the conference by saying: "It is a matter of great inspiration to see the intelligentsia of our continent come together . . . with the serious intention to add to the strengthening of the movement for Africa's renaissance" (Mbeki, 1999: xiii). In 2001 Mbeki addressed the Association of the African Central Bank Governors in Sandton: "There is a new dawn on the African horizon. . . . It portends a rebirth of Africa that can and must occur" (Mbeki, 2002: 131). Not only was there a grandiose comparison between a revived Africa and an epoch of human development unparalleled in history, the fourteenth century Italian Renaissance, but also with the ancient Malian empire in Africa. At a state banquet in Mali in 2001, Mbeki commented: "We are profoundly inspired by the remarkable achievements of Timbuktu . . . at a time when much of the world was still in darkness and backward" (Mbeki, 2002: 158). A "renaissance" project was created to restore the ancient scrolls of Timbuktu. Displays in South Africa's Parliament were set up to demonstrate early African cartography. A Directorate in the presidency was created focusing on the African Renaissance and NEPAD. Mbeki was to be seen as the embodiment of "African renewal" – suave, educated, and able to be a global statesman. However, despite much hubris about creating a better continent, at the center of this was an attempt to "conceal imperial ambition". As Harvey (2005: 50) states: "Much as European imperialism had turned to racism to bridge the tension between nationalism and imperialism, so the US sought to conceal imperial ambition in an abstract universalism". South Africa sought to do this through an abstract notion of "African renewal" that was at once both mutually beneficial and imperialistic. The GBM complex sought to bridge the tension between regional resistance and imperialism through an abstract notion of "African-ness" which was to transcend state boundaries. Harvey (ibid.) goes on to discuss American "universalism" which is not unlike South Africa's broad sweeping "African renewal": "The effect . . . was to deny the significance of territory and geography altogether in an articulation of imperial power".

The new ANC and corporate elite members were instrumental in laying the institutional environment for capital accumulation through the creation of the neoliberal macro-economic project, GEAR, in 1996, and through the creation of its continental equivalent, NEPAD in 2001. NEPAD was the development policy officially adopted by the reconstituted African Union in 2002, with Mbeki as chairman. Much of what the GBM complex was hoping to achieve was to be accomplished through NEPAD. The discourse underpinning NEPAD was that Africa needs to determine its own "destiny" and it represented a marked departure from the dominant African international relations framework. In the last decade of the twentieth century, the International Monetary Fund's (IMF) Structural Adjustment Programme (SAP) was the dominant framework through which Africa was cast. This had the effect of maintaining and "normalising" imperialist power relations. The NEPAD document (n.d.) states: "We will determine our own destiny and call on the rest of the world to complement our efforts". In his weekly online letter titled "NEPAD is Africa's response to globalization", Mbeki (2003: 135) wrote: ". . . NEPAD seeks to achieve the situation . . . [where] African governments do not generate the conditions that result in their having to accept structural adjustment programmes in order to access foreign finance, . . . [to] avoid the collapse of their countries and societies". The notion of an "African century" was often linked to NEPAD in speeches and had the effect of drawing attention to the inevitability of Africa's rise. In 2001, while addressing a Joint Sitting of the National Assembly and the National Council of Provinces on NEPAD, Mbeki commented: "When, at the end of the century historians cast their eyes back over this, the 21st and African century, what will they see?" (Mbeki, 2002: 149). Harvey (2005: 50) noted a similar discourse with American imperialism when Henry Luce wrote an influential article in a

1941 cover editorial in *Life* Magazine entitled "The American Century". Harvey (ibid.) asserts:

> Luce, an isolationist, considered that history had conferred global leadership on the United States and that this role . . . had to be actively embraced. The power conferred was global universal rather than territorially specific, so Luce preferred to talk of an American century rather than empire.

A similar strategy was employed by Mbeki regarding the "natural" historical progression of an African century, and how South Africa's attainment of democracy in the last decade of the twentieth century was exactly the impetus the continent needed to "claim" the following century. NEPAD also included measures to enhance good governance, such as the African Peer Review Mechanism (APRM), largely as a precondition for attracting international donor funds. A NEPAD investment council was established by Mbeki. South Africa and international capital colluded with state elite members as public-private partnerships were the primary vehicle of NEPAD.

The creation of a neoliberal macro-economic policy conducive to South Africa's dominance in continental trade and industry was further complemented by the movements toward a SADC common market. This was to find expression through the Regional Indicative Strategic Development Plan (RISDP). The RISDP was a 15-year plan to be implemented in phases of five years outlining the gradual movement toward a SADC common market by 2015. A Free Trade Area was established in 2008. The deadline for the establishment of a customs union was missed in 2010 (Chipeta and Schade, 2007: 36) and remains indefinitely delayed. Nonetheless, at the time, the movements toward greater economic "integration" through the SADC common market formed part of the NEPAD-driven attempt by the GBM complex to widen and consolidate its regional "spatial fix". According to Dr. Prega Ramsamy, SADC Executive Secretary: "[T]he African Union's NEPAD Programme is embraced as a credible and relevant continental framework, and the RISDP as SADC's regional expression and vehicle for achieving the ideals contained therein" (Chikale, 2005). The drive to consolidate capital accumulation through a SADC common market has also been hastened by competition amongst sub-imperial powers, especially China, as they increase their presence on the African continent. Despite a magnanimous "façade", nagging questions remained over enduring regional inequalities. This was especially relevant in the Southern African Customs Union (SACU) where South Africa's dominance is absolute.

Closely related to the neoliberal macro-economic project was broader "multilateral imperialism". A key feature of this was the South Africa-led restructuring of the OAU into the African Union (AU). South Africa was successful in creating "linkages", linking SADC, the AU, the NAM (Non-Alignment Movement), and the UN (United Nations). At the opening summit of the reconstituted AU hosted at Durban Stadium in South Africa in 2002, Mbeki as chairman stated: "By forming the union, the peoples of our continent have made the unequivocal statement that Africa must unite!" (Mbeki, 2002: 186). Multilateral imperialism was closely linked to the ambitions of the GBM complex to accumulate capital by consolidating its influence over the African "fixed space". Here the various organs created in the AU were of strategic importance for the GBM complex to wield its influence, such as the Pan African Parliament (PAP). South Africa was to host the PAP and used the opportunity to further signal its leadership role. As part of this multilateral project, the South African government also took the lead in peacekeeping and peacemaking throughout Africa. Using the stature it had acquired from the fight against apartheid, South Africa was also to engage in vigorous summit diplomacy as a mediator in global matters by hosting the World Conference Against Racism, Xenophobia and Other Intolerances in 2000, and the World Summit on Sustainable Development in 2002. South Africa also sought to host major international sporting events as a significant strategy to further entrench the interests of the GBM complex.

The plans for African leadership dovetailed perfectly with the broader project of Global South leadership. Inherent in the "multilateral imperialism" was the idea of establishing South Africa as the foremost African power. The India, South Africa and Brazil (IBSA) trilateral initiative founded by Mbeki in 2003 (Alden and Viera, 2005), and South Africa's joining of BRIC (Brazil, Russia, India, China) in 2010, signaled these aspirations. The move to a broader focus on the Global South coincided with a broadening of its business expansion as its multinational corporations looked to expand into emerging markets beyond Africa.

However, around the time of the global financial crisis, the South African success story became problematic. This was due to slower growth and an ignominious (forced) exit of President Mbeki, the primary architect of South Africa's Africanist endeavors, for the more inwardly focused, populist and brazenly corrupt Jacob Zuma. The "Africa rising" narrative, therefore, underwent a spatio-temporal shift from its early days under the stewardship of South Africa, to the rest of Africa more broadly. To overemphasize the matter slightly, the pendulum had swung from "South Africa rising" to "Africa rising". Although the African states were coming off a particularly low base, the narrative proved much more convincing with some countries registering growth more than 6%; mimicking their more prolific Eastern counterparts and in some cases outperforming them in year-on-year growth. This narrative was emblemized by the iconic article in the *Economist* (2011) carrying the name of the phenomenon. A "Lions on the move" report was published by McKinsey (2010) giving further credence to the notion that Africa was on the ascendancy by comparing Africa countries to the well-known "Asian Tigers". This was merely one of a succession of reports and publications exploring the growth potential of African markets.

However, not many analyses have managed to firmly embed this narrative within the bigger rise of the Global South narrative and its most poignant exponent – the BRICS phenomenon. It is contended that these spatio-temporal impulses of global capital are intimately intertwined and should be regarded together, or considered as two faces on the same coin. Based upon at least two decades of incremental growth in the Global South, the "emerging markets" mantra really culminated in the founding of the BRICS concept in 2001 and then was popularized in a series of global investment research reports by the research arm of Goldman Sachs, the American investment bank. Although merely formalizing a growing trend, Jim O'Neil and his team scripted what many had been thinking – but not even the South had got around to penning. It is perhaps no surprise that in the era of finance imperialism the concept of a quintessentially Global Southern emancipatory bloc would be based on an "emerging markets" concept. Sidaway (2012: 53) notes on the archeology of the concept: "Since the term emerging markets entered circulation, cycles of boom and bust have led to modifications in the range of countries it labels. Geographers have registered such shifts, noting, in the words of Lai (2006: 627), 'the intriguing geographical imagineering that goes into the construction and maintenance of emerging markets (EMs) as a category, and the roles played by fund managers, brokers and analysts'".

The "emerging markets" concept was originally mooted in the latter part of the 1980s by an entity of the World Bank, to label equity investments in areas that were more readily called the "Third World" (Sidaway and Pryke, 2000). Buoyed by the signals received concerning their "rising" geographies, Global Southern state, corporate, and media elites were keen to consolidate on the optimism in their markets and the not-so-subtle directives from their Western counterparts. This was followed by the creation of the official political body "BRIC" in 2005 which sought to do exactly that: melded the financial potential of these non-Western geographies with the hard power of their aggregate economic data and population sizes.

The BRIC story is well known and unfolded with a sense of historical justice – as a supposedly great historical subversion of empire. The rationale for a shift to the Global South and Africa more broadly, was well supported by consultancies and think tanks located within the West as it captured the imaginations of corporate and business media. The capital markets editor of the *Financial Times* set out how:

> [I]n the past decade, Bric has become a near ubiquitous financial term, shaping how a generation of investors, financiers and policy makers view the emerging markets. . . . Financial institutions now run Bric funds; business schools have launched Bric courses. . . . Bric . . . has redrawn powerbrokers' cognitive map, helping them to articulate a fundamental shift of influence away from the western world.
>
> (Tett, 2010: 1, in Sidaway, 2012: 56)

Given the mood of investors eager to find alternative avenues in equity markets, the emerging markets mantra was to gain a certain amount of credence leading to a phalanx of similar terms such as MIST (Mexico, Indonesia, South Korea, and Turkey), MINT (Mexico, Indonesia, Nigeria, Turkey), BASIC (Brazil, South Africa, India, and China), CIVETS (Colombia, Indonesia, Vietnam, Egypt, Turkey, South Africa) and the N11 or Next 11, which was the follow-up to the BRIC report outlining other pre-eminent emerging markets. Investors, analysts, and academics clearly taken by the idea, were seemingly trying to outdo each other with their creativity, while subtly pointing to these new geographies of global growth and illustrating the increasing importance of these rising powers in global geopolitics.

However, simultaneously, the infrastructural labor was also being laid down by the BRIC countries within underdeveloped spaces in the Global South. Not least of all was the imprinting of such labor within the African space, as these powers looked to Africa for access to raw minerals for fuel and manufacturing (Carmody, 2011). This was robustly supported by the hubristic discourse of "South-South cooperation" and the usual complementary intertwining of infrastructural and affective labors within these spaces. Following the success of FOCAC (Forum for China-Africa Cooperation), and, more recently, its One Belt One Road Initiative, China's GBM has focused much of its diplomatic and financial resources within the East African space, further signaling its attempted encirclement of Africa's Horn (Kenya to the South acting as the official docking point and regional entrepot, with the Djibouti military base on the northern side). As the geostrategic importance of the East African region has grown, so has China's troop contributions to the African Union and United Nations peacekeeping missions. Generally speaking the "Africa Rising" trope appeared to be closely related to the rise of this region, thanks largely to China, with a country such as Rwanda regularly registering growth greater than 7%. Ethiopia, with its large population and widespread poverty, was a particularly willing recipient of Chinese capital and infrastructure development (Van der Merwe, 2018).

Other BRIC nations followed suit. Mimicking China to an extent, such as through its continent-wide summits, India was successful in fusing South-South rhetoric with its business interests within the African space, thereby allowing its steady accumulation to go relatively unnoticed in relation to its larger neighbor (Taylor et al., 2016). Building on its linguistic and cultural advantage, Brazilian state and corporate elites used official donor aid effectively within Lusophone Africa to then gain access for extraction purposes through large, often state-linked companies (Seifert, 2016; Garcia and Kato, 2015). Russia's mix of anti-imperialism and struggle credentials with certain African countries proved alluring to some African state elites, especially those seeking arms (Arkhangelskaya and Dodd, 2016).

The BRICS were to meet every year since 2005 on a rotational basis and in 2010 asked South Africa to join the bloc, mainly because of what they might gain from the presence of an African representative – and given the already firm fixture of Africa within the bigger spatio-temporal impulses of the rising South narrative. Given his emerging markets frame of reference, Jim O'Neill was allegedly surprised by South Africa's inclusion (Naidoo, 2012), clearly choosing to miss some of the bigger geo-economic overtones of South Africa's inclusion.

The rotating annual BRICS summits attended by each head-of-state, further strengthened the bloc as they sought to pronounce on anything from trade to the environment, and were now seemingly speaking more convincingly on behalf of the dispossessed in the Global South, having widened their membership to include its poorest continent. Various coteries formed around the main summit in the shape of a BRICS Business Council and an official BRICS Academic Forum, locking intellectuals of statecraft into the affective work of BRICS, and carving out further space for BRICS networking and infrastructural labor. Vaguely reminiscent of Mbeki's Business Council linked to NEPAD and its Renaissance motif, the connection between the new BRICS Business Council and the old hubris around African renewal was fairly obvious and seemed a now familiar trope of post-apartheid South Africa's capitalist expansion into Africa, only now, operating in a new, suitably Global Southern and Eastern disguise. This time, the "solution" for Africa was embodied in its growing "Eastwards gaze" to China and India captured in BRICS, and not in its "Westwards gaze" to the United States or United Kingdom as with NEPAD. Like NEPAD, however, BRICS also involved the sourcing of finance and potentially aid for the continent but, dangerously, with none of the conditions relating to good governance and democratic observance, such as with NEPAD's (moderately successful) insistence that African states subscribe to the African Peer Review Mechanism (APRM) (Van der Merwe, 2014a).

Perhaps the defining achievement of the bloc was the creation of a New Development Bank in 2014 to help finance infrastructure projects in the BRICS countries and Africa. This bank, along with the Asian Infrastructure Investment Bank and the Silk Road Fund, supposedly heralded a challenge to the prevailing Washington consensus. This argument follows the logic that the emerging powers led by China, and *vis-à-vis* the BRICS alliance, are attempting to challenge the Western-led system of accumulation by replacing it with a Chinese model of development or Beijing consensus. It is assumed that much of this battle for global influence and experimentation in respect of development models and initiatives, will unfold in Africa (Van der Merwe, 2018).

This was followed by the formation of a string of centers, multi-year projects, and institutes focusing on the BRICS and with a particular focus on their involvement in Africa. The interest in these geographies was further supported by a conference industry giving much "air-time" to the "Africa rising" narrative and rise of the Global South. The conferences that were once only focused on Africa were developing entire panels and themes related to emerging powers in Africa. The BRICS established their own research centers focused on these matters and had a country partner in each of the five countries with an equal and corresponding policy focus. These centers were focused on stimulating the flow of donor funds between their respective governments, and their universities and think tanks. The BRICS summits began to be supported by a complementary suite of academic and policy conferences aimed at further elaborating on their ties and initiatives, and the various political and economic implications of their engagement.

These new growth opportunities were further capitalized upon by the Fédération Internationale de Football Association (FIFA) and the International Olympic Council (IOC). Beijing hosted the Summer Olympics in 2008 followed by Brazil in 2016, while Russia hosted the Winter Olympics in 2014. The Football World Cup was hosted by South Africa in 2010, Brazil in 2014, and Russia in 2018 – which is further testimony to the bonanza at the middle tier of global capital accumulation. South Africa's hosting of the World Cup (at a time when global growth declined due to the global recession) was to further underline the growing success of the African continent as an alternative investment destination. Effectively showcasing its potential to grow during difficult headwinds, and in overcoming the skepticism surrounding an African state's readiness to host such an event (Van der Merwe, 2009). According to *Africa Business*, the World Cup-catalysed infrastructure upgrading and the building of stadia throughout South and southern Africa had sparked the largest construction boom on the continent since the 1970s and had raised the demand for building materials considerably (Letsididi, 2008).

Despite the global slowdown, many believed that the South would sustain global growth during this period – claiming that the South had risen and that the BRICS would create a new global order. These same commentators, politicians, and business people, suggested that Africa was going to finally turn the corner and gain an equal footing globally. Africa was now the fastest growing continent in the world. The pendulum had swung from West to East, and from North to South, and a new East-South axis was rising (Pieterse, 2011).

Sub-imperialism in crisis?

The BRICS spatially expanded rounds of accumulation had reached their peak in the early part of the twenty-first century. Although the previous two decades has seen a steady rise in investment and trade in these geographies (Kiely, 2015), midway through the second decade of the twenty-first century these relationships which had their nerve center in the BRICS started to unravel. Many had begun to wonder whether American quantitative easing (the releasing of easy money into the system by the Federal Reserve) had buoyed the emerging markets artificially and that talk of a rivalry with the West was naïve and premature, possibly in the extreme (Cox, 2012). By 2013 already, three of the BRICS appeared on the Fragile Five list, another emerging markets concept used to denote countries which are particularly vulnerable owing to their dependence on fluctuating foreign investment to drive growth, re-emphasising the shallow nature of their rise (Kuepper, 2017).

This was further exacerbated by a lack of structural reform by the BRICS countries to accommodate the changes in the global political economy. 2015 saw the downgrading of the renminbi and a "rebalancing" of China's economy, causing ripples throughout the world. China's imports from Africa dropped by nearly 40% in 2015 (Mail and Guardian, 2016) although it had been declining steadily before then. All the BRICS outside of India and China went into recession (with South Africa in a virtual if not a real recession).

The likelihood of an enduring BRICS challenge to the prevailing Western-led system of accumulation seemed equally dashed through association with a string of stalling economies. China's growth remained impressive, but even this was down according to previous figures. Equally in trouble was the much hoped-for push to replace the dollar with the renminbi as an alternative global currency. The initiative continued to sink after the New Development Bank, without a hint of irony, chose to trade in US dollars (Johnson, 2015: 209). So did the Contingent Reserve Arrangement (CRA). The CRA is a framework which provides liquidity to the BRICS to help them to manage their short-term balance of payments problems but, paradoxically, ended up empowering the IMF. This is because if a country wanted more than 30% of its borrowing quota, it would be compelled to take out a structural adjustment loan and subject itself to conditionality (Bond, 2016: 613). However, realistically, even such a Development Bank needed some kind of financial prudence from its lenders, which had developed notoriously poor track records. In a broader sense, the viability of the New Development Bank against its lofty ambitions and the scale of required infrastructure, was also questioned as it possessed a total strength of $100 billion against the World Bank's $250 billion (Bertelsmann-Scott et al., 2016). In short, the creation of an alternative financial architecture to substantively challenge the prevailing Western-led one seemed unlikely despite the encouragement by "Third Worldist" intellectuals and possible sincere attempts by some Global Southern elites. Moreover, sensing the opportunities for BRICS accumulation, rapidly emerging elites in these countries became deeply corrupt, dispensing patronage to a small state-connected bourgeoisie, and while working transnationally with BRICS cronies (Van der Merwe, 2016a). It is, therefore, no surprise that none of the BRICS score favorably on Transparency International's Corruption Perceptions Index (Transparency International, 2018), while BRICS state elites are now famous for all the wrong reasons. In February 2018 Jacob Zuma was forced to resign as president of South Africa and is awaiting trial for sixteen charges relating to the country's notorious Arms Deal in the 1990s. These are just 16 of the alleged 700-plus charges against the former president.

The rise of China and Africa is linked in the sense that Africa and some of the BRICS were primarily rising as a result of a commodity boom in China, throwing into question the sustainability and supposed developmental aspects of Africa's rise, as well as that of the Global South more broadly. Taylor has perceptibly linked these processes, emphasizing that during the commodities boom of the early twenty-first century, African countries failed to industrialize sufficiently. The hubris surrounding the "Africa rising" discourse had erroneously led many to believe that this phenomenon was a central plank in the recovery of the global economy after the global recession, instead of correctly attributing it to a rise in demand for commodities in China (Taylor, 2014).

China's OBOR initiative was designed to redeploy some of its accumulated capital and to reorient its surplus of construction materials to grow exports and internationalize the renminbi. The initiative is a continuation of China's "going out" policy launched at the start of the century to increase outbound capital and expand the footprint of Chinese companies (Rolland, 2017: 130). Yet some would argue that it may have to "pull-back" in Africa and that China has become more risk-averse and cautious about committing large amounts of capital to risky ventures. The model of buying a mine and managing an African workforce (with unrealistic expectations of worker discipline, and a keen eye for value-for-money) has often backfired against the purely profit-seeking motives of such an investment. The largest Chinese deal in Africa, a $2-billion oil-for-infrastructure deal with Angola struck in 2004 has not been a total success, leading to a further drying up of liquidity for such measures (Johnson, 2015: 216).

South Africa was also struggling on several fronts and had retracted from Africa when compared to the strong northwards gaze of its capital during the late 1990s and first few years of the twenty-first century. President Zuma's tenure signaled a movement away from the grand African ambitions of the Mbeki era, focusing instead on enriching his party, family members and close business associates, primarily the now-infamous Gupta family. The rampant accumulation by this network had, however, extended into the region penetrating as far as the Democratic Republic of Congo and the Central African Republic (Van der Merwe, 2014b, 2016a). During Zuma's tenure, South Africa had become accustomed to predation by politically connected business elites such as the Guptas who would siphon capital to the United Arab Emirates and India for safekeeping and to avoid detection by the authorities. The Betrayal of the Promise (Public Affairs Research Institute, 2017) report outlined some instances of systemic state corruption in South Africa, but fell short in terms of illustrating the wider systemic mechanisms of South Africa's GBM complex and its transnational links. The fact that an immigrant family from India is now the embodiment of a predatory bourgeoisie in South Africa – historically the preserve of Randlords from Britain – seems fitting in an era of BRICS. The outflow of capital from Africa was now heading for capitals in the Middle East and the East as opposed to Western capitals.

Much of the rhetoric of the GBM complex heralding the supposed rise of Africa and the Global South was being exposed for being hollow. A revised "Lions on the move" report was published in late 2016 by McKinsey, where they cautioned that conditions for growth had weakened since the publishing of the first report in 2010. They attributed this to crises such as the Arab Spring and a downturn in commodity prices (McKinsey, 2016). Of course, the implied association with "Asian Tigers" was hopelessly misleading, especially when one considers that Ghana and South Korea were at a comparable stage of economic development in the 1950s but diverged wildly since then (Shamilov, 2016). The startling realization that a concept conceived of for investment purposes would not be the savior of the non-West, should have been apparent right from the beginning.

In summary, although the initial estimates suggested that the BRICS would outstrip the G7 in the size of their economies, and that the BRICS may be able to alter the face of globalization as we know it – the terms of this transition are yet to be seen and the extent to which systems of neoliberalism embedded in globalization can be effectively re-negotiated, is also unclear. Change moves unequally and unevenly over space and time, and thus, although the West's geopolitical and geo-economic power is waning, its global influence cannot be discounted and is still pervasive. Projected economic forecasts for China may need to be revisited in light of recent economic setbacks, and the lasting legacies of Western global powers generally, should not be underestimated. Although the financial crisis and subsequent global slowdown was cast as signaling the decline of neoliberalism and the Western-led system of accumulation, and that in its place, the emerging markets were rising – the veracity of these claims remains deeply questionable. Under these global circumstances, the future of emerging markets is anything but clear.

A critical outlook toward the BRICS alliance should be adopted now before Africa and the Global South are swept away by unrealistic ambitions, which do very little to ease poverty and underdevelopment. Likewise, history suggests that South Africa's involvements in such cycles of accumulation are the product of international elites engaging with local elites to solicit South Africa as a gateway into the region *vis-à-vis* BRICS as the new NEPAD. BRICS is therefore just the latest version of such a cycle.

References

Ahwireng-Obeng, Fred, and Patrick Jude McGowan (1998a) "Partner or Hegemon? South Africa in Africa." *Journal of Contemporary African Studies*, 16(1): 5–38.

Ahwireng-Obeng, Fred, and Patrick Jude McGowan (1998b) "Partner or Hegemon? South Africa in Africa." *Journal of Contemporary African Studies*, 16(2): 165–195.

Alden, Chris, and Marco Viera (2005) "The New Diplomacy of the South: South Africa, Brazil, India and Trilateralism." *Third World Quarterly*, 26(7): 1077–1095.

Arkhangelskaya, Alexandra, and Nicole Dodd (2016) "Guns and Poseurs: Russia Returns to Africa." In Justin Van der Merwe, Alexandra Arkhangelskaya and Ian Taylor (eds.) *Emerging Powers in Africa: A New Wave in the Relationship*. London: Palgrave Macmillan.

Bertelsmann-Scott, Talitha, Canelle Friis, and Cyril Prinsloo (2016) *Making Sustainable Development the Key Focus of the BRICS New Development Bank*. Pretoria: South African Institute of International Affairs.

Bond, Patrick (2004) "US Empire and South African Sub-Imperialism." In Leo Panitch and Colin Leys (eds.) *Socialist Register 2005: The Empire Reloaded*. New York: Monthly Review Press.

Bond, Patrick (2014) "BRICS and the Tendency to Sub-Imperialism." *Pambazuka*, April 10, p. 1.

Bond, Patrick (2016) "BRICS Banking and the Debate over Sub-Imperialism." *Third World Quarterly*, 37(4): 611–628.

Bond, Patrick (2017) "'Africa Rising' in Retreat: New Signs of Resistance." *Monthly Review*, September 1, 69(4). Available at https://monthlyreview.org/2017/09/01/africa-rising-in-retreat/.

Carmody, Padraig (2011) *The New Scramble for Africa*. Cambridge: Polity Press.

Chikale, Ellen (2005) "Southern Africa: Can SADC Still Be a Building Block for Regional Integration and Development?" *Times of Zambia*, September 9.

Chipeta, Chinyamata, and Klaus Schade (2007) *Deepening Integration in SADC, Macroeconomic Policies and Social Impact: A Comparative Analysis of 10 Country Studies and Surveys of Business and Non-State Actors*. Gaborone: Friedrich Ebert Foundation.

Cox, Michael (2012) "Power Shifts, Economic Change and the Decline of the West." *International Relations*, 26(4): 369–388.

Daniel, John, Jessica Lutchman, and Alex Comninos (2007) "South Africa in Africa: Trends and Forecasts in a Changing African Political Economy." In S. Buhlungu, J. Daniel, R. Southall, and J. Lutchman (eds.) *State of the Nation: South Africa 2007*. Cape Town: HSRC Press.

Daniel, John, Varusha Naidoo, and Sanusha Naidu (2003) "The South African's Have Arrived: Post-Apartheid Corporate Expansion into Africa." In J. Daniel, A. Habib, and R. Southall (eds.) *State of the Nation: South Africa 2003–2004*. Cape Town: HSRC Press: 368–390.

Economist (2011) "Africa Rising: The Hopeful Continent." *The Economist*, December 3. Available at www.economist.com/leaders/2011/12/03/africa-rising.

Garcia, Ana and Karina Kato (2015) "The Story of the Hunter or the Hunted? Brazil's Role in Angola and Mozambique." In Patrick Bond and Ana Garcia (eds.) *BRICS: An Anti-Capitalist Critique*. Chicago: Haymarket Books: 117–134.

Harvey, David (2005) *The New Imperialism*. Chicago: Chicago University Press.

Harvey, David (2007) *A Brief History of Neoliberalism*. New York: Oxford University Press.

Johnson, Robert Wood (2015) *How Long Will South Africa Survive? The Looming Crisis*. Johannesburg: Jonathan Ball.

Kiely, Ray (2015) *The BRICs, US 'Decline' and Global Transformations*. London: Palgrave Macmillan.

Kuepper, Justin (2017) "What Are the Fragile Five?" *The Balance*. Available at www.thebalance.com/what-are-the-fragile-five-1978880.

Lai, Karen (2006) "'Imagineering' Asian Emerging Markets: Financial Knowledge Networks in the Fund Management Industry." *Geoforum*, 37: 627–642.

Letsididi, Bashi (2008) "World Cup 2010 Proving a Bad Experience for Botswana." *Sunday Standard*, July 22. Available at www.sundaystandard.info/world-cup-2010-proving-bad-experience-botswana.

Mail and Guardian (2016) "Ouch! China's Imports from Africa Shrank nearly 40% in 2015: It Could Get Really Painful for These Countries." *Mail and Guardian*, January 13. Available at http://mgafrica.com/article/2016-01-13-chinas-imports-from-africa-plummet-in-2015-officials.

Mbeki, Thabo (1999) *African Renaissance*. Sandton and Cape Town: Mafube and Tafelberg.

Mbeki, Thabo (2002) *Africa, Define Yourself*. Cape Town and Randburg: Mafube and Tafelberg.

Mbeki, Thabo (2003) *Letters from the President: Articles from the First 100 Editions of ANC Today*. Johannesburg: ANC Communications Unit.

Mckinsey (2010) "Lions on the Move: The Progress and Potential of African Economies." Available at www.mckinsey.com/global-themes/middle-east-and-africa/lions-on-the-move.

McKinsey (2016) "Lions on the Move II: Realizing the Potential of Africa's Economies." Available at www.mckinsey.com/global-themes/middle-east-and-africa/lions-on-the-move-realizing-the-potential-of-africas-economies.

Naidoo, Sharda (2012) "South Africa's Presence 'Drags Down BRICS'." *Mail and Guardian*, March 23. Available at https://mg.co.za/article/2012-03-23-sa-presence-drags-down-brics.

NEPAD (n.d.) *NEPAD Framework Document*. [Online] Available at www.nepad.org/resource/nepad-framework-document.

Public Affairs Research Institute (2017) *Betrayal of the Promise: How South Africa Is Being Stolen*. [Online] Available at http://47zhcvti0ul2ftip9rxo9fj9.wpengine.netdna-cdn.com/wp-content/uploads/2017/05/Betrayal-of-the-Promise-25052017.pdf.

Pieterse, Jan Nederven (2011) "Global Rebalancing: Crisis and the East-South Turn." *Development and Change*, 42(1): 22–48.

Rolland, Nadege (2017) "China's 'Belt and Road Initiative': Underwhelming or Game-Changer?" *The Washington Quarterly*, 40(1): 127–142.

Seifert, Tony (2016) "New Dynamics or Old Patterns? South-South Cooperation between Brazil and Angola." In Justin van der Merwe, Alexandra Arkhangelskaya, and Ian Taylor (eds.) *Emerging Powers in Africa: A New Wave in the Relationship*. London: Palgrave Macmillan.

Shamilov, Murad (2016) "South Korea in Africa: Exporting a an 'Economic Miracle' or 'Imperialist Mimicry'." In Justin van der Merwe, Alexandra Arkhangelskaya and Ian Taylor (eds.) *Emerging Powers in Africa: A New Wave in the Relationship*. London: Palgrave Macmillan.

Sidaway, James Derrick (2012) "Geographies of Development: New Maps, New Visions?" *The Professional Geographer*, 64(1): 49–62.

Sidaway, James Derrick, and Michael Pryke (2000) "The Strange Geographies of 'Emerging Markets'." *Transactions of the Institute of British Geographers*, 25(2): 187–201.

The South African Foundation (2004) *South Africa's Business Presence in Africa*. Johannesburg: The South African Foundation.

Taylor, Ian (2014) *Africa Rising? BRICS-Diversifying Dependency*. Oxford: James Curry.

Taylor, Ian (2017) *Global Governance and Transnationalising Capitalist Hegemony: The Myth of the Emerging Powers*. Abingdon: Routledge.

Taylor, Ian, Justin Van der Merwe, and Nicole Dodd (2016) "Nehru's Neoliberals: Draining or Aiding Africa?" In Justin van der Merwe, Alexandra Arkhangelskaya and Ian Taylor (eds.) *Emerging Powers in Africa: A New Wave in the Relationship*. London: Palgrave Macmillan.

Tett, G. 2010. "The Man Who Named the Future." *The Financial Times*, 16 January (Life and Arts section): 1–2.

Transparency International (2018) *Corruption Perceptions Index 2017*. [Online] Available at www.transparency.org/news/feature/corruption_perceptions_index_2017#table (Accessed April 2, 2018).

Van der Merwe, Justin (2009) "The Road to Africa: South Africa's Hosting of the African World Cup." In Udesh Pillay, Richard Tomlinson, and Orli Bass (eds.) *Development and Dreams: The Urban Legacy of the Football World Cup*. Cape Town: HSRC Press.

Van der Merwe, Justin (2014a) "The BRICS Puzzle: Rise of the Non-West or Veiled Sub-Imperialism?" In Tatiana Deych, Alexander Zhukov, Olga Kulkova, and Evgeny Korendyasov (eds.) *Africa's Growing Role in World Politics*. Moscow: Institute for African Studies.

Van der Merwe, Justin (2014b) "Regional Parastatals within South Africa's System of Accumulation." In Devan Pillay, Gilbert Kadiagala, Prishani Naidoo, and Roger Southall (eds.) *New South African Review*. Vol. 4. Johannesburg: Wits University Press.

Van der Merwe, Justin (2016a) "Theorising Emerging Powers in Africa within the Western-Led System of Accumulation." In Justin van der Merwe, Alexandra Arkhangelskaya and Ian Taylor (eds.) *Emerging Powers in Africa: A New Wave in the Relationship*. London: Palgrave Macmillan.

Van der Merwe, Justin (2016b) "An Historical Geographical Analysis of South Africa's System of Accumulation: 1652–1994." *Review of African Political Economy*, 43(147): 58–72.

Van der Merwe, Justin (2018) "The Belt and Road Initiative: Reintegrating Africa and the Middle East into China's System of Accumulation." In Li Xing (ed.) *Mapping China's One Belt One Road Initiative*. London: Palgrave Macmillan.

Van der Merwe, Justin, Alexandra Arkhangelskaya, and Ian Taylor (2016) *Emerging Powers in Africa: A New Wave in the Relationship*. London: Palgrave Macmillan.

Wallerstein, Immanuel (1979) *The Capitalist World-Economy*. New York: Cambridge University Press.

Index

Page numbers in *italics* indicate figures; page numbers in **bold** indicate tables.

For Product Safety Concerns and Information please contact our EU
representative GPSR@taylorandfrancis.com
Taylor & Francis Verlag GmbH, Kaufingerstraße 24, 80331 München, Germany

www.ingramcontent.com/pod-product-compliance
Ingram Content Group UK Ltd.
Pitfield, Milton Keynes, MK11 3LW, UK
UKHW021720240926
475702UK00029BA/1709
9781032093802

AI Marketing

This book explores the dynamic intersection of artificial intelligence (AI) technologies and marketing practices, offering a comprehensive guide to how AI is reshaping the way businesses connect with customers, optimize strategies, and drive sustainable growth. It presents an in-depth analysis of the latest AI applications in marketing, from personalized customer experiences to data-driven decision-making, predictive analytics, and intelligent automation.

Drawing on real-world examples and the latest research, the book examines key innovations such as AI-enhanced personalization, AI-driven content creation, campaign optimization, and the strategic use of predictive analytics. It highlights practical strategies for selecting and integrating AI tools effectively, addresses the ethical challenges surrounding AI use in marketing, and discusses future trends that will shape business success in the digital era.

AI Marketing is written for marketing professionals, business leaders, entrepreneurs, and students who want to stay ahead in a rapidly evolving field. It serves as an essential resource for anyone seeking to understand not just the potential of AI in marketing but how to strategically apply it to achieve measurable results and long-term business growth.